ONE THAT WORKED!

"What is it that you want from us?" the voice snapped.

"Inspiration?" the girl quavered.

"Of course," Calliope sneered witheringly. "May I ask why you need it so soon?"

"College essay," she replied in a near whisper.

"For whom?"

"University of Pennsylvania."

"And the question is?"

"Um"—she grabbed at the sheet—" 'Your sense of imagination and creativity is also important to us. . . Create something on or with an 8½" x 11" piece of paper or other thin, flat material.' "

Then Calliope, colder than ever, hissed, "One does not call upon a muse and order her to inspire . . . And now if you'll excuse me—"

"Wait!" the girl shrieked. "What about Penn?!?"

Calliope snarled. "Tell Penn that creativity can't be forced," she snapped. Click. . . .

This is an excerpt from just one of the creative and original college essays you'll find in this remarkable handbook. With the help of top admissions officers and guidance counselors, as well as students themselves, you'll gain inspiration through example, with 100 actual college essays that worked.

CHRISTOPHER J. GEORGES is a 1987 graduate of Harvard and is the co-editor of the *Harvard Independent Insider's Guide to Prep Schools,* available in a Plume edition. GIGI E. GEORGES is a 1988 Wellesley graduate.

100 SUCCESSFUL COLLEGE APPLICATION ESSAYS

Edited by
Christopher J. Georges and
Gigi E. Georges
with members of the staff
of the *Harvard Independent*

A PLUME BOOK

PLUME
Published by the Penguin Group
Penguin Books USA Inc., 375 Hudson Street, New York,
New York 10014, U.S.A.
Penguin Books Ltd, 27 Wrights Lane, London W8 5TZ, England
Penguin Books Australia Ltd, Ringwood, Victoria, Australia
Penguin Books Canada Ltd, 10 Alcorn Avenue, Toronto, Ontario,
Canada, M4V 3B2
Penguin Books (N.Z.) Ltd, 182–190 Wairau Road, Auckland 10, New Zealand

Penguin Books Ltd, Registered Offices: Harmondsworth, Middlesex, England

Published by Plume, an imprint of New American Library, a division of
Penguin Books USA Inc.

First Printing, December, 1988
10 9 8 7 6 5 4 3

ACKNOWLEDGMENTS
From "The Road Not Taken" by Robert Frost, edited by Edward Connery
Lathem in *The Poetry of Robert Frost*. Copyright © 1979 by the estate of Robert
Frost. Reprinted by permission of Henry Holt and Company, Inc.

From "if everything happens that can't be done" by e. e. cummings in *Complete
Poems 1913–1962*. Copyright © 1923, 1925, 1931, 1935, 1938, 1939, 1940, 1944,
1945, 1946, 1947, 1948, 1949, 1950, 1951, 1952, 1953, 1954, 1955, 1956, 1957, 1958,
1959, 1960, 1961, 1962 by the Trustees for the E.E. Cummings Trust. Copyright ©
1961, 1963, 1968 by Marion Morehouse Cummings. Reprinted by permission of
Liverright Publishing Corporation.

From "Time to Change" by Raymond Bloodworth, Chris Welch and Billy
Meshel. Copyright © 1971 by Famous Music Corporation.

 REGISTERED TRADEMARK—MARCA REGISTRADA

LIBRARY OF CONGRESS CATALOGING IN PUBLICATION DATA:

100 successful college application essays / edited by Christopher J. Georges and
   Gigi E. Georges with members of the staff of the Harvard Independent.
      p. cm.

   1. College applications—United States. 2. Exposition (Rhetoric) 3. Universi-
ties and colleges—United States—Admission.
I. Georges, Christopher J. II. Georges, Gigi E. III. Harvard independent. IV. Title:
One hundred successful college application essays.
LB2351.52.U6A17 1988
378'.1664—dc19   88-21059   CIP

Printed in the United States of America

To Dr. Nicholas T. Macris

—*who, like the essays in this book,
inspires by way of example*

Acknowledgments

We would like to thank many people. First, the hundreds of students who submitted their essays for consideration. Their help, with only the knowledge that their experience might benefit others in return, has been invaluable.

Our appreciation, as always, to Thomas Harvey, for his wise advice, his experience, and his introduction.

Often support comes from a place where it is least expected. Thanks to the partnership of Schafe, Sean, and Now, who now know the true meaning of good jobs at good wages. Thanks also to Mike for providing an opportunity.

Special appreciation to Martha Dustin, for her General Attitude and her reading skills, to our sister Stephanie, who promised that all her friends' children would buy a copy, and to Mary Beth Whitson for always knowing when to break for coffee.

Most of all, we'd like to thank our parents.

And, of course, special thanks to George Bear.

The following editors selected the 100 essays in this book from the hundreds of pieces submitted. Editors-in-chief: Christopher J. Georges (Executive Editor of the *Harvard Crimson*, 1987) Gigi E. Georges (Managing Editor of the *Wellesley News*, 1988); Managing Editor: Shari Rudavsky (Managing Editor of the *Harvard Crimson*, 1988)

Editorial Staff: Keith O. Boykin (Editor-in-chief and Chairman of the *Dartmouth News*, 1987); Sean Dobson (writer for the *Yale Daily News*, 1987); Martha Dustin (staff editor of the

Harvard Independent Insider's Guide to Prep Schools, 1987); Tony Laden (President of the *Harvard Independent*, 1988); David Lee (President of the *Harvard Independent*, 1987); Kevin Park (Publisher of the *Harvard Independent*, 1988); John R. Schafer (Co-Editor-in-chief of *The Williams Record*, 1987); Wade Roush (Editor-in-chief of the *Harvard Independent*, 1988)

The following people provided the comments and remarks which follow the essays: Natalie Aharonian, Director of Admissions, Wellesley College, Wellesley, MA; Stanley A. Bosworth, Headmaster, Saint Ann's School, Brooklyn, NY; Ann A. Frietas, College Counselor, Bellarmine College Prep, San Jose, CA; Ted Grabowski, Director of Guidance, Holy Ghost Prep, Bensalem, PA; Tom Harvey, Assistant Headmaster for External Affairs, Poly Prep Country Day School, Brooklyn, NY; Michael A. Hricko, Director, C.A.C., St. Joseph's Prep, Philadelphia, PA; John McClintoch, College Counselor, Francis W. Parker School, Chicago, IL; John C. Merrill, III, Director of College Counseling, Worcester Academy, Worcester, MA; Robert C. Miller, College Counselor, The Thacher School, Ojai, CA; Joan W. Mudge, College Advisor, Garrison Forest School, Garrison, MD; Richard J. O'Hara, Director of College Counseling, Woodberry Forest School, Woodberry Forest, Virginia; Bryan P. Seese, Director of Placement, Milton Hershey School, Hershey, PA; Hal D. Tayloe, Chairman, English Dept., Hampton Roads Academy, Newport News, VA; Arthur S. Thomas, Director of College Counseling, The Peddie School, Highstown, New Jersey; Peter Taubman, English Teacher, Poly Prep Country Day School, Brooklyn, NY

Contents

Preface

It's early January. College applications are due in 48 hours, and your applications are complete—except for the essay.

Why not? Perhaps you fear writing something that will not match the record displayed throughout the rest of the application. Perhaps because of the difficulty of capturing your personality on a single sheet of paper. Or maybe, you still are waiting for an original idea—something that will prompt the admissions officers to place your application in their "great thinkers of the 21st century" folder.

You call a friend. ". . . Oh, you've already finished your essay," you say. "Me? Oh, I'm almost there. Just have to finish thinking of a topic. . . . What did you write about? . . . No kidding. The electoral college. Nice choice. . . ."

You want to say something about *yourself,* but you don't want to sound pretentious. You want to show them you're different—better even—than the next applicant, and you want to show it on a single sheet of paper. You want to show them you're funny, or creative, or bright, or athletic, or ambitious. You want to let them know that you deserve to go to *their* college.

The intent of this book is not to give advice. Nor is it a how-to guide. Instead, it is intended to inspire by way of example.

With that said, we will now offer three bits of somewhat ambiguous advice—which we hope the rest of this book serves to illustrate:

First, try not to accomplish too much in your essay. Less is more.

1

Second, poor essays make a big deal out of nothing (eg., learn to respect mankind from serving as captain of j.v. basketball), and successful essays take respectable accomplishment and keep it in perspective.

Finally, be loose. This doesn't mean writing a string of jokes. On the other hand, write for admissions officers, not for the law review. Keep it simple, easy to follow, and "be what thou art"—a high school student.

Throughout this book, we have attempted to illustrate that a successful college application essay need not be produced by a gifted writer—otherwise this would be a very short book. We could not, of course, resist including a number of essays written by talented writers; however, we also strove more to include essays that stood out for other reasons. And these, we believe, deserve greater attention simply because they illustrate what can be done with a little creativity and a little thought. And that, more than anything, may be what separates the average essay from the successful one.

After almost every essay, you'll find a "Comment" written by one of the professional admissions officers or counselors who helped us with our selections. In the text, they are identified by their initials; their full names can be found on page viii.

The essays in this book are those that college and high school officials as well as the editors of this book have selected as outstanding, successful, unusual, or exceptionally thoughtful. The purpose of the book is simply to expose students to various techniques in essay writing and to illustrate that there is no one type of essay that should or should not be written.

—THE EDITORS

ON WRITING
THE COLLEGE ESSAY

Advice from the Inside

Someone once calculated that I have read around two hundred thousand applications for admission, give or take a couple thousand, since becoming an admissions dean. Does that make me an expert on the subject of admissions essays? Nope. Does it qualify me to offer a few observations about such essays, based on my experience? Maybe. The editors apparently think so. I promised I'd give it a try.

The essay is the main life-support system of the application. Let's face it, most of a college application is a matter of filling in the blank spaces, listing things. Listing your accomplishments and interests, neatly listing them, sometimes even imaginatively listing them, but listing them nevertheless. Takes about a half hour at the outside. The essay is the applicant's opportunity to breathe some life into the folder, to remind the reader that all of those numbers and letter grades and adjectives and test scores and lists of activities represent, for better or for worse, yet another and different person out there.

When I was an admissions dean and faced the task early each January of reading through some fifteen thousand or so applications, I must confess that I was not thrilled at the prospect of seeing just how many different ways in which the number of varsity letters, or the number of years in the orchestra, or the number of offices held could be expressed. Even the recommendations from teachers and counselors, which, when well done, can bring a candidate to life, frequently fall short of doing so, resorting as they almost invariably must to a rather limited set of adjectives (even the superlatives become routine) to limn the students about whom they are writing. It was the essays I looked forward to, not to give a thumbs up or thumbs down to an applicant, but rather simply to help give a particular shape or outline to the person who garnered the grades and test scores and awards and superlative adjectives I read about in the rest of the folder.

In an age of McRankings and media hype about "hot colleges," there is unfortunately a lemming-like tendency of students with similar abilities and accomplishments to cluster their applications at an unreasonable (or so it seems to me) limited number of particular colleges and universities. The result, alas, is that the range among applicants along any one of these numerical/adjectival dimensions above is, at many colleges, often very narrow. A reader of applications at such colleges can become positively glassy-eyed after the first five hundred or so. More often than not, it is the more personal nature of the essays that breaks the monotony and engages the reader.

Keep in mind that a college application is a set of six or seven hooks, on four or five of which most candidates for admissions are going to hang their hats. The essay is only one such hook. Save for those few instances in which candidates wrote essays so completely lacking in taste as to make us marvel at the fact that they even had bothered to apply, in my experience no one was ever admitted *solely* on the basis of a great essay and no one was ever denied admission *solely* on the basis of a poor essay. (See below on "fit.")

Also keep in mind that good essay topics or questions are often as difficult for the colleges to think up as they are for the applicants to respond to. (Not much solace there, I admit.) Unlike "test" questions, they're not set to elicit (or even to imply) right or wrong answers. Ideally, they simply provide some fertile ground to be plowed by applicants from all sorts of backgrounds and with quite different interests and experiences, while at the same time keeping the area sufficiently fenced in so as to allow for comparability. In some instances, essay topics simply reflect the preferences of those who have to read them. My own preference, for instance, was for questions that I hoped would be fun to answer and that I also hoped would elicit answers fun to read. These are some of the reasons why essay topics not only vary enormously from college to college, but even year to year at the same college. The essay is the one part of the application that allows a student to think out loud. Indeed, when you stop to think about it, it's the only part of the application that usually requires any thinking at all!

Since most readers of application essays (myself included) are not by any stretch of the imagination experts in that particular art form, and indeed frequently disagree among themselves over the merits of one or another essay, my first piece of advice is to write your essays, *not* for some imaginary admissions officer or faculty member at the other end, but for yourselves, or for a favorite avuncular relative, or roommate. Write it for anyone *other* than that admissions person whom you've come to convince yourself holds your life in his or her hands. (I read somewhere that the term "short shrift" originally referred to a brief respite for confession before execution. Don't consider your essay "short shrift." Relax.)

That brings me to my second piece of advice. When you write your essay, consider simply telling a story. I can think of few college application essay topics, including the weightiest, that don't provide the student with an opportunity to tell a story. I'm convinced that storytelling comes more naturally to most of us, and also more accurately expresses our nature, than does essay writing. Ask me to tell a story, no problem. Ask me to write an essay and I break out in a sweat. But I long ago figured out that some of the best essays I've ever read are simply stories well told.

Besides, stories need not be long to be effective, a not inconsequential virtue given that colleges frequently require that an essay be no longer than a single page. Don't consider brevity a limitation. You should be able to tell a story in just one page. It has always struck me that a poem is a really *short* "short story." The art of poetry is in knowing what to leave out. What is left out is often precisely what draws the reader in. That's as true for storytellers as for poets. And what you want to do is draw in the reader of your application. Don't hesitate to risk leaving something to the reader's imagination. (Here I must confess that no matter what kind of writing I'm doing, I try to discipline myself to go back over it and remove the unnecessary baggage that always creeps in, an exercise delightfully taught in William Zinsser's *On Writing Well*.)

My third piece of advice is to invest some time in reading some good writing before sitting down to write your own essay. I find I *have* to do that. I think most of us have a passive vocabulary and even ways of expressing ourselves that are far more intricate and colorful and imaginative than that we're normally required to draw upon to get through an average day. Reading a good book or a good essay can sometimes ignite the same skills in the reader. You probably have your own favorites. Mine include people like E. B. White, Robertson Davies, Stephen Jay Gould, Russell Baker, John McPhee, Joseph Epstein, Garrison Keillor, and Red Smith, to name a few. Good writing is contagious. It can also put you in an appropriate frame of mind for embarking on your essay. Observe how they tell a story. Observe how they tell a story in order to make a point. Observe how they draw the reader in, often from the first sentence. Keep in mind also that there's nothing wrong with imitating a good writer. That is how many writers we now consider "good" started out.

My fourth piece of advice is to be sure that your essay reflects you, and not some idealized version of yourself that you have come to imagine is precisely the kind of person an admissions office will be most favorably disposed toward. In my most plaintive moments as an admissions dean, I could be heard stalking the office corridors shouting, "Where in the hell are the Huckleberry Finns?" Such explosions normally took place after I'd made my way through a long string of applications that left me convinced we had cornered the market on saints and scholars, none of whom had ever stumbled, faltered, or failed at anything, and few of whom seemed real. To a certain extent, the entire admissions process invites that. Applicants are constantly advised to "put their best foot forward." But I must confess that I always liked the ones who put *both* feet forward. Whatever number of feet you plan to put forward or to stand on, make sure that your essay "fits" your application.

An application where the various pieces don't appear to "fit" together stands out like a sore thumb. As with admissions officers, students come in all shapes and sizes, with different personalities and ways of approaching the world. Some are gregarious, some are shy. Some are athletically inclined, and some are more sedentary. Some are more mature in some aspects of their lives than in others. The freshman class at any college in the country will be made up of students who exhibit a mix of all of these traits and many more. What throws off a reader of an application is a sharp and inexplicable contrast between a student's essay and everything that that reader has learned about the student throughout the rest of the application. For instance, an essay that is so highly polished that even a tenured professor would be proud to submit it for publication, from an applicant whom a reader otherwise finds attractive precisely because the evidence throughout the rest of the folder depicts a diamond in the rough, naturally raises questions in the reader's mind about whether the essay is really the work of the student. How does one square this brilliant of brilliantly put essay, not only with comments from the applicant's teachers that poor writing skills constitute his only major weakness, but also with the student's rather modest writing skills that are all too evident throughout the rest of the application?

This is not to say that if you need to you should not have someone else whose judgment you value take a look at your essay in order to point out typos, grammatical errors, or even, ahem, incomprehensibility. But I can't emphasize enough (well, maybe I can) that the style, flavor, and substance of your essay needs to *be* your own and to *look* your own and to *sound* like you. In a word, your essay (in fact, your entire application) should *smell* authentic.

I guess what I am saying here is that essays that appear contrived, either in style or substance, often stand out and can end up working against an otherwise attractive applicant. My hunch is that many students tend to underestimate their attractiveness compared with other applicants, come to imagine (erroneously) that colleges have some single, ideal admissions candidate in mind, and in the course of trying to come off as this imagined "ideal" candidate actually do themselves a disservice in the process. (With only a slight amount of exaggeration involved, the applicant I remember most quickly putting in the "admit" pile was one who wrote: "As you will notice, my test scores are quite low. They are accurate.")

My fifth piece of advice is not to ask of your essay that it carry too heavy a load. Don't use the essay to drop names, or to remind the reader that your parents are alumni of the college, or to rationalize a low grade or a low test score or a lost election for yearbook editor. Essays that are used to tell a college everything you think they should know about you but didn't ask elsewhere in the application come to resemble junk sculptures. Just give the essay question or topic itself your best shot. (If there *is* additional information or an explanation you think is useful for the college to have in considering your application, simply add an extra sheet and attach it to your application papers.)

Also, resist the temptation to write the *all-purpose* essay, to which you then make small adjustments in order to use it for all of your college applications no matter how different the essay questions or topics they set before you. Such essays are painfully obvious, and more often than not engender a negative reaction. Just as applicants want to be treated as individuals by each of the colleges to which they are applying, so, too, do the colleges desire that their applications be treated individually by the applicants. At least that's the way we felt.

My last piece of advice is to tell you to sort and sift any advice you receive (including my own) and to settle only on that which intuitively makes sense to you. As crazy and as varied as the admissions process seems when you are going through it, it's always struck me that one of the virtues of admission to American colleges and universities is precisely the lack of a consensus among even the most selective colleges on what the "perfect" application looks like or who the most desirable applicants are. The observations I've made here are based upon my particular experience in reading the applications at one college and one university over a twenty-year period. They're not offered from on high, but rather simply on the off chance that one or another of them just might ring a bell with you. Whatever, good luck.

—FRED HARGADON
Dean of Admissions,
Princeton University

(Fred Hargadon was Dean of Admissions at Swarthmore College from 1964 to 1969, and Dean of Admissions at Stanford University from 1969 to 1984.)

The Question of the Essay

Should it be catchy or trendy? How about something straightforward yet really specific? Or maybe one should cover broad topics and wander freely in any direction. . . . What would be the most pleasing? What would give them what they really want? Why does it seem that all the good ideas have been taken?

The time has come to change the Haverford College application essay question. We knew that we were dissatisfied—tired of reading the same old answers to the same old question. Students found our essay boring and restrictive. We did, too. Ours was a plain and unadorned question: *Why do you want to go to college; and why do you particularly want to go to Haverford?* Although it fit the honest, direct style of the College, it elicited deadly dull answers and a plethora of "additional essays" that students thought allowed them more creativity. They were right.

What we needed, then, was a straightforward question that was a bit more exciting. How could we expect varied and interesting essays if we insisted on being so restrictive? At the same time, we liked the notion that the question should somehow reflect the style of the College. The challenge was to ask a candid question that would still allow originality and variation in the answers.

What exactly do admissions officers want to know when they ask you to write the college essay? No matter which question, we are asking what is really important to you, who you are, and how did you arrive where you are. The whole college application process is really a self-exploration, and the essay is a way to put your personal adventure into words. It is a summing-up, maybe a catharsis. You need not expose all of your innermost thoughts, but you must share some part of yourself.

We want you to be honest, genuine, and forthright. You could also be witty or clever, if you are skilled at humor. We want you to give a piece of yourself to the project; and we want you to grow in the process. The best essays shine with the personality of the writer and give depth and credibility to the person described in the application. This may be the first time you thought critically about your high school accomplishments, your motivation for a career, or the difficulty you experience with math. Perhaps you have never before articulated your feelings about the pain of leaving home, the love of a grandparent, or the joy of a religious experience. You need not cover every detail or aspect of your life; just a piece of your philosophy or a moment of your experience will do.

What if the question asks you to address something specific? What if you despise being any vegetable, or have no favorite person in the nineteenth century? How can you show your true self if the essay question seems to limit your expression? Keep in mind that the form of the question does not alter the fundamental challenge; we still want to know what is of real importance to you. The metaphor really makes little difference. Some will be easier than others for you, but none should be impossible. Do answer the question that is asked, but gently take it in the direction you want it to go. We would like all essays to be as entertaining and enlightening as the ones in this book, but we are happy to have your best effort, no matter what your writing talent may be.

Finally, we who sit on admissions committees expect that you will have several issues or experiences that are important to you. Sometimes you are able to touch upon most or all in your essay; but other questions will limit your answer and force you to choose just one. Be assured that we know the limits of our own essay questions; our universal expectation is that you will do your best, in both form and content. If you have done self-exploration during the process of choosing colleges to which you will apply, then you should be able to generate a list of topics and ideas that are important to you. As you consider each college's essay question, apply it to the ideas on your list and see which ones fit best.

Getting back to the question of *The Question*, we knew that we wanted to encourage genuine and honest responses about important matters in students' lives. Like the students, we wanted our "personality" to manifest itself. Like *Jeopardy!* we needed the question after we found the answer. Although the solution eluded us far too long, the question, like the best essays, is simple and direct: *We want to know you better. Please write a description of what you are like as a person.* What could be easier? Or more difficult?

—DELSIE Z. PHILLIPS
Acting Director of Admissions,
Haverford College

What *Not* to do ... and Why

I Yam what I Yam.
—Popeye

I urged the *Harvard Independent* not to do this book. I told them that the last thing most high school seniors needed was a collection of superb college essays, exquisitely crafted and boldly imaginative. Most seniors are not going to write great essays, at least not ones that will by themselves get the reader admitted. In fact, I know of college studies in which 3 percent of the essays helped the applicant, 2 percent hurt the applicant, and 95 percent, while perfectly respectable, had no effect whatsoever on the admissions decision. Yet I have seen even good writers crippled by the pressure they put on themselves to write a great essay, one that will get them admitted. I was worried that this book would contribute to the already high anxiety level of most seniors seeking admission to the kinds of colleges that ask for and read the essay.

I suggested that the *Harvard Independent* compile a book of bad essays, examples of the kinds of writing to avoid. They agreed that the book would not contain all faultless examples of essays, and they asked me to write an introduction. Following my advice, I would like to mention some of the more common mistakes seniors make in deciding upon an essay topic, and in writing the essay

First, don't write an essay that any one of a thousand other seniors could write, because they probably will. By the nine-

14

hundred and forty-second time a college person reads about how bad you felt after losing the big game, that essay has lost its emotional impact. You can write about losing the big game, but when you have finished, read it and ask yourself if anyone else could have written the same essay. If you think the college might receive even one other essay like yours, rewrite it. The fact that you cried after losing the big game doesn't distinguish you from all the others who might write this essay. On the other hand, the details—where you cried, who talked to you, exactly what you were thinking—probably will set you apart.

I think you should avoid writing an essay that will embarrass the reader. While you definitely must risk something personally in order to write an effective essay, the risk should not place a burden on the reader. The reader is not your therapist, not your confessor, and not your close friend. If you place the reader in any such role, he or she will be uncomfortable. You certainly want your essay to stand out from the crowd, but it is probably better to be forgotten than to be remembered in a negative manner.

Don't try to sell yourself. The college will exercise its quality-control function using the grades and scores, not the essay. They use the essay to flesh out the numbers, to try to see and hear the person in the application. Rather than persuading the college that you are great, just show them who you are, what you care about, what moves you to anger, what the pivotal points in your life have been so far.

Also don't try to write an important essay . . . the definitive statement on the Middle East crisis or on race relations in America. These essays tend to come across as much more pompous than their authors intend, I suppose because it is unlikely that a high school senior is going to make the definitive statement on a major topic. More to the point, these essays tend to be written from a detached, objective point of view, exactly the opposite of what most college people are looking for in an applicant's essay. They read your essay to find out who you are. When they want an informed opinion, they will go to the editorial pages, not their files of college essays.

Don't set out to write the perfect essay, the one with a huge impact, the one that will blow the doors to the college open for you. It just doesn't happen very often. It is largely a fantasy, and you will be putting enormous pressure on the still-developing writing skills of an eighteen-year-old. Think instead of giving the reader a sample of yourself, a slice of the real you, a snapshot in words. It doesn't have to be an award-winning photograph, it just needs to be really you and reasonably well focused. Imagine that if you wrote the essay next month, it might well be completely different, because you would be different by then. I find regularly that the best essays I read are the result of a concentrated forty-five minutes, not the result of hours and hours of agonizing.

I will give one caveat on the writing itself. Don't have others edit and correct it until you cannot hear your own voice any more. Certainly, you should correct the spelling. Of course, you should rewrite the essay, probably several times. My favorite writer on the subject of writing, William Zinsser, has convinced me that there is no such thing as good writing, only good rewriting. Rewrite to make sure that your words are saying what you intend them to say. That is all. That is the primary goal of rewriting. Word choice and word order must remain yours; even if a more experienced writer might suggest the more precise word, it will not be your word and you will begin to disappear from the essay. And remember that the only reason this essay has for existing is to show the reader who you are.

Finally, relax. Your chances of writing an essay that gets you admitted when you otherwise would not have been are unbelievably remote. Pick something you feel strongly about, for that will give the reader a window into your heart, and just write it. Think of the choice of subject and the first writing as simply sharing some part of yourself with a new friend. This is not usually painful. The work should come in the rewriting stage.

Good luck.

—WILLIAM K. POIROT
College Counselor, Brooks School,
North Andover, MA

How to Use This Book

You will find this book useful if you use it well, but you will not find a formula for success here. The essays included are as varied as the people who wrote them. Some are long. Some are short. Some are deeply moving. Some are hilariously irreverent. Some are profoundly personal and some are wonderfully whimsical. Yet they are all judged effective, or successful.

The message here is a simple one. Be honest and be confident. Be willing to be different by being yourself. Those who read your essays will be looking for reasons to like you. Trust them by writing what you feel, and by writing whatever you feel.

Take chances. If you think you can be funny, be funny. If you think you have a particular skill or personal quality worthy of note, send the message. This is not the time to be cautious.

Your essay will succeed, if you are prepared when you write it.

As you read the essays here, conduct an experiment. Pick out the ones you like best, and then reexamine their openings. You will find that the best essays have the best openings. A good opening is the result of forethought. If you know what you want to write, and you find an effective way to begin, the essay will pour out of your pencil.

—THOMAS D. HARVEY
Assistant Headmaster for External Affairs,
Poly Prep Country Day School,
Brooklyn, NY

ESSAYS ON
APPLYING TO COLLEGE

Charles W. Applegate
College: Ohio Wesleyan University

Here I sit, my pen vying for equal time in my hand as some Connecticut School of Broadcasting flunkie blabbers on and on and my glass of Diet Coke wordlessly whispers of its passage from fizzy to flat. "What am I, Sam?" I beseech of my cat, who is disdainfully picking over the remains of his Tuna Entree and eying the purposeful plummeting of the sky's best snowflakes with the vigorous venom of a cat grown old enough to truly despise winter.

"Ahh," he hisses, lidded eyes coming to bear on my vaguely despondent figure. "You are, oh Grasshopper, what you accomplish. A man (or, in your case, a boy) can only be measured by his achievements."

"Sam, I'd buy it if you were a Siamese, but let's face it. You're a Domestic Shorthair rescued by me from a West Side alley in New York. Now come on. I need this for my Beloit essay."

"Okay, Charles. You want to know what you are? You are an insignificant eighteen-year-old kid pretending to be an adult, trying to write about some aspect of your rather short life and make it seem not only interesting, but significant, too. No offense, but the best thing you ever did in your life was to adopt me."

"That's not quite true, Sam, but you do have a point." Sam disdainfully shook his left front paw and resumed glowering at the snowflake's gently offensive descent.

Snowflakes notwithstanding (for I in my youth still enjoy them greatly), my snide little fur-face is right. As my pen hand evicts my head and my pen begins to romp across the paper, I look back on my life and find a notable paucity of great achievements and memorable experiences. I see, complete with warm feelings of triumph and heightened self-esteem, the earning of my driver's license, my first date, my first (and only) sack in a football game, and other memorabilia of my not-so-distant youth. Not to say that I've had an uneventful life, but there isn't too much to brag about.

21

This is where what Sam just said comes into play. One simple word which explains my aforementioned paucity of experience. That word, if you have not already guessed it, is eighteen. After all, I've been on this earth for but one-quarter of my expected life span, and it's only in the past few years that I have gained leave to explore the world's virginal vistas, so it's no surprise to me that my past is far from chock-full of wondrous life experiences.

Picture if you will the world reduced to the comparative microcosm of a chicken coop, perhaps with Sam playing a role as the Grim Reaper, or the threat of Communism, or the Fuller Brush salesman, or some other such menacing apparition. Following through with the analogy, I have been spending my time in the eggshell of high school. I am soon due to be released into the training ground of the coop's floor, which serves as a college designed to prepare me for the dangers, inconsistencies, and complexities of the adult world outside the barnyard.

While the snowflakes remorselessly mount their attack against my poor, aged cat, I ponder the infinite mysteries of college. Why college? Sam is remarkably uncommunicative, his ears flattened with rage at the sky's vile behavior, and refuses to answer my query.

Sitting here in the kitchen, all the wrong reasons for college are readily apparent, and I chant aloud of money, power, prestige, and the endless others that send people scurrying to the shelter of higher education in the hope that one will show some sign of earning my feline mentor's stamp of approval. Nothing. He sits on the window like a stone meatloaf. Glumly, I stare into the oven, my wave of inspiration having crested and broken on the beach of writer's block.

Now, though, I feel as if I'm being watched. Slowly, I turn to the window and gaze into two deep, burning liquid eyes. Sam has abandoned his snowflakes for my problem.

"You never could see the forest for the trees, could you? What is it that you were complaining about earlier? A lack of experience, wasn't it? Now then, tell me what college is for."

As the words sinuously roll off his tongue, I realize how totally correct he is. I need college to learn, not how to read or add, but how to live.

College is the beginning of real life, of life outside the chicken coop. And it is where I will begin my life.

Jennifer Applegate
College: University of Pennsylvania

MELPOMENE STRIKES

"I don't know yet," she replied. "I'd like to write a poem, since I think that's my forte, but I just can't find the inspiration under this kind of pressure."

"I think I can help you," Martha said slowly. "Call this number and ask for Calliope," she said as she scribbled. "Gotta run."

That night the girl sat for a full hour staring at the blank sheet of 8½" x 11" paper before she dug out the bubblegum wrapper and dialed the number etched on it in #2 pencil. After three rings there was a short silence and a perky voice chirped, "Calliope and Company, may I help you?"

"Uh, yes," the girl stammered. "May I speak to Calliope, please?"

"Calliope is in a board meeting right now," the voice bubbled. "May I connect you with another party?"

"I don't really know," the girl replied, flustered. "I was told to ask for Calliope, but if there's someone covering for her . . ."

"Well, let's see . . ." Sound of pages flipping. "I believe Erato and Thalia are free, but I can't be sure. What is it you would like to write?"

"Um, a poem," she replied, puzzled.

"Wellllll," the voice said, "Calliope deals with overall eloquence, but perhaps Erato could help you. Is this a . . . love poem?"

Is it? the girl wondered furtively. "No, not really."

"Hmmmm . . . Perhaps bucolic poetry? Thalia is free today."

"No, that's not quite right somehow . . . I don't suppose you have a resident expert on prose poetry, do you?"

There was a tinkling laugh. "No, I'm afraid not. Would you like to try your hand at music or dance? I could ring up Euterpe or Terpsichore for you."

Where do they get these names, she smiled to herself. "No, I'm afraid this has to be visual. It has to be done on one sheet of paper."

There was a puzzled silence. "Oh . . . I see. Can you use both sides?"

"Um, I'm not sure. Good question . . . lemme check."

She grabbed at the sheet and quickly scanned it. " '. . . on or with an 8½″ x 11″ piece of paper . . .' Yeah, I guess you can." She was growing desperate, staring at the list of deadlines posted above her desk. "I just need a little inspiration on this poem, that's all. It's very important."

"I could try for Polyhymnia . . . she's the muse of sacred lyric poetry."

"I said important, not sacred . . . did you say muse?"

"Well, of course," the voice bubbled. "You are speaking to Calliope and Company, Muses, an agency designed to help inspire artists of all sorts."

Where did Martha get this number, she wondered. Ready to try anything, she said dully, "Oh. Well, who can inspire me?"

"Well, I'm afraid I don't quite know what to suggest," the voice said sadly. "Please hold while I check with Calliope."

Blowing the stray hairs out of her eyes, the girl slumped back in her chair and sighed, listening with half an ear to the faint strains of lute Muzak. A frosty voice broke the tranquility, shattering her thoughts: "Calliope speaking," it snapped. "Is there a problem?"

"No, ma'am," the girl stammered. "I mean, yes, there is . . . I want to write a poem, and I need it by the first of the year."

"And what is it you want of us?"

"Inspiration?" she quavered.

"Of course," Calliope sneered witheringly. "May I ask why you need this so soon?"

"College essay," she replied in a near-whisper.

"For whom?"

"University of Pennsylvania."

"And the question is?"

"Um . . ." She grabbed once more at the sheet. " '. . . your sense of imagination and creativity are also important to us. . . . Create something on or with an 8½" x 11" piece of paper or other thin, flat material. All means of expression, written or otherwise, are equally encouraged.' "

There was a dead silence on the other end of the line for a minute. Then Calliope, colder than ever, hissed, "You would do better to simply recopy and send a poem that you have already written. One that you created spontaneously, not under a royal command. One does not call upon a muse and order her to inspire. Inspiration does not come when one tries to force it. Do I make myself perfectly clear?"

The light bulb clicked on over her head. "Oh! So that's why I had that mental block! It was the pressure . . . you know, normally I can just sit down and churn out some funny little story or a nice poem with some good images, but this 'Fill up this paper' business just threw me!"

"Wonderful," said Calliope, unenthused. "And now if you'll excuse me—"

"Wait!" the girl shrieked. "What about Penn?!?"

Calliope snarled. "Tell Penn that creativity can't be forced," she snapped. Click.

Buzzzzzzzzzzzzzzzzzzzzzzzzzzzzzzzzzzzzzzzzzzzzzzz. . .

COMMENT:

Terrific! Organized confusion and a spoof on anyone not up on his mythology. The central figure asks, "Where do they get these names" only shortly after the reader asks the same question. There is something dreamlike about the essay. It's very clever. (TH)

Eric A. Maki
College: Brown University

High above the Earth in a starship from the Andromeda Galaxy, two aliens stand gazing out a viewport at the brilliant blue orb below. They are intergalactic scouts, sent from the planet Nerfon to gather information on this strange civilization recently discovered by Nerfonian astronomers. Zilbub, a high-ranking military officer, has the task of gauging the Earth's military strength. Zarkon, a Nerfonian anthropologist, has been assigned to gather all possible information concerning Earth's culture . . .

"Well, Zarkon, my duties are nearly completed. It has been quite an easy task to monitor the military activities of the Earth creatures from here. But your task intrigues me. Just how do you propose to gather information regarding this strange and primitive culture?"

"I have decided that the best way to do this will be to replace an entrant into an Earth 'university' with one of our robotic spy clones. This action will provide us with unlimited acsess to a huge storehouse of information without causing any undue alarm among the Earthmen. Hopefully, they will never notice the switch."

"Am I to assume that you have already found a suitable candidate for replacement?"

"Yes, Zilbub. He is called Eric Maki, and is an applicant to the institute of higher learning the Earthlings call 'Brown University.' "

"Ah, yes . . . 'Brown' . . . I have heard the name mentioned in Earthling transmissions. It would be quite an accomplishment to have one of our agents inside such a place. But are you sure this 'Eric Maki' will be admitted to Brown?"

"Well, Zilbub, we cannot be absolutely certain. The Earthlings who control the 'universities' employ other Earthlings, called 'admissions officers,' to determine such things. In my opinion, however, he seems a most promising candidate."

"Hmmm . . . what are the characteristics of this creature?"

"Physically, he is five and one-half Earth 'feet' tall. He will certainly never be a member of the association of giants the Earthlings call the 'National Basketball Association.' Fortunately, though, extreme height is not a requirement for entry into the place called 'Brown.' "

"Does the creature hold any position of importance among his fellow beings?"

"He is a leader among those of his age, holding a local position they call 'senior class president.' "

"Ah . . . a leader . . . he may be the kind of creature I can identify with . . . tell me, Zarkon—does he use his power to subjugate and conquer other Earthlings?"

"No, Zilbub, you misunderstand. His main function is to organize his fellow beings—'classmates,' to use the Earth term— in preparation for year-end ceremonies called 'the prom' and 'graduation.' He also serves as a representative of his 'class' in dealings with the older Earthlings known as 'school administrators.' He was elected to this position, rather than ready-grown in a test tube, as our leaders are back on Nerfon."

"This 'democratic process' by which they select their leaders is quite amusing to me. Besides, a leader without a military to enforce his decisions seems hopelessly powerless."

"Nevertheless, Zilbub, he is a representative of over one hundred fellow Earthmen. It is a position of great responsibility, even if he has no armies to command. He has, judging by many observations, performed his duties well."

"I am curious, Zarkon . . . as to how these Earth creatures select a leader such as this one; what qualities does this 'Eric Maki' possess which distinguish him from the others?"

"According to the data I have collected, he seems to be of above-average intelligence, doing well in his studies and on the 'Scholastic Aptitude Test,' a much-feared trial among the Earth creatures. Also, he seems to derive much satisfaction from helping his fellow 'students'—an activity I believe is called 'tutoring.' "

" 'Tutoring,' eh? The charity these creatures show toward each other disgusts me. Does he have any other notable characteristics?"

"Yes. The one that interested me the most is what they call a good 'sense of humor,' something quite unknown on our planet since ancient times. It seems that the ability to percieve things in a 'humorous' way and make other creatures 'laugh' is highly prized on the Earth. This ability enables one to make friends and generally put other Earthlings at ease."

"This . . . 'sense of humor,' did you say? seems a most illogical trait. We Nerfonians have advanced quite highly without such a thing. I suppose I should not let it bother me; there are many things about these Earthlings which defy understanding. Besides, you are the cultural expert; if you think we can gain a foothold in 'Brown University' through this 'Eric Maki,' we might as well try it. When shall we instruct the technicains back on Nerfon to begin the construction of an android to replace him?"

"I think it would be wise, Zilbub, to return home and wait awhile. The only possible hitch in my plan would be a 'rejection letter,' a notice to Eric Maki that he has been denied admission."

"And what if he is rejected, Zarkon, what then?"

"Obviously, my dear Zilbub, the next step would be to replace the Brown admissions staff with our androids. We would then be able to admit anyone we wanted. Think of it—we could admit a student body made up entirely of Nerfonian spy clones— what a glorious day that would be! But for the moment, we must be patient; the admissions decision will not be final for several Earth 'months.' "

"I am curious, Zarkon, as to what will become of the original Eric Maki after our android has replaced him?"

"I was contemplating depositing him in the interplanetary zoo on Nerfon. He has several other talents which might be interesting to visitors there. Spends much time attached to a thing called a 'saxophone,' creating weird and chilling sounds. He also rides a device called a 'bicycle' great distances at high velocities for no apparent reason. An exhibit like that could cause a larger sensation than the four-headed grooble from Dorcon IV. We could be two extremely rich Nerfonians for capturing such a one."

"You are shrewder than I had previously thought, Zarkon.

But as you say, we must wait until the 'month' of 'April.' Let us set a course for home."

"Yes, Zilbub. I long to breathe the sweet, fresh methane of our atmosphere again."

Their conversation ended, the two aliens move their craft out of orbit and back out into the inky blackness of space. . .

COMMENT:

Thumbs up for the high degree of creativity displayed here. This will surely grab and hold the attention of the earth creatures on the admissions committee. Eric is a talented writer, with a fine sense of humor, and many other positive things to offer his college. The downside is that most of the information about himself contained in the essay represents information found elsewhere—already—in Eric's application materials. We must applaud this original approach to answering the question— but should also caution against gimmickry for its own sake. There are a few spelling errors Eric should have spotted: "access," "perceive," "technician." (RJO)

William Meyerhofer
College: Harvard University

THE TRIAL

(As the lights slowly rise, a spot distinguishes the suspect alone in the middle of the stage. He is sitting in a rigid, uncomfortable-looking wooden chair. His ankle is handcuffed to a chair leg. High above him, behind a glass booth, such as is the kind used in recording studios, sit three shadowy figures, the judges. There is a great deal of clicking and scratching of the sort made by microphones when they are first turned on. Finally, there is a long, piercing cry of feedback, and a blowing on an overamplified microphone. Judge 1 has the voice of a bored clerk.)

Judge 1: Your name please?

The Suspect: What?

J1: Your name, please?

Suspect: Will Meyerhofer.

J1: Do you know why you're here?

S: Here?

J1: Being judged.

Judge 2: He's playing stupid.

Judge 3: Shhh!

J1: You have been accused of uselessness. How do you plead?

S: Plead?

J2: Really . . .

J3: Shhh!

J1: Please answer the following question in any way you can. Tell us about an extracurricular activity which is important to you and which you think will help us know you better.

S: Well, I write. And I . . .

J2: We've read your writing, Meyerhofer. It's pretty pitiful.

J3: (A *female voice, rather condescending*) Oh, yes, all the adjectives! Cliches galore . . .

J2: Shhh!

J1: Can you think of anything else?

S: (*thinking*) I play the bass . . .

J1: Anything useful?

S: Perhaps less than I'd thought.

J2: Suspect pleads guilty.

J1: We are going to run quickly over a list of your more glaring faults, Mr. Meyerhofer. Please stop us if anything should strike your particular interest. You talk too much. You don't know how to punctuate conversation. You like to sit with your sneakers on the wallpaper. You often forget to walk your dog. You never clean your contact lenses. You curse. You are arrogant, . . . let's see . . . you don't practice the piano . . .

S: Is this really necessary?

J3: We're only doing this for your own good.

S: Just tell me why I'm supposed to be useless.

J2: It's simple, you don't accomplish anything of use to the rest of the world.

J1: You wander around in a haze, Meyerhofer, paying no attention to anyone around you. What's your greatest ambition?

S: To go to Harvard.

J2: You're as good as lost, kid.

J3: Why don't you take up something useful? Like soccer, or student government?

J3: Or speaking Arabic, or Hindi?

J1: Or a varsity letter, or a piano competition.

J3: Make something of yourself. Perfect your character.

J2: Yes, make yourself perfect.

S: But no one is perfect. You couldn't find someone who does everything well.

J2: Of course we could.

J3: We do it all the time.

J1: Do you honestly think that everyone is as useless as yourself?

S: Well, I do believe that no one is perfect.

J2: If you insist, then we'll prove it to you. Call in the last witness.

J1: He's fairly average, but he'll do.

(*There is a short pause, then the witness walks onto the stage. He is every senior's nightmare, the perfect kid. He is immaculately dressed, down to the penny loafers and a wool tie. He sits comfortably beneath the judges.*)

J3: (*In a sickeningly sweet voice*) Good afternoon.

Witness: Hello, and how are you today?

J2: We're just fine. Anything we can get you?

W: No thank you, I'm fine, beautiful day.

J2: Yes, it is lovely.

J1: We called you here to tell us a little something about yourself.

W: Well, I'm terribly modest, but I'm at the top of my class in every subject.

J2: That's just wonderful.

W: I play varsity hockey, tennis, lacrosse, wrestling, cross-country, squash, handball, backgammon, and chess.

J3: That's good to hear.

W: I read Sanskrit fluently, and dance, and star in every

school play, and have bicycled across the country, and won the Tchaikovsky piano competition.

J1: Thank you, that's just grand. We'll see you later.

J2: Yes, bye-bye.

J3: Take care.

(*The witness leaves. There is a silence.*)

S: So that's the competition.

J1: What?

S: I'm a little discouraged, that's all.

J1: Cheer up, we'll make something of you yet. Here's the next question: What's your Social Security number?

S: I don't know. What is it?

J1: This is no time for games, Mr. Meyerhofer.

S: How could my Social Security number possibly have any relevance to this hearing? I object.

J2: Objection denied on the grounds that it may be a good Social Security number or a bad Social Security number. Read the school philosophy concerning such matters to the suspect, if you would.

J3: Ahem. In its effort to maintain a fair and comprehensive admissions policy, the court has found it appropriate to give equal consideration to both the applicant's classroom grades and the numbers, such as SAT scores, ACT scores, school CEEB numbers, Social Security numbers, birthdates, expected dates of graduation from the aforesaid institution, and dates of graduation of the parent or guardian of the accused, which have been assigned and considered appropriate by the institution of assignation. Is that quite clear?

S: Yes, I think so.

J2: You see, Mr. Meyerhofer, these numbers are the only standardized basis on which we can base our considerations. I don't like numbers either, when I dial 'O' on the telephone, I like to talk to a person, not a machine.

J3: Hear, hear.

J2: But these numbers simply must be considered.

J1: Very well put.

J3: Yes, perfectly concise and comprehendable.

J1: Now, what is the birthdate of your maternal grandmother?

Please give us the best date possible. We will discard the lowest date.

S: May 1, 1908.

J2: Thank you. Next question. Please describe how you expect to change during your four years in college.

(*Silence*)

J1: Well?

S: I don't know. I've never gone to college before.

J3: But surely you must know what you're in for.

J2: You must have seen what other people are like when they get out of college?

S: They just seem older, I guess. And they know more.

J2: This is ridiculous. Call in the other witness!

J1: I've never heard of such a thing. What is he going to college for, anyway? Employment?

(*The perfect kid reenters, with a Walkman around his head.*)

W: (*In a bored monotone*) I expect my four years in college to be years of profound personal and intellectual growth, a time when I will have the freedom and resources at my disposal to expand and broaden the scope of my vision of mankind.

J12: Oh, now that was lovely.

S: But what exactly did it all mean? What "scope of vision"?

J3: Please!

J2: If you cannot appreciate another's true superiority, you might as well be quiet.

J1: (*To the witness*) That was very nice. Do say hello to your father for me. He was a Yale man, wasn't he?

W: What?

J1: Well, I'm pretty sure of it. Bye now.

(*Witness leaves.*)

J2: Now, are you going to be helpful, or do we have to sit here all day?

S: (*Bitterly*) I will expand my horizons.

J3: Very good. Next:

J2: Tell us about a book which has changed you, which you have read in the last six weeks, and which was not a required-reading book. It must be between one hundred and fifty and four hundred pages, written between 1830 and 1952, and well known to our admissions staff.

J3: May we suggest *The Catcher in the Rye.*

J2: Or Shakespeare's *Faust.*

J3: Or *Spanish Lace*, by Joyce Dingwell.

S: Well, I remember *Remembrance of Thing Past*, by Proust.

J1: Too long.

S: I read *The Magic Mountain*, by Thomas Mann.

J3: Never heard of it.

S: I read *Crime and Punishment.*

J2: What's that?

S: *Crime and Punishment.*

J1: Isn't that that Russian thing?

J3: I know I've heard of it.

J2: Probably just obscure. Book accepted. Now then, Mr. Meyerhofer, are you applying for very early admission, fairly early admission, earlier than most admission, regular admission, late admission, blueberry admission, guava admission, rectilinear admission, rolling admissions, bouncing admissions, or large green admissions with fur on their teeth?

S: The former, I think.

J2: Excellent choice. You must have your application in by yesterday afternoon.

S: That doesn't give me much time.

J1: We're just trying to treat you like an adult, Mr. Meyerhofer.

J3: The real world isn't a bed of roses, I can tell you that.

S: I'll do my best.

J2: Now for the part of the application process which we are personally very proud of, the personal statement.

J1: Yes, this is the brand-new part of the process which lends us the important final insights into your character which are so vital to a cooperative and successful admissions experience.

(*During the end of the play, perfect students, like the witness, appropriately dressed, are lining up behind the suspect, their dark forms visible, like Macbeth's line of kings.*)

J3: We are very proud of the courage it took to grant our applicants this portion of the application to be creative, personal, and irrelevant.

J2: Mr. Meyerhofer, describe for us, in as many words as you wish, in as personal a way as is possible, the relevance of new-triassic polymers in the reproductive cycle of plasmids.

S: The what!?

J1: I told you that it wouldn't work.

J3: Blasted liberals, what more could we do for these brats. Ungrateful termites!

S: What am I supposed to do with a topic like that?

J1: I think it's perfectly clear.

J2: Write, pig!!!

J1: We couldn't have made it clearer.

J3: Do you think we enjoy our jobs? Do you think we enjoy reading your stupid essays? I drink ten cups of coffee a day just to get through this boring job, and I need a bottle of Valium to get to sleep at night.

J1: You don't have to sit and study adolescents all day for a living. You don't have to read this junk all day. You have to understand her feelings.

J2: He'll never understand what he's done, that his generation is singlehandedly destroying all that mankind has worked so hard for. Just go away, you vicious child.

S: But I'm handcuffed to this chair, I can't go away.

(*The line of perfect students marches slowly toward him, their arms outstretched, ready to kill.*)

Total silence.

(*The lights in the glass booth go out, and the suspect stands alone in a slowly shrinking spotlight. He turns to the audience with a look of complete despair, and the spot blacks out.*)

Curtain

COMMENT:

What is impressive about the essay is not the theme, which is rather pedestrian, but the form. The writer is clearly and admirably in control of his medium. (TH)

Arun Ramanathan
College: Haverford

Mental Block is a nasty old hermit who lives in the gullies and ravines of my mind. He makes a living by slinging nets across my neural canals and catches my thoughts as they swim toward the great spawning grounds where writing is born. M.B. always waits until his nets are full to the point of bursting before he drags them up. Like any experienced fisherman, he saves only the big, healthy, mature thoughts and throws juvenile or diseased thoughts back into the canals to mature or die. Those thoughts he saves, he either eats immediately or freezes and sets aside for use when my stream of creativity slows.

Up until three weeks ago, I had always ignored M.B.; his paltry catch consisted of only a small fraction of my thoughts. Lately, however, with college essays to write, M.B. has become an increasingly irritating problem. Many of my best thoughts begin their journey through my mind only to be poached and eaten before they can breed and create others like them.

So, with college deadlines looming, I set off in search of the old hermit, determined to somehow halt his activities, if only temporarily. Finding him was no problem. The recent flood of thoughts accompanying my latest attempts at creativity had so fattened him that he was uninclined to move about. Instead, he sat in the center of my mind at the junction of a number of important canals, wielding his net with practiced expertise. M.B. pulled in one load after another, emptying them from his nets in a flopping, jumbled tangle.

He frowned when he saw me approaching and shifted to face me, his motion scattering the skeletons of countless thoughts. I picked my way toward him, through heaps of such skeletons, stopping at the base of a particularly large one upon which M.B. was seated. "What cha want?" he snapped, peering down at me over his massive, bloated waistline. Before I could reply, he angrily muttered, "C'mon ya gotta want somethin'; you ain't one ta come visitin' fer no reason."

"I want to make a deal," I replied.

"A deal, with me, how nice of ya, now what kinda deal were ya thinkin' of makin', my boy?" he said, his lips curling into a sneer.

"I want you to stop stealing my thoughts until after college deadlines . . ."

"And if I should do this?" he interjected.

"I'll do whatever you want."

"Well, my boy, let me tell you." He paused, shifting into a more comfortable posture. "I'll make this deal with ya if ye'll do me two things."

"What two things?" I asked, dreading his answer.

M.B. picked up a bone and began to wave it at me in schoolteacher fashion. "You know, my boy, I've been doin' this job fer sometime now, seventeen years at last count, and over this time yer thoughts have been gettin' progressively better. Over these last four years, boy, not only has the fishin' improved, but yer thoughts have been bigger, healthier, and more mature."

"So what are the two things?" I questioned, irritated.

He ignored me. "Especially when ya tried ta write poetry last year, my, that was some good fishin'; and that term paper, 'Richard III and The Prince: the Villain and the Pragmatist,' whooo whee, that was some good eatin.' "

"No wonder I could never write poetry or organize that stupid paper," I muttered under my breath.

"Well, gettin' back to my point, I'll stop my fishin'—fer the time bein'—if ye'll apply to Haverford and take liberal arts if ya get in."

"What??!!"

"See boy, the thing is; if ya get into Haverford, I figure ye'll have so many term papers and suff ta write that I'll be feastin' regular fer more'n four years."

"But what about the liberal arts?"

"Well, boy, in my many years at this fishin', I've caught yer liberal arts thoughts and I've caught yer science and math thoughts, and, when ya get right down to it, yer liberal arts thoughts are just much tastier. They're so much more natural and healthy. Them science and math thoughts just taste so processed and mechanical. It's like the difference between filet mignon and Spam; see?"

"Yeh, I do," I replied. "You got a deal."

M.B. held out his great, pudgy hand, which I grabbed and

shook. "Ye'll know when I'm back in business," he said, giving me a wink.

"And by the way," he shouted, as I walked away. "You better get into Haverford; I ain't starvin' fer nothin'."

━━━━━━━━━━━━━━━━━━━━━━━━━━━━━━━━━━━━

Julie J. Rim
College: Harvard University

Television is the next best thing to being there. I'm watching the fifth game of the World Series—New York Mets versus Boston Red Sox. Let's go Mets!

Full count on Ray Knight. Strawberry on second. Two runs in. Line drive to left field. Strawberry comes home. Conference on the mound.

Baseball's a mental game. Watching the game, keeping my eyes glued to the screen and away from the unwritten college essay glaring at me, I can see an elaborate analogy between baseball and college admissions.

The important thing to note is the ratio of offense (1) to defense (9). The only help the offense has are coaches who aren't really in the game anyway. The defense is, of course, the admissions boards. The offense is . . . me.

Like both teams, I've been working for this time since the beginning of the season. My season has lasted twelve years. I started at five years old. Reaching this point in my career is a goal in itself. Both teams are already their individual league champions.

I have several chances. I can apply to as many schools as I wish. Deadlines limit my time up to bat. I can get balls (acceptances from safety schools) and strikes (rejections from safety schools). In the game I am playing, there are no walks, no free bases. I may even get a hit ("yo-o-ou're in there!") or a strike-out ("yo-o-ou're outta there!").

The ball flies toward me at 100 mph. I have a split second to decide: Do I hit it? I have to; I have to take every chance that comes. How hard do I hit it? To what part of the field? What is the defense expecting?

It was a ball. A strike would really have hurt my morale at this point in the game. The catcher sends signals I can't see to the pitcher. I feel terribly alone.

The count jumps to three-two. The crowd of family and friends grows hushed. The PA system falls silent. The pitcher winds up, the bat goes back . . .

(At this point, the reader may choose an ending. The writer suggests choice B.)

Choice A! And I swing. Whoosh. And nothing. Nada. Rien. I missed. The pitcher jumps up and down, falling to his knees on the mound. The defensive dugout clears. A human pileup forms on the field.

I am left all alone. Maybe I can go abroad for a year, try again. The disappointed fans have gone home. The coaches are closed in their offices. I shower and get dressed. There are no pleas for autographs, no requests for interviews. The empty locker room—

(At this point, the writer breaks off. This is getting too depressing. Go to B.)

Choice B Crack! The bat shatters. I can feel my success. I jog toward first, watching the ball head for the stars. It's outta here!

The crowd goes wild. Ju-lie! Ju-lie! Ju-lie!

I round third, high-five with the coach. My teammates surround me. They know how I felt all along. I was never really alone.

"So, Julie, you did it! What are your thoughts right now?"

"Well, Bob, I have to tell you. It feels great. I'm sorry that anyone had to lose—" a champagne cork explodes "—but . . . well, I'd like to thank my mom and dad and sister . . ."

COMMENTS:

Julie's achievement is impressive. Her style is lively and engaging. Her metaphor has an urgent but perfectly acceptable message, given the facts of college entrance. The reader learns several things to Julie's credit: She can write vividly and well, she has a fine sense of humor, and she's unabashedly ambitious. Well done! (SAB)

This is excellent. It is written well and it's different. Using the analogy between baseball and the admissions process is sure to catch the interest (or at least the attention) of the sleepiest of admissions officers reading those hundreds of essays! (BPS)

Karen Steinig
College: Brown University

Through the wee hours of the morning, during the time between *Late Night with David Letterman* and reruns of *Ben Casey*, I stayed awake, sitting on the carpet and gnawing my pencil. Sane people were sleeping. Yet here I was alone in my room with the television droning in the background, agonizing over "this opportunity to tell us about anything you think we should know." After yet another sales pitch for imported bamboo steamers (just $19.95), something on the TV screen caught my eye. Lights flashed, bells rang, and then . . .

"Hey there, ladies and gentlemen, and welcome to . . . THE ADMISSIONS GAME! You all know the rules: There are none! Our players will be competing for a chance at the Grand Prize: a four-year trip to . . . Providence, Rhode Island!"

"Oooooh . . ." sighed the studio audience. "Aaaaah . . ."

The host continued. "Here are today's players. Why don't you introduce yourselves, kids?"

The three teenagers glanced about nervously. "Ah'm Becky Sue Smith," drawled Player #1.

"I'm Joe Jock," mumbled Player #2.

"And I'm Karen Steinig," said Player #3.

The host went on. "We've got a great mix of opponents here. Let's get under way. First question. Be careful, it's a tricky one: Where do you live?" Player #1 slammed the buzzer. "Yes, Becky Sue?"

"Ah'm from Vandervoort, Arkansas," squealed Player #1 with a knowing grin.

"Good answer! Good answer!" cried the audience.

"All right!" shouted the host. "Ten points to Player #1 for Geographical Diversity! Don't feel bad about not getting to the button first, Karen; Long Island is the wrong answer anyway. Next question: How do you spend your free time?"

This time Player #2 was the first to the buzzer. "I play football," he rumbled. The alumni in the audience stood up, cheered, and threw $20 bills like confetti.

"Excellent!" exclaimed the host. "Ten Endowment Points for Joe Jock! Don't feel bad about not getting to the button first, Karen; badminton is the wrong answer anyway. Well, things are really sizzling here, but Karen seems to be at a bit of a disadvantage. Let's see how she does with question number three. Everyone ready? Okay. Why do you want to attend Brown University? Yes! Player #1, Becky Sue Smith."

"Ah'd like to take all thirty-two courses S/NC." BZZZZ!

"Spare me," groaned the host. "Let's hope for a little more depth from Player #2, Joe Jock."

"Uh, well," he stumbled, sweating beneath his shoulder pads, "I hear those Ivy League women are pretty hot." BZZZZ!

"Not quite what we were looking for. How about you, Karen?" Player #3 cleared her throat and stood up straight. She knew her answer to this one. "I want to be part of Brown University," she began, "because I'm more motivated, more disciplined, when I have the freedom to chose not to be. You see, I am—"

"Thank you, Karen," said the host. "That's just fine. And now, a few words from our—"

"Excuse me, but I'm not finished. As I was saying, I am my own harshest critic; therefore, my biggest challenges are the ones that I alone seek to create, not the ones that are imposed upon me by outside sources. Paradoxically, I'd be roused to take a wide variety of courses at Brown because there are no distribution requirements. Brown would trust me to make responsible choices about my education, and when I'm treated as an adult, I become one."

The crowd roared, whistles blew, balloons fell from the sky. "Well, folks," yelled the host, "it seem as if only Karen Steinig will move on to the big bonus round and try for that Grand Prize . . . four years in Providence (a metaphor if ever I heard one). But we won't let our losers go away empty-handed. For

Becky Sue and Joe Jock, a very nice consolation prize . . . six months' training at Wilfred Beauty Academy! And we'll be right back after these messages."

During this commercial break I went down to the kitchen for a fourth cup of coffee, cursing myself for vegetating in front of a TV game show when I should have been working on my application. November 15 was quickly approaching, and still I had no essay. My little sister's advice made it seem so easy: "Just write something that tells them you're smart, creative, spirited, artistic, and funny." Sure, but how. Frustrated and bleary-eyed, I trudged upstairs.

When I entered my room, I was greeted by the final strains of the national anthem. Apparently I missed the final bonus rounds of that game, so I don't know how it all turned out. To tell you the truth, I'm sort of curious. If you happen to have been up late that night and you saw some unusual programming coming across the airwaves, tell me what went on. Did Player #3 win the Grand Prize trip to Providence, or did she wind up with the dining room furniture and a year's supply of Turtle Wax? Let me know around mid-December, okay? Thanks.

COMMENT:

Nice. Tight, introductory paragraph that sets the mood but doesn't belabor it. The game show section is creatively done, not too involved, and filled with appropriate and funny phrases that have been borrowed from real game shows. The game show format ties into the admissions process, but the writer does not force the connection too far. On the other hand, the writer is clearly writing the essay for Brown, and s/he cleverly, using Karen (contestant #3), presents her rather full understanding of Brown's academic program and the kind of student who will benefit most from it, despite the potentially awkward context. This writer has an excellent ear for dialogue and a very mature sense of what will succeed in being humorous. (AST)

Kristin Ward
College: Dartmouth College

I would like to explain to you how it all happened. The day I took my SATs started out as a perfectly normal January day in New Hampshire. I woke up with icicles hanging off my ears. I swung my feet onto my bedroom floor, which was as warm as a polar ice cap, and then I slunk down to breakfast, harboring the bitter realization that every step I took brought me farther away from the comfort of my pillow and quilt.

As I sat at the kitchen table, I wished that I could discreetly dive into my mug of hot chocolate to combat the frostbite which I had contracted on the way downstairs.

Merely a red blur of scarf, hat, and mittens against the thick white snow, I trudged down the driveway to my car.

I was halfway to Concord, the testing site, when, all of a sudden, I came upon the mind-boggling scene. I coaxed my eyes back in to their sockets and hit the brakes. Less than ten feet away from my Volkswagen, there were three aqua creatures, shaped like gigantic mushrooms with arms and legs. They were seated in the middle of the road and they seemed to be meditating.

My wits were still scattered all over the car when one of the three creatures, having noticed my presence, came over to address me.

The creature raised his arm in what seemed to be a harmless greeting, and began to speak: "I am Sug. I am on a mission from a distant star. One of the masters of our species has died . . ."

"My condolences," I interrupted weakly.

"Thank you," the creature continued. "We have decided to start a new tradition in our culture. We observed it on your planet. I am referring to the custom of engraved tombstones. My associates (he paused and gestured to the two meditating mushrooms) and I stopped at a gas station and we were told to come to New Hampshire, 'the Granite State,' to get a slab for our master's tombstone. So here we are. Can you please assist us?"

Several maxims surfaced in my mind: Don't talk to strangers (especially ones who resemble mushrooms); be hospitable to guests (especially foreigners); be on time for tests (especially SATs).

I glanced at my watch nervously. If I did not get to the test center in ten minutes, I would be late. The creature was leaning on my car, waiting for an answer.

"I'm very sorry," I said. "I would like to help you, but I am taking my SATs today and I can't be late."

The creature looked puzzled. "SATs?," he asked, tilting his head inquisitively.

"They're hard to explain," I said, "and I really must be going."

Sug scratched his head thoughtfully. "No, I'm sorry," he said. "You will have to help us *now*. We must get back to our people soon. They are anxiously awaiting our return. As soon as you have helped us, you can go to your SATs."

I considered my alternatives: I could try to make a break for it and be pummeled by three extraterrestrial beings in search of a tombstone, or I could help them with their mission and then pray that I would be admitted to the testing center a little late.

I noticed that Sug's two associates were now up and walking toward my car, so I quickly decided to go with the latter option.

"I'm not sure, right offhand, where we can get a slab of granite," I said. "I'll have to go back to my house to get a phone book. I am sure there will be a listing in the Yellow Pages."

It was fortunate that the creatures had some invisible flying mechanism, because it was quite obvious that they would not fit into my car. Constantly glancing at my watch, I drove back to my house. To spare my family the shock I had experienced, I politely asked the creatures to wait outside while I consulted the Yellow Pages.

"All right, I've found a place," I said, feigning enthusiasm. "It's about twenty minutes from here."

They flew alongside the car as I drove to the quarry. (You can imagine the stares!)

The man at the quarry was very helpful—even if he was in shock. The creatures were very satisfied with the tombstone, which they had engraved on the premises, and then tied onto

Sug's back for the journey home. Before leaving, they thanked me profusely.

"Thank you so much," Sug said. "Our people will be forever grateful. And good luck on your SATs."

My face turned white as a sheet. I had forgotten all about them. I looked at my watch. The tests would be almost over by now.

I arrived at the testing center in an absolute panic. I tried to tell my story, but my sentences and descriptive gestures got so confused that I communicated nothing more than a very convincing version of a human tornado. In an effort to curb my distracting explanation, the proctor led me to an empty seat and put a test booklet in front of me. He looked doubtfully from me to the clock, and then he walked away.

I tried desperately to make up for lost time, scrambling madly through analogies and sentence completions.

"Fifteen minutes remain," the voice of doom declared from the front of the classroom.

Algebraic equations, arithmetic calculations, geometric diagrams swam before my eyes.

"Time! Pencils down, please."

"Thanks a lot, Sug," I thought, when I saw my math score six weeks later.

Naturally, I attributed the disastrous 480 to him. He had been in a difficult situation, of course, with his people depending on him and all, so I decided, in my mind, to forgive him. I felt a little less gracious, however, when I was halfway to the SAT testing center in June, and there he was *again*, an oversized blue mushroom in the middle of the road. . .

ESSAYS ON COMING TO AMERICA

Anonymous
College: Princeton University

I think I began to grow up that winter night when my parents and I were returning from my aunt's house, and my mother said that we might soon be leaving Leningrad to go to America. We were in the Metro then. I was crying, and some people in the car were turning around to look at me. I remember that I could not bear the thought of never hearing again the radio program for schoolchildren to which I listened every morning before going to school.

I do not remember myself crying for this reason again. In fact, I think I cried very little when I was saying goodbye to my friends, relatives, and even to my father. When we were leaving I thought about all the places I was going to see—the strange and magical countries I had known only from adventure books and pictures in the world atlas; I even learned the names of the fifty states because their sound was so beautifully foreign and mysterious. The country I was leaving never to come back was hardly in my head then.

The four years that followed taught me the importance of optimism, but the notion did not come at once. For the first two years in New York I was really lost—coming from a school in Leningrad to a Brooklyn yeshiva, and then to Chapin, I did not quite know what I was or what I should be. Mother remarried, and things became even more complicated for me. Some time passed before my stepfather and I got used to each other. I was often upset, and saw no end to "the hard times."

My responsibilities in the family increased dramatically since I knew English better than everyone else at home. I wrote letters, filled out forms, translated at interviews with Immigration and Social Security officers, took my grandparents to the doctor and translated there, and even discussed telephone and utilities bills with company representatives. I spent a lot of time at my grandparents' house, and eventually moved in with them.

As a result of my experiences I have learned one very important rule: Ninety-nine percent of all common troubles eventually go away! Something good is bound to happen in the end when you do not give up, and just wait a little!! Of course, troubles need help in getting out of our lives, but I do not mind putting in a little work. For some reason I believe that my life will turn out all right, even though it will not be very easy.

America gave us freedom and independence. It also made us assume the responsibility for ourselves. Nobody can ruin my life unless I let it be ruined. We create our own happiness. It is up to us to use our freedom with responsibility.

When I was twelve I read a book about a girl growing up in tzarist Russia. Her grandfather once told her, "Life is like a zebra. There are whites, and black stripes on it. When you are on a white stripe walk slowly, enjoy it. When you come to a black stripe raise you collar, shut your eyes, and run as fast as you can go to get to a white one. But, remember, there is always a white stripe after a black one!"

COMMENT:

The opening is very powerful because it grabs the reader and creates suspense. She also talks about difficulties without any self-pity or a self-congratulatory attitude. The anecdote at the end is very good too; it ties the essay together. (PT)

Tami Nassiri
College: University of Washington

MY IRAN

I will never forget the greeting that my family received when we arrived in Iran in the spring of 1972. My father, Iranian by birth, took my mother, a native Washingtonian, my two brothers and me, aged two, four, and five respectively, to live in Teheran where he had just accepted employment. Showers of hugs and kisses descended upon us from relatives whom I had never met. Much laughter mingled with tears for my father's joyous return home with a wife and family whom most of his family had never met. It seemed as if thousands of voices were talking all at once to my five-year-old self in a language I could not understand. Frightened by the noise and anxious about the strangeness of the trip and our boisterous reception, I immediately wanted to leave. I tried hard to control my tears. Little did I realize that eight years later I would shed more tears as I left the place which had become my home. I grew to love Iran, its people and its customs, and I now consider it to be my spiritual home.

No, the most significant experience in my life has not been a single event, but those formative years between ages five and thirteen which I spent with my family in Teheran. Not for me were there elementary school years spent in an American grammar school. I attended a British school where the languages were English and Farsi, and I grew proficient in British English as fast as I acquired Farsi. Tacoma and the Puget Sound were forgotten as I roamed native markets and tasted camel's cheese. Memories of a home on a tree-lined city street faded as we came to live in a company compound of giant houses, swimming pools, and tennis courts. In Teheran I was exposed to a lifestyle dramatically different from mine in the United States. Iran is a country of people whose religion and traditions guide them through every aspect of their lives, whose lives center around the family, and for whom happiness does not depend upon material possessions. As I grew comfortable in that Middle Eastern city, I came to accept and to appreciate a people who practiced their Islamic faith with their every gesture of kindness and generosity. My Iran is not that of a deposed Shah, a despotic Ayatollah Khomeni, or of hostages, American or otherwise; my Iran is a people who give of their time, their belongings, their hospitality, and of themselves.

During our time in Iran, we spent a great deal of time with our relatives and friends. We may have lived for a time as a company family, but we went out into the streets, into the villages, and into the countryside. There religious faith creates an atmosphere in which material possessions have little emphasis. The people do the best with what they have. We visited tiny hamlets filled with miniature houses no larger than an average-sized American bedroom and whose inhabitants washed their dishes in the rivers that flowed just outside their front doors. We watched nomads on the outskirts of the town who owned not much more than a camel and a small knapsack of belongings. When we talked to these people, we found their lives to be full of jokes and laughter. Through knowing the Iranians I have grown to be thankful for what my life holds, but I do not pity the people of Iran because I saw their expressions of happiness for the blessings they found in their lives.

The family unit forms a significant part of Iranian life, perhaps because there are so few material possessions for most of them. Through my relatives, I experienced overwhelming affection, true caring, and unceasing generosity. Although their houses were small and their work burdensome, there was always time to prepare enormous meals and the space to make all their relatives comfortable. To them nothing was more important than being surrounded by the people they loved and who loved them. Because of my youth in Iran, as a young woman about to leave home to go to college I can now appreciate the support system with which my family has provided me. They have given me confidence and stability; I have learned to cherish their presence and the love that they have always given me. Iran taught me to be thankful for what I am, and not for what I have. That joyful and fatalistic acceptance of whatever life holds which I found in Iran has shaped me into the person I am today. The Iranian people, their unqualified and unselfish generosity, their optimism, and their joy for life will always remain a part of me. I will never forget my eight years in my father's country, which will always be mine as well.

COMMENT:

The writer shows unashamed honesty. It is a touch verbose, but generally colorful and interesting. It instructs the reader while revealing values that she has thought about. (JMcC)

Thai Pham
College: Brown University

Uproot a tree and replant it. Chances are very high that the tree will have difficulty surviving. If you do the equivalent to a human, the poor person will have the same problem. Yet he could usually overcome it. Though this may have some physiological implications, it is also a matter of will. A person fights both physically and mentally. He never gives up, because by doing so he renounces all chances of a victory. In my case, leaving Vietnam and coming to the U.S. is the equivalence of being uprooted and replanted some place else. In the course of this painful change, I learned that the secret to successfully achieving a goal is tenacity.

At the beginning of my journey, I observed and admired the tenacious quality in my parents. All I could remember in the early stages of our escape is that occasionally I was taken out of the city, only to return the next day. Later, I learned that those were the unsuccessful attempts to escape from communism. Eleven times my family tried; eleven times we were swindled. Eleven times we risked imprisonment, yet eleven times we were lucky. Our family resources were being exhausted at an astonishing rate. Family heirlooms were exchanged for the hope of freedom. The next time could have been the last, but we did not quit. We invested everything in the twelfth attempt. Looking back, I realize that it would have been so easy to quit during any step of the way. Repeated failures could have discouraged us, but we kept on trying. Finally, we were lucky. The people were honest. We thought that we had succeeded.

However, a great ocean still separated us from freedom. Storms with towering waves tossed our small boat about indifferently. A well-equipped vessel would have had problems dealing with such a storm; but we had only a high school world map and Boy Scout compass as navigation tools. Later, even these were taken by pirates. Our food and water supplies became practically nonexistent in the last few days of our journey. Getting lost at sea did not do much for morale. Nevertheless, we held onto our goal though it would have been easier to resign our fate to the currents. With determination, we conquered the elements, and arrived safely at the refugee camp.

When we reached the U.S., new problems surfaced. I had dealt with thirst and hunger on the boat, but humiliation requires an extra something. I entered the third grade with practically no understanding of the English language. At school, I was not well received. The other students looked down at me because of my inability to speak English well. I can still remember the times in spelling class when the teacher went down the list: "Who has one wrong? . . . Two wrong? . . . Thirty wrong . . ." I would always be the last to raise my hand, and the only one to receive zeros on these assignments. Instead of giving up, I became more determined to conquer my problems, both in and out of the classroom.

By the second semester, my hard work was paying off. On the playground, I was making new friends. In the classroom, I was making new friends. The door was finally opened for me, but it took a lot of effort. There were times that I wanted to stay home, times that I did not want to face another day of humiliation, and times that I wished we were back in Vietnam. But I remembered my parents' example: They did not quit when the situation seemed hopeless. My journey to the U.S. has taught me a valuable lesson: "Winners never quit, and quitters never win." I have applied this lesson to solve my problems in adapting to a new environment, and I expect this attitude to help me overcome those problems I may encounter in the future.

COMMENT:

The impact of this essay comes more from the reader's realization of what the writer has experienced than from the "telling of the tale" or the writing. No matter, the impact is a very strong one, and the opening analogy, comparing the uprooting of a person with the uprooting of a tree, is a very powerful image, which sticks with the reader throughout. The rest of the essay conveys, in a poignant way, just how significant a part the values of family, determination, hope, and courage have *already* played in the life of this young person. One can only imagine what a wonderful adult s/he will become. (AST)

<hr>

Nguyen Dong Quan
College: Yale University

It is given to only few candidates to have their talents earn quickly for them the admittances. The others, with their academic records, still succeed in convincing their institutions of their abilities. Myself, I have nothing more than my hard works and a wish of your understanding.

I have nothing to be proud of except the ordeals which I have gained in my survival through what the Americans call "the imaginary world" of George Orwell. His predicted nightmares in 1984 had come to me in reality nine years earlier. I had seen myself the epitaph of the twentieth century since April 30, 1975, after South Vietnam fell in the hands of the Communists.

That year, when I was barely nine years old, my father was exiled to concentration camps. We were then "advised" to give up our home and to come out of the city. In that year, I learned the first lessons of enduring in order to live. Going to school had later become a dream for me and for my other three brothers. Because of our "parents' sins," serving the old army as a medical doctor and working for the former government as a lawyer, the revengeful Communists had never stopped preventing us from getting an education. No matter how talented and diligent a student may be, if his parents are "nguy," the term used by the Communists to classify people who worked for the old government, he would have no chance to get into any university. For him, there remains only one route after he finishes high school: to enlist in the blood-thirsty army. During the following hopeless years, I had grown up and fought for living without the love, the protection, and the guidance of a father. With my broken family, I had managed to pass through all obstacles and suffered every atrocity from the Communists. Our home was regularly searched by the police; they thought that we still hid our fortunes somewhere even though they had already "borrowed" almost all our properties. My mother did not have to go to concentration camps, but she could not find a permanent job because she was a "criminal." If there were no help coming from our relatives, we could not have survived through all those years.

Fortunately, I was able to see back my father in the spring of 1978. Our last impulse of love was not smashed yet. Few months after the reunion, I shared with my family the risk of life: We decided to escape. During that period, the Vietnamese originated from China who wanted to flee from Vietnam could leave "semi-official" if they could pay a certain amount of money. The true Vietnameses, on the other hand, had no such privilege. Their escape had to be a secret or their lives would end in prison. After three years of enduring within the Communist hells, my father was terrified thinking if he would ever be caught again. Yet, he continuously looked for a way to escape because of the futures of his sons. Fortunately, God had granted us His mercy at the last minute: Some of my father's old Chinese patients produced for us fake Chinese identities and took us along with them. They wanted to have a doctor with them and my father happened to be the right one.

The "Mayflower" which carried 365 of us to the free land was a small 18-meter boat, a ragged craft with an antiquated engine. We were the only Vietnamese family aboard. Although my father had cut his hair, my brothers had taken off their glasses (we tried to look like Chinese as much as possible!), we were still horrified when two middle-aged soldiers walked back and forth along the aisle of the boat, checking each passenger for the last time before we took off from the Soc Trang, an harbor in South Vietnam. Our hearts were striking 200 beats per minute. The men could have identified us at any moment and asked us to get off. I used to wonder what would our lives be like then.

After five days and four nights struggling with hurricanes, starvation, and thirstiness, and the Pacific Ocean itself, we landed in an isle in southern Malaysia: Pulau Bidong. Never-theless, we were probably among the luckiest boat people who could ever touch land for the second time. It took us less than a week to reach Malaysia while other boats may spend one or two months in the sea. Only an old man and a young girl did not have the fortune to enjoy again freedom although their deaths came on the last night of the journey. Leaving in October, a storm month for the sea, had saved us from meeting any Thai pirates, which could lead to more tragedy. In the 50,000-inhabited island, we had lived "the miserable and inconvenient life of Robinson Crusoe" for seven months before we were granted the permission to choose the United States as our political asylum.

In the summer of 1979, we arrived in the New World with nothing but our souls. The land did not seem to be much different from ours, but we all know that it has the ONE that our does not: the freedom. Yet, America has given us more than what we have sacrificed for: "the freedom to be discriminated." In this new land, I have found out the true value of "boat people." When I went to school, I was thought as a retarded boy, but I was treated as a scornful yellow refugee. The instruc-tors, the students, all seemed to despise me. Every day, going to lunch was like a punishment. I sat quietly and tried not to look at anyone; yet, they did not leave me alone. They looked at me in disgust, talked to the friends in a language that I had not yet mastered, and all started to laugh. It hurt.

Depressions after depressions, at last, time has permitted me to earn the love from my teachers and the reputation among my friends. When I received my first award, in an American high school, I had back my confidence. I am as intelligent as anyone else, but I am better because I work harder. Eventually, I found almost no challenge left at my hometown high school. This was when my father decided to send me to a demanding private school; he wants me to always work as hard as I could. At Exeter, the challenge is tough, but I have prepared for it; the courses are hard, the teachers expect a lot more from the students, but I do not think that it is impossible to get an "A."

I believe that at Yale University, I can build up the strong, permanent base for my future. The admittance to Yale is still my dream, but I understand that the success or failure of my life is depending on it. I feel sad that I have not had enough opportunities to prove my true ability. All I wish to have now is your understanding.

COMMENT:

The writer earns not only my understanding but total interest in what he expresses, and true admiration. Simply put, this is just a great story! The obvious difficulties with the language make for occasionally awkward moments in reading the essay, but do not stand in the way of the message. The writer shares his life with us; we get the sense that no other Yale applicant (or very few, at least) could have written this; it sets the candidate apart as a tremendously unique applicant. There is real passion here, as well; the irony contained in the quoted phrases (e.g., "parents' sins," "borrowed" property) is especially effective. I also like the almost poetic touch of a phrase such as "Our hearts were striking 200 beats per minute," when the writer could have stated simply, "We were scared." He effectively draws the reader into his/her thoughts, emotions, reflections, and personal history. Very well done; I'd feel compelled to make this candidate's "dream" a reality. (RJO)

DRAWINGS
AND CARTOONS

Paul K. Min
College: Yale University

PART III ...COMMUNICATION

COMMUNICATION IS IMPORTANT. JUST IMAGINE "MY DINNER WITH ANDRÉ" WITHOUT IT AND YOU'LL SEE MY POINT.

PRINTED FOR THE HEARING IMPAIRED

MANY MODES OF COMMUNICATION EXIST. THE ORAL ORIFICE IS OFTEN USED. MUSIC, AS WELL AS BOOKS ARE OTHER BIGGIES. LARGE, BLUNT OBJECTS ARE ALSO USED, OFTEN TO EXPRESS EMOTION.

CARTOONING IS YET ANOTHER MODE, AND THE BEST AT THAT. OH, YOU DOUBT MY WORDS? WHO GETS MORE READERS, MALRAUX OR GARRY TRUDEAU? SEE ANY "KILLING FIELDS" CALENDARS NEXT TO THE "FAR SIDE" ONES? NEED I CONTINUE?

CARTOONING ALLOWS ME TO COMMUNICATE WHAT MERE WORDS CANNOT... ...FOR EXAMPLE —

MAKING FUN OF PHYSICS TEACHERS WHO HAVE COMPRESSED MANKIND'S EXISTENCE INTO THREE MATHEMATICAL EQUATIONS, THESE SAME FOLK WHO WEAR STRANGE BELT BUCKLES.

THE WORLD IS SHAPED LIKE MY HEAD. I PROVED IT.

...PET

BUT DO YOU KNOW WHAT I LOVE THE MOST ABOUT CARTOONS? I MEAN ASIDE FROM THE ESCAPISM, FIAT AND COMMUNICATION VALUE?

...THE THING I LOVE THE MOST IS —

THE COMPANY!

WAIT UP, GARFIELD, I'LL GO WITH YOU.

OH MY... THIS IS THE END!

MOM! DAD! PJ! WHERE IS EVERYBODY?

OH... A BED... A BED...

EASY, ZONK...

SUCH TALL FOLK!

GOOD GRIEF! I'M IN THE WRONG CARTOON!

WELL— IT'S HARDLY TRUDEAU.

COMMENTS:

A very creative, attention-getting yet risky approach to the essay question. It reveals a witty, imaginative, and daring personality. The cartoon essay appears a bit disjointed at times. The cartoons help to mask the occasional lack of creativity. (TG)

How can the reader not be impressed with Paul's talent, imagination, and willingness to take a risk? So many students feel bound by words and an 8½" x 11" page—not Paul, who clearly reveals his personality through cartoons. (JWM)

Zoe Mulford
College: Harvard University

THERE ARE COMPLICATIONS, OF COURSE.

A CASE STUDY: ZOE'S MUSICAL EDUCATION

DO LA SO... SOL LA SI DO MI RE...

← BY EAR
two ways to make music
SOLFÈGE →

1) **Improvisation** — what sounds good?
2) **Repetition & Mutation** — let's play it again and see if it comes out the same.
3) **Solidity** — after a while, it develops a beginning, a middle, and an end.
4) **The Tough Part** — if absolutely necessary, we write it down.

Sounds Like MUSIC

Looks Like MUSIC

1) **Syllables** — we go through chanting the notes on a uniform tone and beat.
2) **Rhythm** — we give the notes their proper value.
3) **Speed** — we take it up to tempo.
4) **The Fun Part** — we sing it all the way through with the real notes, phrasing, dynamics, etc.

The **DISCIPLINE**-FIRST METHOD IS TOUGH AT THE BEGINNING AND CAN LEAD PEOPLE WHO WANT IMMEDIATE RESULTS TO AN "I DON'T LIKE THIS" REACTION EARLY ON. IT CAN ALSO LEAD TO A SLAVISH DEVOTION TO CONVENTION THAT HINDERS SPONTANEITY. THE **CREATIVITY**-FIRST APPROACH LEAVES ALL THE HARD STUFF FOR THE END, THUS OFTEN PRODUCING BRILLIANT BEGINNINGS THAT STOP HALF-WAY THROUGH. IT ALSO TAKES A LONG TIME TO GET PAST THE MESSING AROUND STAGE, AS ONE SPENDS SO MUCH TIME RE-INVENTING THE WHEEL, AS IT WERE.

right hand — high singers

I THINK THE MOST EFFECTIVE PRODUCTS ARE OBTAINED THROUGH FREQUENT — SOMETIMES SPLIT-SECOND — SWITCHES BETWEEN **CREATIVITY** AND **DISCIPLINE**. LONG PROBLEM-SOLVING PRACTICE HELPS ONE TO KNOW WHICH IS NEEDED IN WHAT SITUATIONS. GETTING THIS PRACTICE REQUIRES THE **CREATIVITY** TO EXPERIMENT AND THE **DISCIPLINE** TO STICK AT IT UNTIL IT WORKS...

...AND EVEN THEN THEY CAN BE CAPRICIOUS.

Well, I finally got around to starting this damned Smith thing... but I can't think of anything to write!

What a fantastic idea! ...I suppose I oughta get out of the tub and ...ugh... write it down...

CREATIVITY FAILURE

LACK OF **DISCIPLINE**

As TO WORKING CREATIVELY ON SCHEDULE, ALL I CAN SAY IS I THOROUGHLY AGREE WITH AGNES DE MILLE. IN AUGUST OF 1986 I LEFT FOR BELGIUM WITH A HALF-WRITTEN COLLEGE ESSAY IN MY SUITCASE. FIVE MONTHS LATER, I'M JUST FINISHING SOMETHING WHICH BEARS VERY LITTLE RESEMBLANCE TO WHAT I STARTED WITH. I GUESS EVERYBODY HAS TO FIND FOR THEMSELVES THEIR PERSONAL **CREATIVITY**/**DISCIPLINE** BALANCE; I'M STILL LOOKING FOR MINE. COLLEGE IS NOT THE ONLY PLACE TO LOOK FOR THIS, BUT IT DOES PRESENT A LOT OF OPPORTUNITIES TO PRACTICE.

WE CAN ALWAYS HOPE.

24/1/87
Zoe Mulford
PÂTURAGES, BELGIUM

COMMENT:

The real success of this wonderful essay lies in the fact that its very creation is a combination of discipline and creativity. The discipline shows in the substance of the message, the simplicity and clarity of the presentation, and the careful choice of the details and issues presented. The creativity shows in the clever drawings of the figures, whose body shapes, facial expressions, and "thoughts" are so appropriate to the stereotypes the creator is trying to evoke. Ms. Milford not only demonstrates she has a profound understanding of the "apparent" incongruity between discipline and creativity, she demonstrates she also knows how to reconcile the two and use the benefits of each to her great advantage. This essay is a masterful job and a thoroughly enjoyable one to savor. (AST)

Jaeyong So
College: Yale University

COMMENT:

Obvious strengths of the "essay": extraordinary creativity revealed, as well as excellent sense of humor and superior artistic talent (he *does* bring out his real strengths). Drawbacks: This is not an *essay*! We're not sure if he can write at all well. Jaeyung So has placed all his chips in one pile—namely, his artistic gifts. I would question whether or not we as readers have developed any real sense of who this person is, how he thinks, what is important to him, etc. In fact, we should even be a bit concerned if, as the comic strip Jaeyong laments, "I have nothing to write about. I have nothing." How effective this response is would depend on how much about himself (or how little) the writer has included elsewhere in the application. (RJO)

ESSAYS ON DEATH AND DYING

Ann-Marie Breaux
College: Harvard University

VALENTIN DESIRÉ BREAUX, SR.

My grandfather, Valentin Desiré Breaux, Sr., lived with my family from Thanksgiving of 1981 until his death in March of 1983. His short time with us affected my life and ideas more than any other single incident in recent years. Over a period of a few months, I grew to love a senile old man whom all of his children (except my father) had wanted to commit to a nursing home.

We called him Papa. He was eighty-four when he first came to live with us. He had lived all of his life from the age of about twenty-five in a small Louisiana town of two thousand residents called Gueydan. I can remember wondering as I waited for my parents to bring him home what could be so terrible about him to make his children dislike him so. When he arrived, I discovered that he was merely an old man who could not walk or function very well and was slowly breaking down. My parents gave him their master bedroom, which was right next to my room. They moved downstairs to a bedroom on the ground floor along with my brothers' bedrooms. Consequently, whenever Papa would yell for help during the night—whether he had fallen while struggling to the bathroom or merely wanted a drink of water—I was the only one who could hear him. As corny as it may sound, a special bond grew between us when I would go into his room at two to find him sitting up in bed or even once on the floor rolled up in the drapes clutching to his chest a broken windowpane divider in the shape of a cross and crying, "Oh Saint Mary, help me!" Or when I was helping him down a step from the kitchen and he grabbed the wine rack and sent it crashing down on top of both of us.

He was extremely fastidious in his appearance and grooming. One of his major embarrassments was when he was no longer able to control his bladder. He slowly, carefully combed his hair

77

several times each day. Every morning before leaving for work, Dad would bathe and dress him, and often gave him a shave. About once a month, we would all bundle into the car and take Papa to the barber whether he needed a haircut or not. He loved to go places. Once when my mother and brother took him to a shopping mall, he remarked that it was the biggest store that he had ever seen. There he talked to Santa Claus and received two candy canes which he would not eat because he thought that they were pencils.

Eventually, when he became too sick to walk more than a few steps, we rented a hospital bed and made him a small room just beside the kitchen. He died peacefully on Thursday, March 24, 1983. That day there was a freak snow in Birmingham, and we children were out of school. At 2:30 P.M., we were all with him when he just slowly stopped breathing. We all told him we loved him, and then about ten minutes later when Papa was beginning to get cold and stiff, I called my father to tell him what had happened. I recall sitting on the attic stairs and looking down on his body on the bed and thinking all of it was a dream. When the ambulance came to get him, they put a blue crushed-velvet drape over him. We had a very nice memorial service for him in Birmingham which was conducted by Father Sexton, the priest who had come to the house once a week to give Papa communion. Then the body was flown down to Gueydan and, on the following Monday, his funeral was held. The young priest who conducted the mass had never known Papa, and as a last irony, said that it was good now that Papa was dead because he was no longer a burden on anyone. As a member of VFW, Papa was given a full military funeral, complete with a twenty-one-gun salute, a full honor guard, and a flag draped over his coffin. He would have loved to have seen such a sight. For you see, Papa never hurt; he never felt sick; least of all, did he wish to be a burden on anyone.

When we arrived home from Gueydan, everything in the house was the same. His chair was still in its place. His wheelchair and ramp were still in the corner of the den. But something important was missing. The dogs kept looking for the man who had scratched their backs patiently for hours on end. There were little marks where the wall paper had been worn away by his fingernails when he hoisted himself up the step to the bathroom. Most of all, I missed not saying, "Good morning Papa" and "Hey, hey!" when I would walk into the den in the morning. I respected and admired him so much that when he died, I was not sad; there is merely a void in my life now that can only be filled with memories.

COMMENTS:

This essay is appealing in that it speaks to a personal relationship in a simple and direct style. It also reflects the sensitivity of the writer toward her grandfather and her discovery of her love for him, thereby providing the reader with some insight into her character. Its weakness may be in that it does not prove how and why her life and ideas were affected by the experience, which she mentions in the first paragraph. Further, she makes a statement about his children disliking their father, meaning her grandfather, without any evidence except possibly because they wanted to put him in a nursing home. In spite of these points, the essay held my attention because it described a real-life situation with feeling and humor. (NA)

There is extraordinary sensitivity and poise in this essay. The writer makes it very clear that she was all the old man had; and yet it is not self-promoting or egocentric. The style is straightforward and measured. The reader is anxious to know what happened. The central point, that the aged disadvantaged need not forfeit dignity, respect, or admiration, is made beautifully. (TH)

Julie C. Cantor
College: Yale University

Annie was short, white-haired, and about ninety. She had none of the usual signs of age—veined hands, withered appearance, liver-spotted skin. Instead, Annie could have been a friend's grandmother.

Each time I brought her up to therapy, I had to explain to her that Occupational Therapy was the place where she worked on her knitting with Doris. She remembered the knitting, but not Doris, the therapist, or me either. One day when I came to take her to O.T., she said she could not go because her daughter was coming to visit. I told the nursing staff where Annie and I were going so that her daughter could find us. Even so, she asked me five times if her daughter would be able to locate her.

Whenever she saw me she asked if I worked at the home. When I answered no, I was a volunteer, she sweetly replied, "Then you give your time freely. God will bless you and your family." Annie frequently asked if I was still in school. When I told her I was and would be a senior, she said, "How long have you been in school?"

Annie always insisted that she had forgotten how to knit. Yet she knitted beautifully. Puzzled, she would squint and demand that I check to see if she was knitting correctly. She said, "You know, I once dropped a stitch and had to do a whole row over again." I asked her what she wanted to do with the scarf when she had finished. She scrunched up her face and answered. "I don't know. I've made others, but they always take them."

"No, Annie, Doris told me you gave them to your children and grandchildren." I watched as she strained to remember. Annie knew she had lost some of her memory, for she often said, "I'm old and can't remember things the way I used to."

Each time she struggled to see her knitting, until I suggested she wear her glasses. She never knew where they were, even when they hung on a chain around her neck.

When I had to leave her in the middle of a therapy session, she would drop her knitting and beg, "Don't leave me alone. I hate being alone. I need you to help me with my knitting. You won't leave me here, will you? You'll come back?"

Annie frequently wrung her hands in pain, pulling at each joint. Sometimes she dropped her face in her hands. Then she rubbed her watery eyes, lifted her head, knit a few more stitches, and stopped, letting her head fall into her hands again. I wish I could have done something for Annie, but I knew the doctors had already tried everything they could. I hoped her younger years had been happier.

___

COMMENT:

This is nice work. A heavily descriptive piece, the author does not make an editorial comment until the very end. Only then do we learn what she has taught us to expect, that the woman is about to die. The final reflection is poignant and compelling. (TH)

___

Stephen Gripkey
College: Yale University

Beyond salvation in this world, she lay slowly dying on a cheap mattress, her emaciated frame almost incapable of movement. A victim of malnourishment beyond medical help, she lay in agony, not romantic acceptance. No music played in the background; no trumpets heralded her pain-filled exit from this world. No poets commemorated her in song. She was nothing more than a human skeleton, and yet she strained forward to mutter greetings to a visiting nun. I watched but for a moment, and then turned and strode away, gripped with oblivion. I felt no true shock or pain, or even sorrow; I felt only numbness and emptiness. I could not even cry.

During my summer-volunteer service in the Dominican Republic, such horrible sights of malnourishment and sickness taught me the dispassionate brutality of human life. I saw babies who are crippled for life because a $2 box of nutritious oatmeal came too late to save their weak limbs . . . decrepit mendicants who spend an entire day begging so that they may face another day of slow death . . . and children who have no hope for the future and only pain and suffering in the past and present.

When I was capable of having one, my reaction to such sights was anger. I was not angry with God because such people are allowed to suffer, but angry with man. We Americans have enough capital to feed the entire world, yet gluttony prevents us from doing anything.

And what of education? Philosophy, literature, classics, music—all are worthless to a starving man. Have you ever tried to explain the theory of relativity to a jobless man with eight children to feed? Or the laws of motion to a child without functioning arms or legs? All our technology and knowledge mean nothing if we are not prepared to use them to end such needless human suffering. Philosophy and knowledge can only be appreciated on a full stomach.

As for me, I intend to use my education and skills to help put an end to such suffering. Granted, the goal is probably naïve. But as Robert Browning once said, "Ah, but a man's reach should exceed his grasp. Or what's a heaven for?"

Juliet Siler
College: Harvard University

My brother Tommy died when he was four and I was six, so I never knew him well; however, I do have certain definite memories of him. Although two years younger than I, he was much stronger, built like a bulldozer, or at least a small ox. I was a scrawny coward in those days and he would chase me unmercifully, head lowered and a glint in his eyes—he had light hair and his grandfather's intensely blue eyes—and I would cry and he would laugh and get spanked and laugh even louder. He was fearless in the pursuit of his sister. Yet deep down, he admired me very much, more than I appreciated at the time. Whatever I was drawing, he would want to draw; whatever game I was playing, he would want to play, too. He always wanted to be with me, and he would enlist me in his own games, assigning me the American toy soldiers and himself the British. He never stopped moving; he was either energetically chasing me or running his toy cars along the floor. In all of his photos he is grinning his toothy widest, happy, ready to conquer worlds of bandits and bad guys, a cheerful little hurricane.

A lot changed when he got sick with leukemia. The illness sapped his energy and happiness and often led to fatigue and crankiness. Chemotherapy made his hair fall out and he had to wear a brown wig that didn't at all resemble his shining, golden hair. His fearless and trusting nature was—must have been— assailed by unspeakable bewilderment and terror. Yet he managed to smile when he saw me, laugh at television cartoons, and run his toy cars along the sheets. In his own childish way he was making the best of his life. Near his death, he asked my mother if there would be toy trucks for him to play with in the sky. She answered yes, and I know she is right.

COMMENTS:

This is a very affecting piece of writing. Without being overly sentimental, it invites an emotional response. In the process of learning a great deal about the writer's little brother, we learn a great deal about her as well. The vocabulary, the sentence structure, and ordering of ideas all contribute effectively to the overall impression. There is a great deal more I would like to know about this particular writer, and I expect that those matters would come clear elsewhere in her application. In any event, this piece does a good job of making clear one particular facet of her personality. (RCM)

A well-written description of Juliet's brother. I get a glimpse of her compassion and hope, but not much else. The essay is so focused on him that she gets blurred out of the picture. (AAF)

ESSAYS
ON FAMILY

Anonymous
College: Harvard University

TOO EASY TO REBEL

In my mother's more angry and disillusioned moods, she often declares that my sisters and I are "smarter than is good" for us, by which she means we are too ambitious, too independent-minded, and somehow, subtly un-Chinese. At such times, I do not argue, for I realize how difficult it must be for her and my father—having to deal with children who reject their simple idea of life and threaten to drag them into a future they do not understand.

For my parents, plans for our futures were very simple. We were to get good grades, go to good colleges, and become good scientists, mathematicians, or engineers. It had to do with being Chinese. But my sisters and I rejected that future, and the year I came home with Honors in English, History, and Debate was a year of disillusion for my parents. It was not that they weren't proud of my accomplishments, but merely that they had certain ideas of what was *safe* and *solid*, what *we* did in life. Physics, math, turning in homework, and crossing the street when Hare Krishnas were on our side—those things were safe. But the Humanities we left for Pure Americans.

Unfortunately for my parents, however, the security of that world is simply not enough for me, and I have scared them more than once with what they call my "wild" treks into unfamiliar areas. I spent one afternoon interviewing the Hare Krishnas for our school newspaper—and they nearly called the police. Then, to make things worse, I decided to enter the Crystal Springs Drama contest. For my parents, acting was something Chinese girls did not do. It smacked of the bohemian, and was but a short step to drugs, debauchery, and all the dark, illicit facets of life. They never did approve of the experience—even despite my second place at Crystal Springs and my assurances that acting was, after all, no more than a whim.

87

What I was doing then was moving away from the security my parents prescribed. I was motivated by my own desire to see more of what life had to offer, and by ideas I'd picked up at my Curriculum Committee meetings. This committee consisted of teachers who felt that students should learn to understand life, not memorize formulas; that somehow our college preparatory curriculum had to be made less rigid. There were English teachers who wanted to integrate Math into other more "important" science courses, and Math teachers who wanted to abolish English entirely. There were even some teachers who suggested making Transcendental Meditation a requirement. But the common denominator behind these slightly eccentric ideas was a feeling that the school should produce more *thoughtful* individuals, for whom life meant more than good grades and Ivy League futures. Their values were precisely the opposite of those my parents had instilled in me.

It has been a difficult task indeed for me to reconcile these two opposing impulses. It would be simple enough just to rebel against all my parents expect. But I cannot afford to rebel. There is too much that is fragile—the world my parents have worked so hard to build, the security that comes with it, and a fading Chinese heritage. I realize it must be immensely frustrating for my parents, with children who are persistently "too smart" for them and their simple idea of life, living in a land they have come to consider *home*, and yet can never fully understand. In a way, they have stopped *trying* to understand it, content with their own little microcosms. It is my burden now to build my own, new world without shattering theirs; to plunge into the future without completely letting go of the past. And that is a challenge I am not at all certain I can meet.

COMMENTS:

This is a good, strong statement about the dilemma of being a part of two different cultures. The theme is backed by excellent examples of the conflict and the writing is clear, clean, and crisp. The essay then concludes with a compelling summary of the dilemma and the challenge it presents to the student. (NA)

A masterful job of explaining the conflict of being a child of two cultures. The writer feels strongly about the burden of being a first-generation American, but struggles to understand her parents' perspective. Ultimately she confesses implicitly that she cannot understand them and faces her own future. The language is particularly impressive: "It smacked of the Bohemian," "subtly un-Chinese," and "a fading Chinese heritage." That she is not kinder to her parents does not make her unkind, just determined. (TH)

Lydia Bassett
College: Harvard University

Family legends passed down through generations grow more incredible each time they are told. Sitting at my grandmother's feet listening to her tell of my great-great-grandmother, Kate Travis, I knew *that* story would never change. The ideal of it was too important to be stretched and exaggerated, too important to be tampered with for the sake of a happy tale.

My great-great-grandmother was born an enslaved person in about 1845. She lived in a small, rural community, Horse Pasture, Virginia. She was allowed to keep part of her wages and when she was freed she had money saved to buy a restaurant in nearby Martinsville. With freedom a great desire to succeed came to Kate Travis. Money was not the important part of her dream. She wanted to raise her children with pride. She wanted them to be educated and have a chance to become what they wanted to be.

The restaurant was a success. Two of Kate's children died of smallpox. Her remaining son, Raleigh, went to school and grew up into an ambitious young man. But the dream of Reconstruction was dying. Martinsville was changing; Kate was constantly being hounded to sell her restaurant. There was no place for Raleigh there. With high hopes Kate traveled North with her son to help him establish a business in Chicago. She returned to Martinsville to find that Jim Crow laws had become more oppressive. A sturdy partition was constructed down the center of the restaurant and she was forced to run a segregated business.

Kate learned to live within the new laws, but that was not enough. Close by the courthouse, her land was desirable property. A victim of legal manipulations and her own illiteracy, she finally lost her restaurant, forced to accept as compensation land on the outskirts of town. Raleigh returned to Virginia, his ambition crushed. Chicago was not what he had dreamt it to be. He died, leaving a baby daughter for Kate to raise. She earned a living working as a cook.

I wish I could have known my great-great-grandmother in her later years, her bitter years. I would tell her that her dreams were not lost, they lived on in her granddaughter, my grandmother, who grew up into a woman with the same strong convictions as Kate Travis.

COMMENT:

Direct, strong, and simple, the style here reflects the content. She takes a family legend and without sentimentalizing it or politicizing it, without editorializing she takes the reader back in time and tells a story. She does exactly what she says. She doesn't "tamper with the story." The end works because it brings the story into the present and suggests themes of continuity, continuation, and generation. (PT)

Kelley P. Bordon
College: Barnard College

> Somewhere ages and ages hence:
> two roads diverged in a wood,
> and I—
> I took the one less traveled by,
> and that has made all the difference.
> Robert Frost

I have chosen to take roads less traveled by. I have chosen to be different than other members of my family.

My family is one of backwoods heritage—down-to-earth, good-hearted people who value hard work and integrity. We did not step off the farm until my parents' generation, and then, only for economic reasons. In the past, members of my family chose to take the downtrodden path, the safe, well-known highway traveled by their ancestors. Some, I am sure did not have a choice, but others I believe chose the familiar path out of fear. I understand this fear, for I too experience it. It is a distrust of the new and of the different. My curiosity, however, helps me to overcome this fear, it entices me to look for bigger things and not to be content with what I already have.

Throughout my life I have chosen less traveled roads. I chose the road of an artist, the road of a dancer—a choice requiring hard work and total dedication, things family and friends do not always understand. While it causes me pain that my father does not approve of this choice, it has also taught me responsibility, independence, and survival.

Another road I decided to travel was that of a scholar, a path tough to walk on and easy to be pushed off of. Again it is an option which few of my family members and friends understand or dare to take. Peers pressure me to step off that path and follow theirs. Admittedly there are times, especially in this past year, when I succumb to the pressures and walk off of that path. Yet, I know not to stray far for good things lie ahead for me on the road of scholarship. The door to a world better than one my parents are living in. This is what I am fighting for.

So far the roads I have traveled have been rocky, I guess because they are the less traveled, the lesser understood roads. Yet, I continue to travel them knowing it is worth the risk and the heartache, for one day it will all be rewarded. In many ways I could even say I already have. Dance has brought me the joy of movement and the freedom of self-expression. Scholarship has given me knowledge, an open mind, and a new perspective on life.

I do not condemn my family for not helping me down roads different from the ones they would have liked me to take, I just hope one day they will understand my choices.

COMMENTS:

This writer took a risk in writing this essay. It comes across a little negative—she obviously does not have her family to support her in this venture. On the other hand she is very open about herself and her goals even though she has "traveled the road less traveled by." She demonstrates her independence and determination to succeed on her own. (BPS)

There is a sort of churlish self-aggrandizement in this essay which leans, too heavily in this writer's opinion, on Frost's beautiful poem. It would have been far more effective had Ms. Borden separated her positive vision of her life from the lingering hurt and resentment of her parents whom she cannot stop accusing. (SAB)

Ellen L. Chubin
College: Harvard University

MARLENE

I have never before attempted to collect and write down my thoughts about my sister and her effect on my life—probably because it's so difficult for me to talk about—but as I turn it all over in my mind, I begin to see what a profound impact she has had on me.

Marlene, now age twenty-two, was born with learning disabilities and a lower than "dull normal" I.Q. that to this day prevent her from functioning at a normal mental capacity. When she was first tested, her I.Q. was found to be 60% of an average child's, and though she now tests at 85% of normal, she continues to have severe gross and fine motor coordination problems, reading and speaking difficulties, and poor rhythm and balance. She is destined to remain socially and academically backward despite her efforts and those of my entire family.

Those efforts have been tremendous ever since I can remember, and I am told that they appeared even more shocking and unrelenting before my birth. When my parents initially realized that Marlene's unresponsiveness and lethargy signified mental handicap, they suffered a crushing blow that threw my mother into a severe mental depression, but they were determined that Marlene should reach her potential no matter how limited it may be. Throughout Marlene's life my parents have always sought out the latest information, techniques, and educational opportunities available for the learning disabled, and as a result of these efforts combined with her willingness to engage in the struggle to achieve, Marlene has made slow but steady progress toward emotional and intellectual maturity.

She began her formal education in private schools for the mentally deficient, switched to special education classes in public school, and progressed to a mainstream academic program in high school. Though such success might have been ample for the family of another L.D., Marlene's education did not end upon the receipt of her diploma. My parents again endeavored to find the seemingly unthinkable option for their mentally handicapped daughter—a post-secondary educational opportunity—and they discovered one. Marlene became a member of the first class of the two-year Threshold program—a specially designed college experience for high school graduates with significant learning disabilities—at Lesley College in Cambridge, Massachussetts. Upon graduation from Threshold, she entered the third-year transitional program to aid her with her full-time job in child care and her independent living arrangement in a Cambridge apartment with another Threshold graduate.

Though I do not spend nearly as much time with Marlene as I once did, we continue to share a close, caring relationship. When we were younger, our relationship was surprisingly mutually beneficial on the whole. The many things I tried to teach her in more recent years, after my accumulated knowledge had far surpassed hers, are balanced by the direct and indirect aid she gave me as a young child. Rather ironically, it was Marlene who first taught me how to read and write when I was two and three years old. She was seven and eight years old at the time and had just begun to develop these skills herself, but my parents verify that she imparted to me her knowledge in these basic academic areas through playful use of her educational books and toys.

I am also grateful to Marlene for a significant occurrence in my life which she indirectly brought about. My parents' hunt for a special summer camp program for Marlene led them to the Tikvah program at Camp Ramah in Palmer, Massachussetts, and my sister's first summer there was so successful, both socially and educationally, that consequently I began attending Ramah. This camp aroused my interest in Judaism and equipped me with the liturgical expertise that enable me to serve as a cantor several years later.

Now Marlene lives with two other Threshold graduates, works as a stock girl in a Boston department store (since our realization that she could not succeed in day care, though Threshold had trained her for such work), has a steady L.D. boyfriend, and relentlessly maintains a nearly independent existence, except for the continued support of family, friends, and hired social workers and other professionals. I wish to assist her as she struggles toward independence, and attending Harvard University would enable me to do so.

Marlene has taught me to be the best that I can be because that is what she is. Her kind, generous disposition has not become embittered by her endless battle in life. She has had to overcome so many more obstacles than the average person in order to satisfactorily perform ordinary tasks, and she continues that struggle although she knows she will never be totally successful. In that sense the struggle is hopeless, but she never stops—she never gives up. She is fighting the unbeatable foe. If she can achieve that much, can I be any less? I have to live up to her standard.

Lissa Elhindi
College: Colby College

The most important influence on my character has been my Arabic father, a most traditional Middle Eastern man. While he has been a stabilizing influence at home as a central wage-earning figure, as a model for relationships, particularly familial and marital, he has failed. Through his failure to be a loving father and parent, I have learned that love must be freely given without obligation or guilt. There is a further benefit, however, to my negative upbringing, because, through his opposition to education for women, specifically for me, his first daughter, he has made me all the more eager to go to college and to graduate school. His rejection of the worth of higher education for women has created in me a determination not only to attend the college of my choice but also to become a self-educating, independent woman.

My father, Mohammad Yassar Elhindi, at times can be a positive force in our family. If there is a problem or argument, he decides it; his is always the final decision. He supports our family because supporting the family is the chief role of the Arab male. He also holds the family together. We children are all extremely different individuals, my brother Robert, my sister Suehaad, and I are all potentially fiercely independent. Unfortunately my mother has lost all her individuality. His is the hand that keeps us from flying off to the four corners of the world; his is the down-to-earth influence on the family.

My father's behavior, however, has had an intense effect on my views on relationships, especially marriage. He believes that all relationships should have a superior and inferior person. Usually the man dominates the woman, or the elders dominate the youngsters. During my growing up years, my father has constantly berated the rest of my family, trying to ruin any self-respect and independence we may have had. My mother has lost hers completely, but we children have managed to hang on to at least part of ours. My father despises what he has created in my mother, but at the same time tries to create the same thing in his children. I believe that people in a relationship are equals and should support each other. Instead of attempting to stifle self-respect and independence, they should try to foster more. My father tries to use people to get what he wants by manipulating their emotions. In his mind games, he tries to make people feel guilty enough to accede to his wishes. He allows me to attend Annie Wright only so that I will be the perfect, loving, daughter when in his presence. My education and training at a girl's college preparatory school enable him to look better to his business associates. I have had to learn to play my father's games while under his roof, but I try not to play them outside of our house.

My parents' marriage is a shambles; it is neither based on mutual love nor respect. It is based on the fact that neither parent believes in divorce, especially with children in the home. My mother has been conditioned to be extremely dependent upon my father, another reason for remaining together. When my father threatens to leave, another mind game to remind us how much we need him, my mother begs him to stay, not because she loves him, but, rather, because she could not support herself without his money. I would never engage in a relationship or marriage that has the remotest resemblance to that of my parents.

My negative experience has convinced me that the foundation for a moderately successful marriage, loving or loveless, is compatibility, friendship, and understanding. The second necessary ingredient is respect for your spouse, and the third is equality. No one adult person should be totally dependent upon another. Love in my family is a tool used to get what one wants, whether it be money or revenge. Love and compassion are weaknesses to be used against the weaker individual. Paradoxically, my parents believe it to be the child's obligation to love the parents. We do not give love in my household, we barter it for favors rendered. Love is not like this, it should be a choice, not a reflection of blood-kinships, not a series of guilt-ridden obligations.

My father, although now an American citizen, grew up in Syria, and still harbors many Arabic ideas; chief among them is that the women should not be as well educated as men. He married a woman who had more inferior education, and he opposed my going to the Annie Wright School three and a half years ago. It was only through my mother's insistence and her financial support that I was able to leave home as a freshman in high school. Over the years, my father's opposition to my education has hardened while my resolve to attend college has been tempered by his inflexibility. I had to prove that I wanted and needed to come to Annie Wright: I had to learn to work and fight for which I feel entitled. My brother supported me in my resolve to attend a private college preparatory school. Because he is the eldest son of an Arab family, he has an incredible amount of influence in the way the finances are distributed, although my father still has the final say, in this, as in most, family matters.

Hardened by unhappy family experiences, I have been nourished by my education at Annie Wright. Here I have been taught to believe in myself and in my potential, both academic and personal. As a resident of a boarding community, I have found a refuge as well as a place to heal and to grow into myself. I will never repeat the mistakes of my mother who sought security and a refuge from abusive parents through marriage. I have been blessed with a good mind, and need to continue in college what I have begun at Annie Wright. I am resolved to become independent, skilled, and professional, whatever my future career.

Julia D. Kyle
College: Princeton University

IN THE BARN

To the casual observer, my family might have seemed fragmented. My older brother Josh and I lived with our mother in Philadelphia. My two younger half-brothers, Allan and Kent, lived with their mother in the small town of Pipersville. The four of us spent every weekend together with our father, who lived in a nineteenth-century farmhouse near Doylestown. The

farm hadn't been worked for decades, but the huge, slightly
decaying barn still stood.

Whenever I think of my childhood, that barn looms large in
my memory. Adults almost never went in there. I think they
were a little afraid of it—and with good reason, too. The
floorboards had rotted in some places, and unless you knew
exactly where to walk, you risked falling through onto the
concrete area below which had once housed the cows. In some
rooms, ceilings were half caved in, and the superstition developed among us children that if we spoke above a whisper in
those rooms, the ceilings would fall in on us.

But for the fours of us, the barn held more than fear.
Sometimes the barn was awe-full, almost holy. We would stand
quietly in the still of the afternoon and watch myriad particles of
dust glitter in the rays of the sun that slanted through the cracks
in the walls. We could hear the almost inaudible creakings and
moanings of beams which had held together for a century and
were trying to last yet another day.

Sometimes the barn was interesting. Josh (whom we considered omniscient) would tell us how farmers used to build without nails, show us barn swallows' nests, or explain how bats can
fly without sight.

Sometimes it was challenging. Josh would lead us on expedi-
tions to the top of the rickety silo, or to the uppermost windows
which could only be reached by creeping precariously along the
beams.

Sometimes it was terrifying. We would go into the barn at
night and tell ghost stories. Some, I later found out, were
well-known, like the Tell-Tale Heart, but the ones that still
send a shiver up my spine were those we created just for
ourselves. I remember one dark night when the wind was
blowing through some wire, making a high-pitched wailing
noise that sounded like demented laughter. The story that night
was about four children (three boys and a girl, of course) who
were killed, one by one, by the barn. Each time, just before it
killed the next child, the barn started laughing. After that,
whenever the barn "laughed," we would remember that night.

My father moved to another house several years ago. The
barn has been boarded up so "children won't wander in and get

hurt." Josh has married, and we're all too old now to be frightened by ghost stories. Yet sometimes we drive past the barn and those memories flood back, and I know that inside its crumbling exterior, the barn holds a part of us intact forever.

COMMENTS:

This is an excellent essay. I don't know if the essay hints at the character of the writer or whether she'll do well in college, but she should do well in a writing course! (BPS)

Brava! Julia, Princeton would be lucky to have you. What beautiful tension is created here, what understated home truths are revealed by the barn! This is a writer. She is also someone who manages to reflect in a way that is fiercely independent. She is truly transcendent and, best of all, she writes so well that instead of having to take her word that she is a writer the readers know it to be true. (SAB)

Jade Deon Larrabee
College: Whitman College

JEFF

The experience I want to share with the Whitman Admissions Committee is the joy my brother Jeff has brought into our family. Jeff is special. Since birth he has been mentally retarded, a Down's Syndrome child. To our family, my parents and my sister and myself, he is just Jeff. We treat him as a normal family member, not as an outsider or some sort of handicapped liability to be hidden from the rest of the world. But the experiences and lessons he has given to all of us Larrabees are far from normal.

I have never wanted a better brother. As a child, I never thought of him as different. I grew up loving him as my older brother and accepting him for the wonderful human being I knew him to be. As a young boy, Jeff was always smilingly content, never seeming to want anything more than he was given nor appearing dissatisfied with his life. Of all his many admirable qualities, I most appreciate his enduring strength and self-will. I remember one incident from our childhood at the neighborhood playground. As we entered the play area, all of the children stopped, stared, and gawked at him. After a brief moment of fright, Jeff realized that he was all right and began again to play. I was probably four and he nine, but I will never forget his courage, which has always given me the courage to believe that he *is* all right.

Another lesson that Jeff has taught me and all those around him is a greater awareness. Jeff is sensitive to the fragile and delicate feelings of others. Once, when my aunt was doodling on a note pad, drawing sad faces and happy faces, Jeff insisted that only happy faces should be drawn and the sad crossed out. My brother Jeff has his own charisma, and a special way of sharing his love for us. All of those who have the privilege of knowing him well are better people because our lives have been touched by him. I love him and all he has added to our family. My parents have never treated him as a mentally handicapped person and my sister and I grew up without concentrating on his "difference" and without feeling that his condition was a disgrace to our family. He has always just been Jeff and my special brother.

Jeff is a very successful twenty-five-year-old young man. At present, he lives in a group-home sponsored by REACH with many others as special as he is. He and his housemates have an advisor who lives with them, but they are practically self-sufficient. Jeff and his fellows support their basic needs through working; all of the members of the home do their share of the housekeeping, cooking, and cleaning chores. Jeff is exceedingly independent and is deeply involved with the Special Olympics. Competing for the last seven years, his talents range from basketball, to track, and to skiing, and he is now the number one athlete on his Alaskan downhill ski team. The most rewarding experience shared among our entire family was our venture to Louisiana for the International Special Olympics in the summer of 1983. Among the many outstanding retarded athletes in Juneau, Jeff was chosen to represent his hometown. At the Louisiana meet, there were representatives from forty-nine other countries and some four thousand contestants. The brave and dedicated attitudes of all of the participants enriched all of us who watched them compete for twelve days.

We are very proud of our special brother.

Ron Lee
College: Harvard University

> As far as I could tell, Ted Williams, Dom DiMaggio, Walt Dropo, Birdie Tebbets, Billy Goodman and all the rest came from humble backgrounds. On that basis I used to think there was some connection between rough childhoods and good batting averages, which is why I sometimes wished my own house would burn down, to give me an edge.
>
> Laurence Sheehan, "How to Play Second Base"

Things I will always remember about my family: my father showing up for soccer games in out-of-the-way places; my mother driving me to a Little League practice she really didn't want to go to; doing my homework at my desk and being interrupted by my sister who comes in, lies on my bed, and talks with me while "You know?" and "I know," go back and forth like a responsive reading in church . . . I will leave all these things next year. No matter where I go to college, I will never again be with my family as much as I have been—as much as I would like to be.

Dad started coming to soccer games when I played freshman soccer. He stood on the sidelines, alone, and watched the game attentively, hands clasped behind his back. I never told him how to get to a game; he just showed up. When I left the field at the end of a period, he would call me over with his hands. Not quite sure of what he was talking about, he always said the same thing, "You're playing good, Ron. Bend your knees a little more. Are you tired? You look tired." I would utter some witless remark and respond to his comments by bending my knees more and running harder when I got back in the game.

When I was eleven, my mother came to visit me at Boy Scout Camp. I knew everyone else's parents would be there, but I was still comforted by my mistaken belief that my parents weren't coming. Looking back, I realize how touchy I was about being the only Korean, the only non-white, at the camp. Undaunted by any of the self-consciousness that burdened me, mom showed up with my sister Michelle, Kentucky fried chicken, and some things to help me through the week. She did not embarrass me with her poor English, as I was sure she would. My mother's confidence and love made me ashamed of my own unfounded insecurities. I am thankful to my family for giving me a sense of identity in being Korean, something that has proved to be a blessing, not an embarrassment or obstacle as it has been for other first-generation Korean-Americans I have known.

Now and then Michelle will say with a sigh, "God, Ron, you're going to college next year." I respond with a forlorn "I know." I have gotten an "edge" in exactly the opposite way Laurence Sheehan hoped he could: I haven't had a "rough childhood"; God has blessed me with an amount of talent, but as college draws near I realize He has blessed me with a family I will miss a great deal.

Recently, I have realized how profoundly a child is shaped by his parents and his environment. My family has helped me to become secure, appreciative, confident, and independent. If I am accepted to Harvard, perhaps the letter of acceptance should be addressed to me and my family.

COMMENT:

It's a poignant conclusion. Again what works here is the use of specific examples. The closing makes the "sincere" tone authentic. (PT)

Kimberly D. Morgan
College: Harvard University

GROWING UP ON THE JERSEY TURNPIKE

"Howard, slow down, you're tailing that blue car!" We switch lanes. "Danielle, move your leg!" demands one voice. "How much longer," demands another.

This is common banter on my family's frequent drives to New York. The route to my grandparents' house isn't "over the river and through the woods" as in the stereotype of Americana; but over bridges, turnpikes, and highways. In fact, their house isn't even a house; it's an apartment. Once every six weeks or so, my family makes the pilgrimage to a far off land called Queens, New York. The journey takes over three hours and although it is usually an ordeal, it allows me to spend a significant amount of time with my family. We have been making the same trip since I was about three and it has become a family tradition of a sort, and one which I have found myself looking forward to.

The first fifteen minutes of the drive is always crazy. My mother worries about how late we will be while my sisters and I fight over our seating positions. Then the inevitable battle begins: the war between the radio stations. It is the "Sinatras" against the "New Wavers." Eventually an armistice is called and a compromise is reached. The "New Wavers" may have their station until it is overtaken by static and then they must relinquish control to the "Sinatras" for the remainder of the ride. Oddly enough, the static appears after about 45 minutes and we are stuck in a car with the big band sound.

We have also developed our own rules and regulations for these rides. The most important ones govern food. The "Constitution" is as follows: no pretzels until the first toll booth, two cookies each while in Pennsylvania, and the rest must be divided equally after we reach the N.J. Turnpike. Most importantly, NO throwing trash on the floor.

Usually after we have passed exit 7A (the one for Great Adventure) and we've divided up our snacks, my sisters fall asleep. This is one of the best parts of the trip for me. For an hour or so I am an only child. I lean over the front seat and turn off Frank, abruptly ending "That's Why the Lady Is a Tramp."

"So where am I going to college?" "Wherever we can bribe them to take you," teases my father without missing a beat. Lately all of our discussions seem to concern college. Where do I want to spend the next four years? What interests should I pursue? What are my long-term goals? Although it is hard to admit, talking it out with them has helped me to focus on the sort of experience I want for my undergraduate years. Essay topics also take up a lot of our time. What is there about me that distinguishes me from the thousands of other bright Harvard applicants? "Emphasize leadership," suggests my father, taking both hands off the wheel to gesture. "Make sure you mention the grant," adds my mother. "Just don't mention the trips to Europe," they add in stereo.

"Why don't you tell them that you always wear my clothes without asking." My sisters wake up and again, I am part of a trio of girls who strive to spend equal time fighting and having fun. When we pass Newark, we all talk in nasal voices as if we were holding our noses. We do the same thing when we sense a skunk near Cranbury and when we drive through Secaucus. We play the alphabet game and twenty questions. And, when we reach the Elizabeth exit, my sister declares, "We are now going through the town with the most awesome name in the world. Mine!" While passing a service area, we note its obscure name. "Who the hell is Richard Stockton?" "He was a New Jersey signer of the Declaration of Independence," answers my father, the world's authority on everything.

The ride continues. We see ships at the piers in Brooklyn and keep up our quest for unusual license plates. In my fourteen years on the turnpike I have spotted all except Alaska. We cross the bridge, see the abandoned car that's been in the same spot on the B.Q.E. for thirteen months, and finally hit Queens Boulevard. The green sign for Lefrak Towers is the signal that it's time for the socked feet and footless shoes to become one. As the car circles the block for a parking space we rapidly gather our belongings. When all is in place my father ceremoniously declares, "We're here!"

Our car rides are really a microcosm of our life together as a family: teasing, advising, arguing, joking, and caring. Some of my funniest moments, loudest discussions, and soundest advice have been shared between the tolls of the New Jersey Turnpike. Perhaps it is because I have taken so many comfortable car rides with my family that I can now travel to college as an inquisitive, confident, eager person armed with humor and a realistic sense of self. Now, if only I could convince the "Sinatras" that New Wave is the REAL music those trips would be truly worthwhile.

COMMENTS:

Wonderfully irreverent, honest, and observant! Underneath the pull and tug of family life there is a sense of bonding: of "teasing, advising, arguing, joking, and caring." She should have resisted the temptation to draw the too obvious connection between the family and college, but it was probably her father's idea. (TH)

I like the essay, for sure. I've driven the route myself often enough. But the essay is too long for an application, I think. It sustained my interest because of my familiarity with the route, and I wanted to compare notes with her. She has a great feel for her family and conveys it well. The phrase "for an hour or so I am an only child" is quite poignant, and many of her quips are quite cleverly expressed. I reacted negatively to the use of "Who the hell . . ." and wonder if "B.Q.E." is comprehensible as such. Overall, well written and interesting. (MAH)

While the essay is well written, and there is depth, it tends to labor along the turnpike. There is almost a travelogue quality about the essay. To her credit there is a definite sensitivity and family being which comes out. (JCM)

William S. Plache
College: Haverford College

When my brother, Alex, was in law school a few years ago, he lived at home with us. But he always did his studying at my grandma's house. He said there were fewer distractions and he could concentrate more on his work. So after several unsuccessful attempts to write the great college admissions essay at home, I have decided to see if I can do any better over here. Instead of using my own desk at home, I am sitting at Grandma's kitchen table.

I came over alone this time, as I usually do lately. But I can remember when our whole family would go together to see Grandma. The holiday occasions when we would all come for dinner are still vivid in my memory. Christmas Eve at Grandma's house was an annual event. Just getting there was an experience in itself.

My father would make it clear to the whole family that we were to leave our house by five o'clock. But as it turned out every year, he and I were the only ones ready to leave at that time. Dad was always on time, and I had nothing to do to get ready. The youngest didn't have to get dressed up to go to Grandma's, and nobody expected him to wear a tie. The others, however, were in a mad rush to put on their formal outfits.

Finally, when everybody was ready to leave, at quarter after five, we would all pack into the Citroen. Our positions in the car were pretty well established. Dad always drove. No matter where we were headed, Dad was behind the wheel. Next to him, in the passenger seat, was my mother. The back seat was left for the four boys. Alex, Dave, Matt, and me. Darwin proposed his theory of the survival of the fittest, and such journeys were no exception to this idea. I always ended up in the middle of the back seat, forced to contend with the hump that runs along the floor. As the youngest of them all, I never thought of complaining.

The first moments of our ten-minute trip were filled by the harsh yet familiar lecture of my father. "For crying out loud,

Marilyn, I said we had to leave by five. We're a half hour late!" Over his shoulder, he would exclaim, "You always wait until the last minute to get ready! Why can't we ever get anywhere on time for Pete's sake?" Nobody cared to mention that we were not a half hour late, but rather only fifteen minutes late. And dinner would not be ready until six o'clock anyway.

The rest of our drive consisted mostly of silence, except for some occasional jostling in the back seat, which was immediately extinguished by the emergence of Dad's proverbial hand of discipline reaching around from his own seat.

When we arrived, Grandma was busily at work in the kitchen. Mom would stay to help mash the potatoes, while we went into the other room to wait. The dinner was always great, but what I looked forward to was the dessert. Every year Grandma makes thirteen different kinds of Christmas cookies, and when she brought them out, we would each grab our favorites. After dinner, we all assembled in the living room, where Grandma had her artificial tree set up. I would eat one of the candy canes that were hanging from its branches. Then Grandma walked in bearing six envelopes, one for each of us. I opened mine to find a fifty-dollar bill. Alex would shout, "A hundred dollars, thanks Grandma!" We all anticipated this annual quote, and we knew that everybody's gift was equal.

Today, as I sit here it is quiet except for the sewing machine Grandma is using in the other room. The Citroen broke in half ten years ago, and has been replaced by a succession of odd cars over the years. Alex, Dave, and Matt have all moved out. They visit occasionally, but they are never all home at the same time, and when they do return, their wives usually tag along. Grandma still makes her famous cookies, but she has to mail them to her out-of-town grandchildren.

COMMENT:

The beginning is promising, but his memories are not well tied to his present task nor are they particularly unusual. It bothers me that the only emotion expressed is anger. (JMcC)

Jacob Press
College: Harvard University

Sunday was the day we went visiting. Just about every sun-baked, suffocating, summer Sunday during the period known as my childhood, extending as far back as I can remember and rapidly coming to a close, we packed ourselves up in the car and drove down to "the Beach House," my grandparents' summer home.

This weekly pilgrimage was not simply a trip, like a drive to the shopping mall, the butcher, or the Chinese restaurant. It was nothing less than a journey to a different culture, like a weekly student exchange program. Gone were the elaborate landscaping and fancy cars sunning themselves in driveways. Here there were no driveways and, as you gazed up, it was obvious that the trees had been here long before the people. All the homes on this street were similar: small frame houses with large front porches and shingles that had once been shiny and bright but were now faded by the saltwater air into softer, friendly pastels, so that no matter what color a house might have been when it started out, it eventually fit in perfectly with the others.

It was the same with the people. They had entered this block as independent individuals, but over time their facades, like those of their houses, had faded together. As they aged together they became closer, and a community was formed where the phone wasn't used to call neighbors who were just a short walk away and one could drop in next door for dinner unannounced (and frequently did). The women shared recipes and the men shared financial advice and they all joined in the powerful and mysterious cult of the Grandchildren which, through its powers, forced otherwise rational people to swear that their five-year-old grandsons were taking college-level classes.

The drive was just long enough to be massively miserable, but was immediately forgiven as we drove up the street and spotted Grandpa waving hello. He must have been waiting on the front porch for hours, but time meant very little to this octogenarian. My Grandpa was a slight short, usually quiet gray man. He preferred bow ties, and gave perfect hugs: not very powerful, and not lasting very long, but covering you from head to toe with a feeling of well-being that made you feel at home. I've been told that in his day he had quite a temper, which I find hard to believe, but if so, he had certainly mellowed. He took just about everything in stride, including Grandma, which was quite an accomplishment.

We would all make our way inside and shortly Grandma would come trotting out of the kitchen, drying her hands on the apron that covered her stout, slightly plumpish body. She seemed always to be washing dishes, in spite of the fact that she had owned a dishwasher for a number of years. She "rinsed" the dishes before she put them in, explaining that it was absolutely necessary. In a loud voice she greeted us all, gave a hug, and said, "So, why are you so late, you said you would be here at twelve?" as she took some packages and my mother back to the kitchen. "Sam, I think you should go warm up the barbeque," she shouted across the house, "it might need some new coals. Kids, you won't believe how cold the water is, I couldn't even put my feet in. On Wednesday, Aunt Pearl and Uncle Herman were here and they were saying, well actually Aunt Pearl was saying, Herman wasn't really paying attention, so what else is new, Pearl was saying that she remembered that the water in Florida . . ." Grandma was rarely at a loss for words. Whether on line at the bakers or on a bus full of strangers she had enough to say for everyone, but especially her family.

So it was to these warm surroundings we went in the warm weather. Little did we know that we were being filled with memories of people and an atmosphere that were almost extinct. These visits helped me understand much about what a community should be, what a family is, and where values and priorities should be placed. No matter what I do or where I go, I will always keep these Sundays in mind. And maybe someday young children will come to visit me in my beach house.

COMMENT:
This is well written. When given a choice write about that which is known or familiar. This is written about a childhood

experience that obviously left a deep impression on the writer. (BPS)

Leah S. Schanzer
College: Swarthmore College

WASHING UP

Recently my grandfather showed me a photograph of my grandmother when she was just eight-year-old Eva Littwin, living a little girl's life in post-World War One Brooklyn; she stands in the courtyard of a tenement building, hanging a laundry to dry (perhaps this is her regular Monday afternoon chore, and when it rains, are the wet sheets and underthings hung in the kitchen, to drip and run in thin rivers over the linoleum floor? On rainy Mondays, does my great-grandfather joke that dinner is cooked at sea?). Smiling roundly, she holds a grubby dishtowel before her stocky little body with a dainty turn of wrist, as if it were a heavily draped evening gown.

During my own eighth summer, my sister and I established a tradition of eating breakfast with my grandparents Eva and Max. Each morning we would race across the wide lawn which separated our house from our grandparents', nightgowns flashing about our legs, night-tangled hair flying straight behind, to trip onto the wet, cold flagstone path which led directly to their front door. The first thing my grandfather always did when he got up was to turn his radio on to a classical music station—the memory of that announcer's voice, gentle and without inflection, as familiar as an old friend, was a great comfort to me in my times of eight-year-old trouble.

My grandmother always made my grandfather a single fried egg, sunny-side-up, and served it to him in a heavy old cast-iron frying pan, while my sister and I looked on in distaste: It was our job to do the washing up. As soon as breakfast was finished, we hurried to clear the table, for we usually liked to be quick as possible, and very efficient. But sometimes, if it were a rainy day and Bach spoke to me eloquently from the speakers in my grandparents' bedroom, I would put the sponge to one side in preparation for my special Sink Dance.

My grandma's nylon peds became beautiful worn toe shoes which transformed my feet into the strong, bony feet of a dancer, and conjured for me the breathlessness of a dancer's life. My sink dance was an expression of what I felt looking around at the smiling faces of my sister and my grandparents, there in that summer kitchen—lifetimes of experience. Urged on by Bach and the steady, quiet rush of tapwater beneath, my dance took me across rooms, around corners, careening and leaping through the whole house. When it was all over, my sister giggled knowingly, but my grandparents always kissed me and told each other, low, that I was a graceful girl, wasn't I?

Afterward, I was ready to get to my chore. I could appreciate the feel of the musical water running over my hands, and I squeezed liquid soap onto the sponge with a will as I looked out the little window above the sink at the bright sodden flower beds my grandma had planted long ago to line the walk. Beside me, in companionable silence, my sister stacked everything in the drainboard and when we were through, we stood back to admire the way the dishes slouched orderly, gleaming, against one another. Just as eight-year-old Eva Littwin must have admired the rows of sheets and dishtowels which billowed and danced on their line in the tenement courtyard.

COMMENT:

It's very atmospheric, and I like very much the first part of the opening paragraph and the closing. There's a lovely sense of the way generations echo each other. What is particularly good are the images. They are concrete and emotive. I thought the weakest part was the parenthetical section in the first part. (PT)

Annelise K. Skor
College: Wellesley College

Ever since Emily was born when I was five I've known what it feels like to be a big sister—always full of pride, often wanting to share, and sometimes just wishing I could lock my door. I loved having a little sister and was ecstatic in seventh grade when my mom had Margaret. At fifteen I was content with two sisters who were a lot of fun and just a little pain. I felt our family was complete. I guess my parents didn't, because I got a big surprise that fall!

One night in October I came home, slamming the door, late from swim practice, tired, and in a particularly bad mood. In an attempt to cheer me up, my mom asked, "Guess what I just found out?!"

Being in rotten humor, I sarcastically replied, "You're going to have a baby!"

"Yes!" she answered in delight.

Of course I knew she was kidding. I tried to ignore her but she wouldn't leave me alone. She insisted she was pregnant! I just couldn't believe her. My parents had joked with me before, and I knew (or at least hoped) they were trying to get me excited or make me laugh. I finally gave in and smiled, but they persisted. My mom showed me a doctor's appointment written on our calendar, and then the appointment card itself. The truth slapped me in the face. Next spring I would have another younger sibling. I cried. I didn't want another sister or brother. I cried some more.

The months went by, and even though I never said another word against my new family member, I still had angry feelings. I convinced myself many times over I didn't want that baby. Looking back, I now realize it was selfishness. First of all, I didn't want to share my parents, who spent enough time as it was with Emily and Margaret. In fact Margaret, who was two at the time, was one of the main reasons I didn't want another baby. In my opinion, as much as I loved her, Margaret was a difficult kid. She spit up on everyone, was awful to babysit, and refused to go to sleep. I felt like this new child might, as Margaret had done, disrupt our family. I'd have to give up my time to babysit two babies! I might even have to move my room to the third floor! My personal sacrifices weren't the only factor, though. What about our family? It would be another year before we could take a ski trip. Not only that, but my mom was forty. Wasn't that too old to have a baby? And I was fifteen. Wasn't that too old to have a newborn baby sister? The more I contemplated my life, the less I looked forward to it.

This resentment continued up to June fourth, the day Stephanie was born. But everything changed at the hospital when I held my five-hour-old sister. Suddenly, looking at her precious face that seemed to smile at my touch, I understood what being a big sister meant. I wasn't going to lose anything; I was gaining everything. My parents and I didn't have to share what love we had; we were simply going to give, and get, more. I had another chance to see a baby learn to talk and grow. Because I was so much older, I knew Stephanie and I would have a special relationship. Not many kids my age have a little person who looks up to and trusts them. I thought to myself, "I'm going to teach my little Stephanie everything I know and love her as much as I can."

Stephanie is now two and a half and a real angel. She calls me "Eela" ("Annelise" is really a mouthful). I love it the most when she climbs out of bed, comes up to my room, and has me sing to her. Never once, not even the time she emptied my favorite bottle of perfume, have I regretted being her big sister.

Rosetta Stockwell
College: University of Pennsylvania

GROWING UP WITH EWICK

When I was a toddler, the name Eric was too difficult for me
to pronounce: I called him Bubala. Later, as my speaking ability
improved, I was able to say Ewick, and that became his name
for a few years. Thinking back, I'm disappointed that I didn't
have someone to bully, teach, and be a friend to as Ewick was
and is to me.

I grew up with Ewick more than with anybody else in my
family. Being the baby of the family, I latched on to the next in
line. That was Ewick, who was eight years older than me.
Naturally I was like any other naive sister, always wondering
why I couldn't join in the games of cops and robbers. I longed
to chase around as he did on his bike, even though I only had a
tricycle. I looked up to Ewick. He was cool.

When Ewick hit the Monopoly, Payday, and card game
stage, it affected me, too, because I desired to do everything he
did. Patiently, Ewick taught me how to play Monopoly. But he
used a different set of rules when he played with me. In fact, I
remember being in debt to him in one Monopoly game some
$2,000. Later he regretted ever teaching me how to play board
games because as soon as he had grown out of the phase, I was
headway into it. Many Friday nights, when Ewick got ready for
the Pirate football games, I stood before him, the Monopoly
game in my hands, begging him to play.

I was a pest to Ewick, and he still put up with me. But, I
suppose he had to. I had a reign over him. I had the power of
"I'm telling!" which was very strong and which I frequently
used. I remember Ewick laughing hysterically as he twisted the
arms of my fur bear. I would run out of the room screaming,
"I'm telling!" and Ewick would grab me, his face solemn and
apologetic. I guess he was right when he jested that I had the
biggest mouth of anyone he knew.

Thinking back on it all, I wonder why he put so much effort into a bratty little sister. I recall memories of sitting on the step leading into the green, shaggy carpeted family room, Ewick, word for word, teaching me how to read. No, we didn't launch into Freud's *Group Psychology and the Analyses of the Ego*, but rather Dr. Seuss's *Green Eggs and Ham*. I never tired of phrases like, *Sam I am and I don't like green eggs and ham*, but poor Ewick must have.

One time, at our family's Pismo Beach vacation spot on the California coast, he treated me to an entire day of rides, food, and fun at the Carnival. I remember seeing him give the ticket person a ten-dollar bill so we could go on all the rides. I don't know how many tickets he bought, but the flashing of that ten-dollar bill made a great impression on me. With the remains of pink cotton candy smothered on my cheeks, we rode the ferris wheel and banged bumper cars all day long. That was the first time that I, as a kid, appreciated him, the first time that I realized what a kind brother Ewick truly was.

As years passed, Ewick became less of a leader for me, and more a rowdy teenager. His life became controlled by tubular waves. Nothing mattered but surfboard wax, and the white sands and blue waters of California. I was stuck in lonely grade school while he and my other brother and sister experienced high school. Instead of a gap growing between us though, he took on the role of big brother. In this Clint Eastwood image he enjoyed acting tough. If a male voice was on the other end of the telephone line, he instantly had to know who it was. He interrogated every one of my friends while my cheeks slowly turned beet red. My theory is that he had finally seen the radical world of teenagers . . . namely sex, drugs, and rock'n'roll, and he didn't want his little sis involved in that stuff. He became very protective of me, giving me tidbits of brotherly advice which I, as a smart junior high schooler, thought I didn't need. He thought he was a parent, and I surely didn't need a third.

One day, when I as usual didn't care to listen to his advice to me, our tempers erupted. I was upset with him for treating me as a child. He was upset with me for thinking I knew so much when I really didn't. My face red-hot and streaming with tears, I desperately tried to show him that I was an adult.

"I know a lot more about the real world than you think, Eric! You think I'm stupid and naive!"

"You are, Rose!!" His rudeness slapped me in the face and I fell silent. Then Eric hurled at me, "I'm only telling you these things because I love you, Rose!" and it hit me. Everything fell into place.

These words meant that all those Monopoly games were important to him. I realized that he was just poking fun when he told me that I ought to go play in the highway. I was (and still am) Ewick's little sister . . . someone whose purpose on earth was to be pushed around by big brother.

Michael Wechsler
College: Harvard University

I have often thought that the fictional character Hawkeye, the lead role in the popular television show MASH, is based on a "real-life" individual: my grandmother. What—you may ask— does a gentle, gray-haired little lady, who is more familiar with the layout of her kitchen than with the battlezones of Korea, and whose skill is with knitting needles rather than with a scalpel, have in common with the sardonic, perennially unshaven, lanky surgeon of the infamous 4077th army unit? The answer is character; the strength and nobility of character that manifest themselves best under conditions of adversity, which made their presence felt, and which leave a lasting impression.

Like Benjamin "Hawkeye" Pierce, my grandmother has had a war against which to rage. In fact, she has had many: the two World Wars spent in Eastern Europe, experiencing inhuman conditions, unimaginable horrors, and senseless losses; later the struggle against poverty and hardships that faced her as a new immigrant to America; and more recently, the long personal battle against an illness that has confined her to a wheelchair. But, for both the fictional character and his living prototype, the raging is simply the manifestation of an indomitable spirit, of an

unwillingness to accept as unsurmountable the problems created by the madness of human conflict or the unpredictability of
fate. Both have been successful in tempering this rage and
channeling this frustration into positive, useful action. Both
have survived with dignity and earned the affection and respect
of those around them.

The prime moving force for each is a fundamental love of
life, with an enormous capacity to care for others. Hawkeye
spends his time patching up fragmented bodies with his sutures
and encouragement. He risks his life on numerous occasions to
save his comrades and patients; she has always placed the well-
being and happiness of others above her own needs and desires.
Even now, despite her infirmity, she does volunteer work regularly, teaching arts and crafts to severly handicapped adults.
What does it matter that he comforts his friends with homemade gin and a pat on the back, while she uses homemade
chicken soup and a hearty hug? The common bond is the
willingness to take the time to give of oneself, to stop and
alleviate the misery in someone else's life.

Both Hawkeye and my grandmother consider frankness of
paramount importance. Forthright and outspoken, they will
stand up for a belief, defend a value, or protest an injustice. In
the same way that Hawkeye does not hesitate to challenge an
unreasonable order or a corrupt decision—even one emanating
from a general—my grandmother has not shied away from
questioning the excessive rigidity of an official regulation, or
from objecting to the prejudicial treatment of a minority group.
He does not tolerate the abuse of a subordinate; she has taken
the cause of the elderly and handicapped, and fights for their
rights.

The ability to laugh and to make others laugh is another
attribute they share. Endowed with a superb sense of humor,
they are quick to dispel a gloomy mood or diffuse a moment of
tension, raising the most flagging of spirits. They have a knack
for detecting the absurd in affectedly grandiose situations, for
deflating pomposity with a subtle jest, and for disarming anger
with a wink and a smile. It is this ability that has allowed them
to deal more easily with the crises and disasters of life, for the
poking of fun extends to their own predicaments: ready to

receive the anesthetic prior to her seventh major bout of leg surgery, my grandmother extracted the promise of a dancing date from her handsome young physician. Hawkeye, who flirts with the nurses to hide his fear of loneliness, would have understood, and rushed to hire the band.

The fictional young doctor from Crabapple Cove, Maine, and the very real eighty-year-old lady that I love share many qualities: sensitivity, warmth, compassion. Having experienced my grandmother's gentle care, I readily recognized the tenderness with which Hawkeye looked after a pet hamster; watching Hawkeye's tears on witnessing the suffering of a friend, I was reminded of my grandmother's gentle sorrow under similar circumstances. Their touch has made a difference in many lives.

To me they represent the essence of being human.

COMMENTS:

The writing here is of a high order. The vocabulary is excellent, and so is the sentence structure. Most important, the comparison of Hawkeye and the grandmother works, from beginning to end. The similarities are clearly delineated and effectively supported with examples. Learning about what he admires in these two characters tells us a good deal about the writer himself. (RCM)

Although his last sentence lacks the punch I expected, this student draws an excellent parallel between his grandmother and Hawkeye Pierce. He joins two unlike persons into harmony by skillfully describing their common attributes and values. His insight and sympathetic portrayal of his two models indicate a strong appreciation of the values a person of intelligence, wit, and moral perspective would cherish. I believe it is a self-portrait. I like him! (AAF)

OFFBEAT
AND OTHER ESSAYS

Anonymous
College: Wellesley College

Sitting in my doctor's office, I vaguely heard the distant remark, "You're so thin you could have a heart attack while walking down the street. Don't you care?"

No. As I ran my index finger along the cave between the blades of my pelvic bones, all I could think was how revolted I felt at the thought of my former weight. My doctor's remark did not affect me, for I feared food a thousand times more than I feared death. During my ninth-grade year, I suffered from anorexia nervosa. After taking fifty-three pounds off my five-foot nine-inch frame, I was left with ninety-six pounds. It was not enough to be thin. I had to be the thinnest. Now, however, fully recovered, I can reflect back and realize that my wishes were more complex that fitting into size five pants. Many of my subconscious emotions were related to my relationship with my father. I hardly knew him because as I was growing up, his work always came first; as he often left the house before six in the morning and came home after eleven at night, I would not see him for up to two weeks. Not only did he devote his whole self to his work, but he expected me to do the same ("You cannot get anywhere unless you go to Yale or Harvard"). Consciously, however, I never felt pressure to please him, nor did I miss a close father-daughter relationship. But it never occurred to me to recall that I began dieting after the first time he told me I looked fat; always in the back of my mind lay that element of trying to please him, to achieve a goal that would earn his pride, and to do it better than anyone else.

Games were for winning. I played starvation. Society urges us to stay slim at all costs, but many people have trouble restricting the size of the number on the scale. I could: I was a winner! I compared myself to my classmates, people in the street, and, of course, my hottest competition, the *Vogue* models, who always beat me. But Daddy knew I was struggling to win; with every shirt that became too large for me, his remarks went from sincere compliments to anxious threats of punishment if I did not eat. He noticed me.

At the time, however, I had no awareness of those underlying emotions or desires to achieve for Daddy. All I knew was that I had to be skinny; skinnier than anyone else. Every month or so my father went to lecture in Europe for a week or two and on the days he left, sorrow and emptiness consumed me; Daddy was leaving. But I just considered my feelings—"the blues." I also enjoyed a mysterious frail, helpless childlike emotion that came from starving. I liked to know that I needed to be taken care of; maybe Daddy would take care of me.

Now, two years later and thirty-eight pounds heavier, I realized that I cannot alter my father's inability to express his feelings. Instead, I must accept myself. I finally realize that I am a valuable person who strives to accomplish. But I cannot strive solely for others. By starving, I attempted to gain pride in myself by attaining my father's approval or acknowledgment of my value as a person. Of course, I gladly accept applause and attention from others, but the primary approval must come from me, and I feel secure now that I can live with that knowledge safely locked in my mind.

COMMENTS:

This strikes me as a gutsy piece of writing. Anorexia is a hard rap to beat, and the writer is entitled to feel proud of the fact that she has. Furthermore, she describes the struggle in compelling terms. I wish it had been possible for her to do so without making a villain of her father—perhaps because I am a father myself—but no doubt that is an important part of her story. It seems to me that the essay fulfills the two basic requirements for such writing: It provides significant information about the applicant as a person, and it clearly demonstrates that she is able to write effectively. (RCM)

The essay avoids what could be the inevitable pitfall: self-pity—or, even worse, a maudlin description. As a reader my strongest reaction was to examine in my own life—who it was that I was seeking to please. Rather than focus on the anorexia problem, the writer effectively describes the reasons at the basis of the problem. The cognitive explanation was so insightfully presented along with the writer's affective reaction that they result in a very successful outcome. The reader comes to know the author very personally. (AAF)

Sarah H. Bayliss
College: Harvard University

WHY I WEAR UNDERWEAR

I yanked open the top bureau drawer. No underwear, only tube socks, wadded into tight balls and packed in. I now owned seventeen pairs of tube socks and six pairs of underwear. The washing machine had a habit of "eating" my panties. I reached my fingers into the back of the drawer, finding only emptiness where my last-resort pairs were usually stashed.

"We're leaving in ten minutes!" My older sister Alice shrieked from the kitchen as she did every morning.

After selecting a pair of socks, I shut the drawer and tugged open the next two. I took out my orange corduroys and my green-and-purple striped sweater. I pulled the first over my bare bottom and the second over my uncombed head.

"Coming!" I shouted back. Snatching up my unfinished third-grade homework, I dashed into the kitchen.

My sister, dressed in a denim shirt and clogs, looked at her watch five times as I gulped my cereal.

Barbara was playing jacks by herself outside the music room during recess. Her round hazel eyes were flecked with bits of brown, and tan freckles spilled across her cheeks and nose. She was in fifth grade and was a friend of Alice's. I decided I was going to look like her when I got older.

"What's up, Shrimpo?" she said as I snuck up behind her. I

was planning on "boo!"ing her, but she saw me first and twisted my arm.

"Uncle!" I gave in after a few moments, and she released me. I hadn't realized my elbow could bend that far without breaking. The joint creaked as I straightened my arm and tried to laugh.

"There you are!" a husky voice boomed from the other end of the hall. It was Lisa ("Obesa"). Her toothy smile made me shiver.

I said, "Oh, hi."

"Why weren't you outside the lunchroom? I told you to meet me there!"

"Um. I forgot."

Lisa had flabby white arms and pierced ears. She always wore complicated earrings which, combined with her abundant wavy hair, made her look enormous.

"Well, that was dumb," she said. She stepped behind me, pressed her palms on either side of my chin, and picked me up by the head, I kicked the air until she set me down again.

"We'll just have to give her a wedgie then, won't we, Barbara?" Wedgies involved being hauled up by the back of one's underwear. Lisa's eyes glittered; her sausagey fingers reached for me again. She locked my neck in the crook of her elbow. I threw Barbara a pleading look. She answered me by gripping me around the waist and pulling up my sweater in the back. Her fingernails tickled my spine as her fingers crept downward. As I struggled, I was held up again by the head.

"What's the matter? Aren't you wearing any underwear?" Barbara joked and grunted as I elbowed her in the stomach. I would be destroyed if they got down my pants and found no underwear. I would have to switch schools. I sweated through my gritted teeth and thrashed my arms. Squeezing my eyes shut, I squirmed as hard as I could. Someone ripped my belt loop. My arms, swinging in wild rotations, smacked into something. I kept swinging, twisting, squirming, striking . . .

Suddenly, Lisa unclamped. Still kicking, I landed on the cold tiles. When I unshut my eyes, she was clutching her nose and facing the door to the girls' bathroom. She turned around slowly. At her feet, a pool of blood was collecting from her dripping nose. Riveted, I stared at Lisa's bloody face.

A bell rang. My fly had come undone. I zipped it up and tore down the hall.

I ripped my new sheet of arithmetic homework in half.

"Hey, Shrimp!" My sister sounded excited. Her voice came from the other side of my bedroom door. I blew my nose and tossed the tissue on the Kleenex-littered floor next to my bed.

"What!" My locked door knob jiggled back and forth.

"Why'd you give Lisa Obesa a bloody nose?"

"I din't!"

"We saw her in the nurse's office! Everybody knows about it." She giggled and whispered something I couldn't understand. I heard Barbara's muffled voice cackle in response. I wouldn't tag along with Alice and Barbara today. I decided not to look like Barbara after all.

"Well, I didn't mean to!" I walked over to kick the door.

As Alice's clogs clomped off, I crumpled my homework and hurled it at the wall.

Later that evening I noticed that someone had shut my top drawer. I opened it and found four new packages of Carter's underwear tucked in among the socks.

COMMENT:

The reader gets involved in her childishness, her embarrassment, her struggle. She handles the ending sensitively. It has a nice pace and rhythm and fine structure. (JMcC)

Paula Bernstein
College: Wellesley College

LESSON IN SELF-EDUCATION

"Identify these quotations from *Hamlet*," read the instructions. My stomach tightened my palms sweat. "Calm down. This is only a test," I reassured myself. I was in English class surrounded by twenty grim-faced students who were busily pouring ink onto their papers while I watched the tree through the window grow and the hands on the wall clock tick-tock.

My eyes raced down the page. "Hamlet said this to Ophelia during the 'Nunnery Scene' . . ." I thought to myself. I knew the answers, at least some of them. But time was fading and my classmates' heads continued to sag and the tree continued to grow into the sun. I began to identify and explain one of the quotes before I stopped myself. "You could write a great poem on this moment. Taking a test. Watching robots suffer to achieve. Seeing the sun shine on the carpeting unnoticed. Not wanting to explain what I know. Wanting to write . . ." So I did.

"Carpe diem," explained my English teacher in a previous class, "means to seize the moment." So I did. I turned over the test and wrote a poem about Hamlet, me, the tree, the clock, and why I felt the urge to write a poem on the back of my test.

"This can't be your test," my usually placid English teacher said in an unusually harsh voice as I handed the test to him. "No, that's it," I replied, trying to repress a grin.

My teacher called each of us to his desk about a week later to tell us our grades. "I already know what I got," I said to him. He smiled ear to ear and said, "I have no doubt that you do." "Well, did you at least enjoy my poem?" I queried. "Yes," he replied. I explained why I wrote it and why I felt that it was a legitimate reason to leave a test blank. "I felt that it was something I had to do, something I had to prove," I explained. He agreed halfheartedly with my excuse. "But," he argued, "you should be able to write poems *and* take tests." I knew he was right, but at that moment something inside me seemed to laugh at life and although no one appeared to notice, my eyes seemed brighter, my cheeks seemed rosier, and I seemed to strut proudly through the halls the rest of the day.

I only regret that my teacher lost our exams before he could hand them back to us. I keep thinking that someone at this moment may have my Hamlet exam with an "F" on the top and a limited edition poem of mine on the back.

NOTE: This essay was written in response to a question asking my views on active learning and risk-taking in education.

COMMENTS:

I find this a weak last paragraph for the essay. It doesn't help me to sympathize with the type of "risk-taking in education" she's written about. The earlier paragraphs don't build my confidence in her academic values either. I don't think this essay was to her as it might have been—it wasn't helpful to me. (MAH)

Very nice. She writes about something we all would like to do. Succinct, serious, witty—all with a purpose. We are able to identify with the writer. Also, we see the serious side to her, in a short span of time. (JLM)

Matthew Brady
College: University of Chicago

I love small children. For the past three summers I have worked as a counselor at a playgroup for children from three to seven years old. Kids at that age are both sweet-looking and incredibly rambunctious. Each weekday that the children were left off at the Convent of the Sacred Heart in Manhattan, two teachers and I looked after them. It was my responsibility to keep the children occupied and out of trouble, not an easy undertaking as we had just a classroom and a rooftop on which to play. I invented games for them that would employ their imagination, told them stories, and tried to avoid being their punching bag. I enjoyed my work so much that, starting in my junior year at Exeter, I became a volunteer teacher's assistant at the local Montessori school. My duties there vary from those in New York in that I also act as a tutor to individual preschoolers. Whether it is helping them learn to pronounce the alphabet or to count up to twenty, I receive such pleasure that I look forward to each Tuesday morning session throughout the week.

My experience with small children leaves me with more than good feelings; from my dealings with them I have equipped myself with some basic rules and observations, called Brady's Laws for Understanding the Young:

I. Kids always say it's theirs when it isn't (i.e. cookies), and claim it's not theirs when it is (i.e., a mess).

II. The ability of kids to do as they're told is inversely proportionate to the number of kids in the group.

III. The worse you feel, the friskier they act.

IV. The brattiness of kids is directly proportionate to the number of weeks he joins the group.

V. The smaller they are, the louder they shriek. Corollary: The louder they shriek, the harder they fall.

Finally, the short but true realization:

VI. The cuter they are, the harder they hit.

I know this early wisdom will be helpful to me when I have my own kids; I'd like to continue to work with small children in some capacity during college.

COMMENT:

The essay section does not necessarily tell us that Matthew is a highly skilled writer, put perhaps that can be revealed elsewhere. I find "Brady's Laws" to be quite clever—in my estimation the best part of his answer. *This guy does know about kids!!* A rather informal style (use of word "kids," frequent use of abbreviations), but this doesn't seem to deter from the quality of the response. The opening statement "I love small children" is very direct and immediately wins me over to Matthew—especially when he is able to document that love by relating his involvement with "the kids." It would have been better had Matthew related details of his work with one or two individual children—to make his experience "come alive" to a greater extent. (RJO)

Adam Candeub
College: Yale University

I have been telling lies all my life. It's not as if my lies are malicious or even self-serving. I just like to test people's credulity with fantastic stories of my own invention which I am somehow able to tell with a very straight face.

I told my first fib in Sunday school at age five. I had ignored the teacher and when she scolded me for not listening, I answered meekly that I was hard of hearing. My poor Sunday school teacher was moved with remorse and sympathy toward her disabled student, and afforded me special attention to make up for my disadvantage. Unfortunately, this idyllic state of affairs ended two weeks later in Bonwit Teller where my teacher met my mother and asked her what was being done about my hearing problem.

My grade school friend, Neil, was fascinated by the very strange old lady who once lived in our house and honeycombed it with peepholes. They had all been sealed except for one which looked into my older sister's bathroom. Neil never came to my house without furtively inspecting the walls near that room. When after two years, I finally confessed the truth, our friendship ended, since Neil had no sense of humor.

I heard many lectures of the evils of making up stories and many renditions of that children's classic, *The Boy Who Cried Wolf*. These warnings did not prevent me from telling Todd about my maternal grandmother who played contrabassoon for the Philadelphia Orchestra or Amy about my pet parakeet, Louise, whose eggs we ate regularly for breakfast.

Junior High marked the creation of my greatest fib, my dear, beloved, and nonexistent sister, Adalgisa Candeub, named after the Druid temple virgin in Bellini's opera *Norma*. She attended

Oberlin College where she studied art-anthropology and fell in love with the French art historian Thierry de Beauharnais, a direct descendent of Josephine, Empress of France. They lived in France where they researched the Neanderthal paintings in the Lascaux caves. When Adalgisa became bored with Thierry she ran away to the Antarctic with Haakon Lagerlof, a Swedish ornithologist. Together, they studied the migratory patterns of Emperor penguins on the Ross Ice Shelf. Mrs. Kaplan, the woman who used to carpool to tennis clinic, still inquires about Adalgisa's health whenever I see her and is amazed that she has yet to catch a cold in the Antarctic.

After Adalgisa I resolved never to fib again, but last summer at the University of Pennsylvania, while I listened to some students whine about their awful parents, the uncontrollable, creative impulse overwhelmed me, and off I went. I never see my parents, I told them. My mom, an archeologist, is always on digs in the Yucatan Peninsula; my dad does research on acid rain for the Canadian government in a lakeside cabin in Northern Ontario. I have to stay home with my evil guardian, Mrs. Crumbschurtz, a free-lance artist, who designs the decorations on Dixie paper cups. She is so mean that I am only allowed out once every three weeks. These kids were aghast, and they invited me to live with them. That night my resident teaching assistant told me that if I wanted to discuss any personal or family problems, his door was always open.

Why do I make up these stories? My favorite English teacher once offered an explanation that appeals to me. According to her, storytelling is the first step to literature. The hallmark of any literary person is, therefore, an interest in stories. In any case, I no longer fib to people; I save my stories for my writing, and I would never lie about important things like college applications . . . honest.

COMMENT:

After eight years of reading "practice" application essays written by college prep juniors I would have to say, this is almost the very best one I have read. My greatest sense of relief came in the last paragraph, when Adam admits to the motivation that underlies his fibbing. I believe that many readers would engage themselves with his works (fiction or nonfiction) in the future, because of the talent he possesses. Any individual who can tell five stories in one essay is extraordinary! (AAF)

Theodore Grossman
College: Brown University

AT HOME

What is written here is not what I had intended to write. I'm sitting in my home alone. My parents, my younger brother and sister, and our two dogs all packed their bags and went to our cabin in Wisconsin. They left me alone so I could work on my application. I was all set to really get rolling. I had a couple of friends over the night before to relax. And I went to bed early so I could get a fresh start in the morning. Only I had a foreign visitor in the house. A very good-looking dog. He had sat at the front door all day, howling. It was so cold at night I let him in. He crouched in the corner and went to sleep. When I woke up I gave him some food and let him out. As he had a collar, I assumed he had a home. Then I started thinking about all the things I could say in my essay which would typify Ted Grossman. But the dog kept coming back and sprinting away. Finally I let him in. He sat a couple of feet away and licked the snow from his feet.

We can't keep him. We have two dogs and my father barely tolerates them. I was going to take him to the Anti-Cruelty Society, but he should have a home, and so we will try to find him one.

The dog may not be the best thing to write about, but to me he's important. And this situation is similar to so much of life. Everything seems to be going somewhat on track and then a dog walks in. I only have a little time to finish this application and mail it. But how can I not worry about this dog. I could talk about all the reasons I'm so cool, and so bright and did this or that. But the fact is, that's not all of me. Aside from being the guy who dressed up as a girl, or played soccer, or edited the school paper, I'm also the guy who lets stray dogs in.

There is a passage from Sherwood Anderson's *Wineburg, Ohio*, which also captures some of my feelings. It's long, but here are a few of the lines: "There is a time in the life . . . Ghosts of old things creep into his consciousness. The voices outside of himself whisper to him concerning the limitations of life . . . If he be an imaginative boy, a door is torn open and for the first time he looks out upon the world, seeing as though they marched in procession of nothingness, lived their lives, and again disappeared into nothingness. The sadness of sophistication has come to the boy . . . He wants, most of all, the love and understanding of others."

The boy in Anderson's passage may feel as though his life is meaningless. And at times it's impossible not to feel that way, and not to question life, and not to want a why, even where there isn't one. The dog reminds me that even though there are questions that can't be answered, there are other things in life that give meaning. And this helps me have confidence that I have the ability to excel and succeed, and should take advantage of life, however it comes.

In ten years college will matter more than the dog, and I know that. But I can't feel it, not now. Watching the dog, caring for him, I feel a sense of satisfaction and worth. That is more important to me than ultimate answers.

COMMENT:

Writing from the moment and in the moment can be dangerous. In this essay the appearance of the dog and the transition from the dog as real object to metaphor and symbol makes the essay work. The way he slides into the quotation from *Wineburg, Ohio* was wonderful! (PT)

J. Daniel Janzen
College: Harvard University

(Introductory note: I was intrigued by this essay. I decided that it would be shortsighted to trace my personal development through high school. After all, it would be impossible to put on paper a tenth of the important experiences in my life during this period, and without a more personal perspective going further back, it would be nothing more than words on paper. Therefore, I have gone a bit further back to get the essence of my person and the way I grow, if not an inch-by-inch chart of my development.)

I have had considerable difficulty in writing this essay. How does one begin to take inventory of his life and sum it up in one page? Well, here goes. I began my life as a child. Then I grew up. This may seem to go without saying, but you'd be surprised at how many people leave out this important step, without which any significant contribution to the world as we know it is highly unlikely. My first major step was learning how to talk. I saw this as a difficult problem. Everyone else seems to know how to do it, but I didn't know where to begin. Oh, I could make noise to be sure—although I always felt a bit apprehensive that I didn't have anything important to say, and so would be regarded as presumptuous and overbearing. I recognized that, without a mastery of a modern language, my life would be empty of meaning. I had a plan. My sister attended school and both my parents worked. My mother took time off from her career to raise me (this added significantly to my early sense of self-sacrifice, as well as to my recognition of the plight of the working woman). However, there were inevitably periods of time when I would be left alone. I would rush into the family room, switch on the television, and watch anything of meaning I could find. MacNeil/Lehrer, This Week in Washington, David Brinkley—these were my teachers. The Watergate Hearings were a bonanza. My learning to speak as I learned about political ethics and Machiavellian power, as well as the Rousseauesque attitudes of my playground contemporaries, I was instilled with a deep understanding of the relationship between language and communicative arts and the expression of abstract thought in the form of verbal enunciation.

I was bursting with ideas, and I planned out several critical and speculative essays for submission to a major publication. Because of my as yet immature sense of journalistic integrity and my ignorance of the relative merits of possible publishers, I decided to contact a literary agent. This presented a twofold problem. Not only was I unable to write a letter, I was incapable of putting my ideas on paper in order to have a précis to present to the editors for consideration. I recognized that the next step was literacy. I had to choose the author I felt could best acquaint me with the English language and prose, as well as a sense of style. I dismissed Shakespeare, wary of his often wordy and overly clever or histrionic writings. I toyed with the idea of J. R. R. Tolkien, but decided that the profusion of words not in common English usage might confuse my still limited vocabulary. I finally settled on Ray Bradbury and Tom Wolfe, for their different approaches to the literary task. I found Bradbury's unencumbered style refreshing, and his representation of traditional American values without viewing the nation through a rosy mist gave me a deep appreciation of the difference between the potential of our nation for good and its actual situation, without disputing the paramount innocence of our still immature culture. Similarly, Tom Wolfe gave me a new perspective on popular American mores and trends without condemning them. His more frank style enabled me to be frank when necessary.

Armed with this new tool of letters, I prepared to begin my career. I mulled over a variety of possible fields of specialization, such as law or psychology, but found the moral questions involved in each area to be too much for the preschool mentality I was cursed to retain, despite having begun kindergarten the previous year. I chose business. I felt that a strong liberal arts background was essential to any enterprise in the modern world, so I decided to obtain a B.A. before applying to a business school. I attended several college interviews, but was never taken seriously; in fact, I rarely got past the receptionist. I was tempted to put this down to the deterioration of social skills in the clerical industry, but soon realized that it was my lack of ability to give a historical perspective to my application. I was increasingly aware of my cadet status as a member of the human race. I was socially embryonic. I had to get a grasp on the idiosyncrasies of modern society by studying the history of Western civilization in general, and the history of organized science in specific.

Taking the logical next step, I applied for admissions to an elementary school. The thought of a public school was entertained, but I saw a trend toward attention to the group rather than the individual, as well as a relaxation of criteria for teachers' licenses. I investigated local parochial schools, but I found the concept of an exteriorly applied sense of ethics repulsive. I was attracted to one school in particular, largely due to advertisements in local magazines claiming an emphasis on the individual. That this would actually be the case, I had no illusions. I may have been six years old, but I was no fool. However, I saw the recognition of this important facet of education by the school as promising. Once in the school, I was surprised to realize the true inadequacy of my previous education. My eyes had been opened to a world of knowledge I had only guessed at before. Such fields as math and applied science which I had no previous experience with intrigued me, and I resolved to satisfy fully my intellectual curiosity in elementary and secondary school before applying to college. As I grew in my understanding of the nature of the educational system as well as a new awareness of my own inner motivation, I realized that I would never be able to completely shake my thirst for knowledge, that I would have to make do with a rudimentary familiarity with the majority of fields, and that I would be able to fully acquaint myself with a very limited number of fields. I was convinced that, while secondary school could provide the general knowledge which would give me a background on which to build, college would best serve my interest in specialization. It is for this reason that I am applying, twelve years later, to your institution. It represents the final step in my maturation as a fully competent member of society.

Terence P. Kelley
College: Princeton University

BALD LIKE ME

For years the question had haunted me: What is it like, really like, to be a bald man in America today? Early in the summer of 1985 I decided to find out for myself. I resolved to cross the hair line and personally experience the world of the bald man. The following is a brief account of my fourteen hairless months.

Shortly after having my scalp scraped smooth in a local barber shop, my mother saw me bald for the first time. At first, she said nothing. Then she regained consciousness. I soon discovered that not all bald men lead glamorous lives like Kojak and Yul Brynner. I found, though, that a naked head can be financially lucrative; garbed in an old bedsheet, I could make a fortune in a matter of hours selling flowers outside the Holland Tunnel.

Protracted baldness does, however, have its drawbacks; until I invested in a Temmington Micro-Screen Electric Shaver (which, by the way, isn't quite as close as a blade) my head was often peppered with Band-Aids from the proverbial "gotcha!" phenomenon, and sunburn was a particularly painful side effect during the summer months. On bright days, people in my immediate vicinity often suffer from something akin to snow blindness, owing to the intense glare my scalp radiated (in a letter of recommendation for me, one of my teachers wrote, "Terence is by far the brightest student I've ever taught; he glows like no other member of his class"). Although a hairless head might appear to be easy to care for, baldness actually entails a hygienic trade-off: less hair to comb, in exchange for more face to wash.

As my hair gradually grew back after I stopped shaving regularly some weeks ago, I noticed that during the early stubble stage my head was useful for sanding irregularly shaped objects and for scouring pots, pans, bowls, and the like. Now, as my naturally curly hair grows in more fully, I find that my head readily clings to nearly every kind of fur, fabric, and coarse material. For lack of a better term, I call this phenomenon "The Velcro Effect."

COMMENTS:

Cute—this sounds like a really gutsy fellow, independent, and funny. He sustained interest through some light humor, and revealed an interesting character. (MAH)

This essay is a nice one which unfortunately falls a little short. The topic is fun to read about, but the ending leaves a great deal to be desired. I am left with—what was the subject? Didn't he have another paragraph? (JLM)

Cassandra Kniffin
College: Yale University

He stood there in his ragged blue jeans, his black T-shirt with "rock and roll" in silver italics across the front, and a cigarette hanging out of the corner of his mouth. He was about five feet four inches tall, one hundred pounds, and probably no older than fifteen. Jack, our boss, had picked him up hitchhiking down the coastal highway and, unable to obtain any information concerning his origin, had brought him back to the restaurant.

We were all on our own, living in Ocean City for the summer, working at the "Galley," and we did not want trouble. After a few days of Earl underfoot in the restaurant kitchen, eating french fries and divulging to us all his observations about the world, we began to object.

He constantly bragged about everything: from smoking six packs of cigarettes a day, to having seventeen tapes of the same record album, to his sixteen-year-old sister's pregnancy. He tried so hard to impress us and to get attention that we could not even feel sorry for him. One day he came in with his ear pierced and his head half-shaved and proudly informed us of his sexual conquests of the previous night. Exhausted with trying to reason with him, we resorted to indifference.

But the day arrived when I finally understood Earl's problem. I was wearing a T-shirt that said "Vermont" on it when Earl approached.

"What's Vermont?" I stopped dead in the middle of frying a cheesesteak sub.

"It's a state," I replied cautiously. He had never heard of it, or Maine, or of Canada, and worse, he did not care. I was stunned. What surprised me the most was that he did not try to cover his ignorance, or even to overcome it by asking more questions. I could not figure out why.

As the youngest by about two years of those who worked at the "Galley," I often kept my thoughts to myself. There was one person, however, Kurt, with whom I discussed Earl. Kurt had grown up in a poor section of town and told me that Earl was just like a lot of street kids who thought they knew it all and had no desire to learn more. "Earl is bad news and will never change."

A few days later, Earl caught me reading a newspaper.

"Newspapers are dumb," he informed me. I knew there was no use arguing. Earl's mind and ideas were inflexible.

About a month after he appeared, Earl disappeared. He took some of Jack's money and clothes and vanished. He called us once at the restaurant, collect, and told us that he had been accused of murder. We rolled our eyes. That was the last I ever heard of Earl.

I was not shocked by his lack of education, his unfortunate life, or his family situation, but rather by his insistence that he knew everything about people and life. Barely fifteen years old, he had already formed his values. I realized that true ignorance stems from rigid refusal to open oneself to new ideas and knowledge. I never had to live on the streets, and perhaps from the point of view of survival, a closed mind is a necessity. But it seems that although there is a risk in admitting ignorance and making oneself vulnerable, the possibilities for growth and reward that arise from a willingness to learn more turn the risk into an adventure.

Sam Liu
College: Harvard University

You strain to be able to see just one more line of the chart sitting twenty feet in front of you as if your fate depended upon it. "Z!" you cry out confidently, but what is the next letter? Is it "C" or "G"? By now your eyes are sore from squinting. It is no use. You resign yourself to your destiny, telling the doctor, "I can't see any farther." You are myopic, destined to be among the one out of every four people in need of glasses.

At the age of fourteen, I was brought to an optometrist because I could not see the blackboard. I had always assumed that what was fuzzy to me was fuzzy to everyone. I discovered that I did not see the world as others did. "You did the wrong problems for homework again," my science teacher would tell me. He would then go over the correct problems on the board, which seemed to be miles away. I had my eyes examined, found that I was nearsighted, and received my first pair of corrective lenses.

Fiat lux! I was now Superman, with x-ray vision. There would be no more doing the wrong problems for homework, no more missing fly balls in baseball, and no more wondering why everyone thought that the girl who sat in the first row of English class was such a beauty. Spectacles opened a new world.

The reaction of my friends was mixed. Some thought that I looked rather handsome with glasses. There were those who were amused by the way the combination of sweat and gravity sometimes pulled the frames down my nose. On the other hand, other people did not like them. "The eyes are the windows to the soul." Is it right to hide behind glasses? Some complained that I looked different. The natural reply was, of course, that they looked different also: They were no longer out of focus.

When someone is said to be nearsighted, it carries negative connotations of being absentminded and unable to think ahead. However, this is not true. Naturally, people who must wear glasses sometimes have to put up with inconveniences. Protective goggles worn in shop class must be oversized to accommodate the extra lenses. One has to be careful in sports. (I find that basketballs have a way of "homing in" on spectacles.) There are always those who ask to look through your glasses. Obligingly, you hand them over, sometimes to be passed around through several persons. The glasses are often returned with the comment, "I can't see through these. You must be blind." This is due to the forgivable, but probably false, assumption that corrective lenses give a person with normal vision an idea of what uncorrected vision is like. In addition, after being handled by twenty pairs of hands, the lenses were usually opaque.

Strangely, some people have enjoyed the view through my glasses. One friend has told me that he thought the world looked more "peaceful" through my lenses. There is the expression, "looking at the world through rose-colored lenses." Perhaps my friend was right. Can it be that myopia is actually a state of mind? (Could I but see myself as another sees me!)

Uncorrected vision has its advantages. As stated earlier, nearsightedness should not carry negative connotations. Nearsighted people have to get closer and are forced to examine things more carefully. In addition, there is a certain privacy to myopia. When I study, I do not usually wear glasses. There are fewer distractions.

Finally, much beauty arises from "imperfect vision." It has been speculated that Vincent van Gogh's fondness of yellow was due to a physical condition that caused the world to look yellow to him. Everyone sees differently. Who is to say what is perfect and what is imperfect? For example, the beautiful twinkling of the stars is caused by the atmosphere and our astigmatism. Otherwise, they would appear as drab, perfectly round dots of light. Some people see with their hands, ears, and other senses. These people have an added perspective that people with "normal vision" don't have. In the final analysis, "seeing" is a mental rather than a physical act. To see through another's eyes is to truly get into his mind.

COMMENTS:

The idea is original and well-executed, although a little long-winded. The descriptions are the strength of the essay—giving strong impressions of the person as well as the incidents. His sense of humore, sensitivity, and insight are clearly reflected. The essay leaves the reader with a sense of who Sam Liu is. (JWM)

An excellent, clever, sometimes humorous analysis of a common problem. The student uses basic but very adequately descriptive vocabulary. It is a well-organized, nicely developed essay that is presented from an apparently original perspective. (TG)

Scott Locke
College: Brown University

I went through a C.I.T. program this past summer which taught me how to work with children: teaching them to be independent, while learning how to grow as part of a group. During the course of the summer I grew attached to many of the children. This attachment was one of the most meaningful experiences of my life. I grew attached to one child in particular, because of this I hope to work with children often in the future. His name is Jason. Jason is only eight, but he and I developed a bond that is incomparable to any I've experienced with anyone else.

Jason and I developed a sort of symbiotic relationship that produced much more than either of us consciously put into it. He wanted someone older who could care enough to spend time with him. When I came along he was thrilled. In turn he offered his love and complete trust. This bond is very similar to that between brothers yet different in that it lacked the sibling rivalry aspect.

Through working with Jason I learned to accept responsibility for and to be aware of the needs of children. Jason's being only eight years old made him seem so innocent; he appeared to be vulnerable and I sought to protect him from harm in the way a parent would for his or her own child. Despite my good intentions there was one time when I failed.

I was coaching a baseball team on which Jason was playing. To convince him to play the outfield, I told him that his team needed him there. This was completely true. I must have "laid it on" a little too thick. When a crucial play came his way he was nervous and the ball rolled through his legs. This was followed up by a grand slam home run. By the time the inning was over, Jason was crying hysterically. He told me that he let "*me*" and the team down. When he said that, I felt rotten. To think that he was so worried about letting me down touched me. It was this feeling of affection that has made me decide to work with children in the future.

Recently my brother, who is a friend of Jason's brother, told me that Jason was upset because he hadn't heard from me and thought that I did not love him anymore. When I heard this, I immediately wrote to him telling him that I still love him and always will. When I learned that I had such a lasting effect on a child I was on a self high. I got such satisfaction knowing that I could bring joy to others and form a lasting bond of love.

COMMENTS:

Scott means well and probably does a lot of good. The problem here concerns both the writing style and the thinking. Both are clichés. Every upper-middle-class Counselor in Training wants to tell how he/she climbed the mountain. They didn't. They were pleasant and helpful. Unfortunately this piece aggandizes all that. Using godawful expressions such as "meaningful experience" and "from this . . . I learned" our writer attempts to sanctify the trivial. (SAB)

This writer, while giving something of himself to others, really perhaps gained more than the children. The writer was asked to give the college more information about himself not shown on the application. The writer demonstrates through this experience his concern and sensitivity to others. Most colleges are looking for people who can relate to others and are not just scholars. (BPS)

Jamie F. Metzl
College: Brown University

I do not have a father on the alumni board of Brown, I don't even have an uncle there. All right, I was not elected to the presidency of some huge, national corporation. I can't (if you promise to keep it a secret) tell you of my Olympic trial in the javelin throw. (Probably because I've never seen one of those long, wormy things.) I do, however, have a seven-inch-tall plastic Godzilla.

Godzilla hasn't always been with me though; he was born and raised in the wilds of a Taiwanese rain forest. When he was only a small monster, his mother sent him for a dental appointment in Taipei. Godzilla, whose family was inbred (for obvious reasons), suffered from dyslexia. On his way, he passed by a large factory which had a sign reading LETTAM. Little did he know that this was his family's most feared spot. He was instantly grabbed, priced, and boxed for shipment. (Once his brother, who also had dyslexia, had wandered onto a ship headed for SOIDUTS LASREVINU, but that's a completely different story.)

Godzilla was sent to the United States, where he was imprisoned in a shiny glass case for three years. Then came his emancipation; I bought him. I took him to his new home: my shelf. There he now proudly stands between books of Thoreau and Emerson, and Kermit the Frog.

Godzilla is not the tough exterior he portrays. The true Godzilla lies within. Through my interaction with this paragon of monsterness, I have come to understand his meaning. Godzilla was born in the wild, yet he was pulled away from this by the forces of society. He has never, and will never abandon, his natural view of the world. His truth is only what is true to himself, not to any toy company or movie studio, or anything else for that matter. He believes imposed truth to be a monstrosity.

Godzilla has been given a pretty bad rap by the press, but I'll be the first to admit that he's really a sensitive monster. This is because he has huge eyes which allow him to really look around. He wants to use this vision to understand as much of the world around him as possible, so that he can be honest with himself and not only be influenced by the immediate.

I have given Godzilla a new home, but even with this foundation, he is an eternal dreamer. He dreams of the ideal, of true beauty. Once, when I woke up, Godzilla had done a strange thing. He had ripped a page out of one of my books of Thoreau. It read:

> If you have built castles
> in the air, your work need
> not be lost, that is where they
> should be. Now put the
> foundations under them.

Godzilla wants to be free to explore and strive for his dreams. To do this, he needs to be free from all but his own restrictions. He wants to use this freedom as a means of exploring himself, not only as a dreamer, but as a monster.

And so as I curl up in bed each night. I look over at Godzilla who speaks to me of myself. He speaks of truth, he speaks of understanding, he speaks of dreams, and he speaks of freedom. He also speaks of being a plastic-covered monster in the middle of the Midwest.

COMMENTS:

This essay is a thoroughly entertaining escape into the author's imaginary yet real world. The freedom, joie de vivre, and creative expertise the author reflects in this essay validate qualities that, I believe, are important to a college community. (AAF)

This is another offbeat essay that certainly achieves the goal of making the writer stand out from the crowd; and the juxtaposition of Godzilla and Thoreau is an arresting one. There is a certain amount of cuteness, such as describing a javelin as "wormy" and the monster as dyslexic. Some of the sentiments about truth, beauty, and freedom are a bit top-lofty, too. On the other hand, such ideals are a part of the dreams of youth, and the final sentence is quite simply a lovely change of pace. (RCM)

Eric Pulier
College: Harvard University

I've been offered advice for every conceivable situation. Relatives, friends, teachers, enemies, even strangers, have bits of wisdom to pass on to me. This is not to say I accept anyone's counsel lightly. I evaluate advice carefully before adopting it.

There is serious information that others have given me in the hope that I may avoid having to discover it for myself. In this category is the advice of my grandfather, whose last words to me were to live my life with hard work and honesty. I have no doubt of the merit of these sentiments, as he was living proof of their success.

Separating this class of advice from the less somber, such as my grandmother's, "Don't eat standing up or you'll get fat toes," is not as easy as it may first appear. Only after much experience can I now keep the different categories of advice apart in my mind, and even now clarification of further explanation is often needed before a final judgment is possible.

When I was younger, the very idea of questioning the advice of elders was foreign. When my mother was cold, she advised me to put on a sweater. Not until the sweat began to flow did I suspect that the advice might be flawed. Could it be that the thermal identity I had shared with her as a fetus had ended? The implications of this train of thought was staggering. I took off my sweater and told my disbelieving mother the reason. In this case the advice had not been offered for reflection but obedience, and she put the sweater back on me. The line that divides advice from rules is often indistinct.

Advice from strangers is quite easy to come by. My experiences with this kind of advice have taught me a great deal. There was the man who exclaimed, "Bet Silver Slew in the Fourth, kid, ya' can't lose!" Needless to say, I could. Then there was the stranger with the fantastic tip on Southern Pacific Petroleum stock. It seemed that the Iranian hostage crisis was going to create a demand for Australian shale oil. After I thanked him heartily and bought the stock, it plummeted to one-hundredth its value. The lesson is obvious: Ignore the advice of a stranger unless he's paying.

Advice on marriage is the most sensitive kind. Any objections to this advice are met with a flood of supportive examples. Marriage advice ranges from my parents' "marry the girl that you love," to my grandfather's "marry the Jewish girl that you love," to my grandmother's "marry the Jewish girl that you love who will wash your socks for you." As I said, some advice is not meant for reflection.

Unfortunately, a great deal of the advice I get is forgotten immediately and is consequently unavailable for further discussion.

Certain advice does lurk in my mind, however, and springs forth when I'm presented with an applicable situation. Notable is that of the wise old lady of the Teaneck Townhouse Scrabble Club, who spoke these fateful words: "Son," said she, "never use a blank for less than forty points."

COMMENT:

I like the way the student gets right to the point of what he wants to say. His is a one-sentence introduction that avoids too much flowery establishment of a thesis statement, and thereby is a welcome sight to committee readers already red-eyed. He comes up with clever, quite original witticisms ("ignore the advice of a stranger unless he's paying"), and the generally humorous tone makes for enjoyable reading. It tells us much about Eric in the process. Reading this I had the feeling I was watching a good stand-up comedian, who illustrated points of everyday wisdom with pertinent anecdotes—and whose next one-liner I awaited eagerly. The only criticism I would make is of the rather abrupt ending, which prevents the essay from concluding with true impact. (RJO)

Erin Ryan
College: Harvard University

I guess the whole thing is kind of ironic. Ironic or not, however, it saved his life—and warmed mine.

The Aaron Copland Music and Arts Program (ACMAP) is a small summer program in upper Westchester in which I have participated for five years, as both a camper and a staff member. The program offers major and minor programs in theater, music, the fine arts, and recently in dance. Over my four years as a theater major I performed in numerous productions. There is one, though, that stands out foremost in my mind. It opened during my second summer; in fact, I can even remember the date: August 2.

On August 2, 1983, I was thirteen years old, and had just climbed off stage from performing in my second major role in a drama. The ACMAP people, a wonderfully supportive bunch, rushed the actors with heaps of hugs and congratulations, as was customary after an ACMAP show. On this particular night, however, I felt distant from people for some reason; my friends seemed strangers, and I was overcome with loneliness. I slipped away from the crowds and wandered back to my bunk, still in costume and still flustered with the usual post-performance emotions. The tension of the oncoming show had withered my energy over the last week. I realized, as I struggled up the darkened path that cut through the woods to my cabin, how utterly sad I was—and had been for quite some time. I wondered why it was so dark this evening; it then occurred to me that there was no moon . . .

The darkness was so cold, and though it was August, I suffered a terrible chill—accompanied by terrible fear. I was tall for a thirteen-year-old, but in the nocturnal vastness of the forest I suddenly felt smaller than anyone I had ever known. My pace slowed until it stopped; I was suddenly surrounded by silence and blackness, with only a sickly wind about my ankles to remind me that I indeed existed in a corporeal world. I suddenly decided that I absolutely could not make it to my cabin alive in this nightmarish manner and turned ninety degrees to my left, heading blindly toward the closest familiar location at hand.

When I finally reached the lake, I was exhausted. The water was very still; I could barely discern its surface from the blurred edge of the forest. There was almost no light, and all was obscured by a murky vapor of some sort. I stepped carefully over the bed of cedar and pine needles which fastened the lake to the woods and then suddenly halted. My fear of being alone in the forest quickly dissolved and was replaced by a new fear of *not* being alone—there was someone else at the lake. In darkness I could just distinguish a huddled figure perched on the gnarled rock which stood guard beside the lake. I crept closer, and the dim reflection of starlight off the water showed me the face of David, the quiet artist.

I didn't know him well; he had always been rather introverted. I remembered that when I had once looked into his face, I had been frightened by the anger in his eyes. But now my fears vanished; I was even glad to see him. As I had felt strangely alienated by my other friends earlier, I somehow felt an affinity for him—as we were both, for our own particular reasons, trying to escape that evening. I climbed beside him on the rock and sat down. He had lately been making efforts to talk to me, I suppose because I seemed like someone who would listen. Ashamed as I am to say it now, I retreated from his pursuit, feeling already overburdened with my own problems and with the problems of my other friends, some of whom were stable—while others were not. My act of selfishness, of course, served only to worsen my feelings of guilt, and his of rejection.

I sighed as I felt the tiredness creep over my body. I think some words passed between us; they must have been mine, and were probably meaningless. He remained almost motionless, wrapped in the fog that rose soundlessly over the water. His manner was strange, but such was not unusual, and therefore did not faze me. I asked him whether he had seen my play, and he meekly answered that he had. I went on to groan about various catastrophic events that had passed during the evening and began to relate my experience in the woods when in the middle of my sentence he croaked something unintelligible. "What?" I asked.

"I almost just tried to kill myself."

—Oh, Jesus Christ—I thought, my mind reeling. It wasn't that I didn't have experience dealing with suicide; God—after dealing with some of my friends I felt like a professional. But I didn't know David very well—I was a little frightened by him. And the absolute last thing I needed at the moment was suicide . . .

Then, in the following instant, all such thoughts evaporated and I suddenly switched into emergency mode. For a split second my mind groped for a course of action, found one, and clung to it. He told me that he had almost tried to commit suicide. He was still sitting intact beside me; obviously something had prevented him from completing his plans. In a very casual but reassuring way, I asked, "What made you stop?"

"Huh?"

"Why did you stop? Why did you change your mind?"

"Oh . . . I don't know, um—" And so we began. I knew there had to be some things in life that were important to him and that kept him holding on, with however thinly strung threads. As I held him back, he began to understand just what those important things were and why they were so important. Upon reflection, he realized that the knowledge of how much pain such an act of violence would have caused his family had heavily influenced his refrain. Thus the importance of his family members to him was unearthed—his love for them and their love for him. He apparently had many miserable family problems. Usually he thought only of the problems, but now the genuine love shone through in his mind. Such an incredible thing followed: I wish that every struggling teenager could have the kind of—almost spiritual experience that we took part in. If all the troubled kids could only take the time to explore the significance of their existences and the beautiful aspects of life for them and life in general, teenage suicide would be obsolete . . .

We pooled our consciousness to isolate exactly what was so meaningful and wonderful in life, to find out why we really should want to live. David was neither hostile nor uncommunicative toward the experiment; he was entirely eager to find inspiration for living. As is often the case, David never wanted to die—he only needed help and attention. All other attempts at getting the support he needed had failed, and he was forced to resort to a final outcry. We spoke about his family, and his love—a warm abundance waiting for reception but finding no place in a violently broken home. But we also spoke about his love of art and music, about all the visible ways of improving the situation at home now. We spoke about the beautiful things in life—and the little things. We remembered how beautiful simple things can be and can make you feel, like lying in the sunshine in the morning, or writing a poem, or reading one. We began to really understand the importance of so many small actions that we performed daily and never truly considered. We took the time to think about the people we cared about and who cared for us, and marked ways of showing that love and perhaps making them a little happier. So many wonderful things existing in nature occurred to us—we felt honestly ashamed at not having paid enough attention to them before. Life would be so much more beautiful, it seemed, if we stopped in the midst of sleepwalking through our daily routines to witness the myriads of beautiful and completely natural events that take place day after day. Watching small children play in the park and seeing their fresh innocence was beautiful. So was taking a long hot bath, or listening to music with eyes closed at two o'clock in the morning. And so was hugging another human being. Or helping one. There were so many people in the world who needed help. What could be more beautiful than giving parts of oneself to helping them.

We cried a lot, and then laughed at ourselves for probably looking like a terrible cliché. Somewhere along the line, we had both received a dose of inspiration—something both of us had needed badly in our own separate degrees.

David had attempted to asphyxiate himself by pouring ginger ale into his lungs, an act we sometimes perform accidentally and refer to as "swallowing (the drink) the wrong way." His act had been planned and deliberate, he had even undergone self-relaxation exercises in order to prevent a reflexive muscle spasm which would have forced him to cough the liquid forth again.

He had been succeeding rather well. Something that was non-physical, however, suddenly overwhelmed him and coerced him to cough, soon rendering all the relaxation useless. He retched until his system was free of the alien substance, and weakly sobbed atop the rock until minutes before I arrived.

In an act maybe of triumph, or maybe of defiance, we strolled off to the camp canteen and bought some soda to drink.

Brian C. Smith
College: Pomona College

ONE TERRIFIC TASK: JUST THE MORALS

The selection of a quotation with a special significance to me is a difficult task because I feel that I have to tell you everything about my hopes and aspirations in just a few lines. I consider myself somewhat more complex than that, so I decided to concentrate my efforts on a quotation which I believe has had a significant effect upon my moral development.

Quotation: Alice the Maid

Every boy's a man inside—
Every girl's a woman, too
C'mon take a lesson from Mother Nature
Here's what you've got to do

When it's time to change
You've got to rearrange
Who you are into
What you want to be
*Sha Na Na Na Na Na Na Na
    Sha Na Na Na Na
              *[repeat]

Perhaps before I begin to speak about this quotation I should familiarize you with its origins. This bridge and refrain, from a song originally performed by The Brady Six, are two parts of a terribly deep and deeply moving song I heard first on a television show of the early 1970s, *The Brady Bunch*. This show was (and still is for millions of others and myself) the story of a lovely lady (Carol) who was bringing up three very lovely girls. She, a widow, met Mike Brady, a widower, who was raising three boys of his own. Well the one day that the lady met this fellow, they both knew it was more than a hunch, and were wed. Alice, the maid, and Tiger, the dog, rounded out the cast, and with a team of brilliant writers behind them, they produced the most winning combination of pointed social commentary and good ol' down-home fun this country's networks had ever seen.

They're Not Just Beautiful; No Panacea

The Bradys have given me many treasured memories, but their rendition of this song is the one I hold most dear. The simple, gentle, and loping lyricism of the song makes it aesthetically beautiful, and its traditional structural setting hides furtively the more important questions posed. The Bradys forced me to face the political and social upheaval of the times—the Nixonian presidency, the feminist insurgency, the self-centeredness of the generation, and the final disintegration of the Vietnam policy. Although I did not make it through this period unscathed, thanks to the Bradys I did not end up glassy-eyed and directionless. The Bradys possessed incredible foresight, but even they could in no shape or form offer a panacea to cure all the world's ills. They realized that both political and social change would be gradual, offering steps to follow so that change could come about ("Change . . . Who you are into What you want to be"). The Bradys were optimists, and they were extremely enthusiastic about what man could inevitably accomplish with the proper guidelines. Ever-changing man, when exposed to change, is capable of almost any task set before him. Practical methods need not be presented when the solution is this universal. Life is a far simpler endeavor with the Bradys leading my way.

True Solution Is Mine; Reach the Refrain

Do the Bradys offer the only quotation that encompasses all that my morals have been built upon? I give answer in this manner, "Yes, I say, Yes!" Most quotes I could disregard easily, their meanings being too distant from my inner self. Actually, the only two families other than the Bradys to whom I seriously gave consideration were the Kennedys and the Partridges. All three families dealt extensively with art and social consciousness, and both of these are of special importance to me. Yet, ultimately, I found their theories on life too reliant upon the upper classes dragging the rest of the world through man's progress, too pessimistic about the capabilities of your average "Joe." Where these two families can project only stagnancy, the Bradys have given the people of the world a chance at glorious triumph. For these reasons, the Bradys' influence on my person has been all-pervasive, they have made me a more complete individual.

COMMENTS:

An original approach although a bit lengthy—a good message from a bright, intense young man. It works because he writes well. (JWM)

This student expands well on an unusual "quotation," thus revealing his equally unusual choice of a model family. Although the writer touches upon what this show did for him I feel he could have gone into more depth to explain more fully the true effects the show had upon his life. (TG)

SELF-PORTRAITS

Ellen L. Beckerman
College: Princeton University

It is a very difficult thing, to define one's self on a piece of paper. Can anyone, through one example, reveal his essence? Whatever words I can grasp will never have the richness of the emotion they are meant to convey. On the page my words look hollow, inadequate: "beauty," "pride," "pain," the words do not hold the intensity of the actual feelings. The image may be there, but the feeling, the feeling must be experienced, and in each person it will be different. And whatever two hundred words I use will be scrutinized, will be ME in your eyes. How can I show you who I am in ten minutes when it has taken me every breath of the last seventeen years to even begin to ask myself the same question?

I am the honey-colored sounds of my grandmother's grand piano on a Saturday morning when the family has gone out for breakfast.
I am the scent of burning leaves and smashed pumpkin, and I am the foggy breath off the top of the pond next door.
I am the scintillation of colored city lights as the car cradles across the bridge, the skidding of windshield wipers across drizzled glass, the streaking of each light into lines of pink.
I am the smack of a spinning volleyball against sweaty forearms, the burning of elbow skin against a newly waxed gym floor.
I am the clean sting of chlorine and the tickle of freshly cut grass which clings to wet feet in summertime.
I am a kaleidoscope of every breath, every shadow, every tone I have ever sensed.

I went on a canoe trip and stood under a pine tree watching the rain patter against the lake and felt the warm summer wind and thought that I had found absolute peace and perfection in one droplet of water.
I sang at a school talent show for the first time in my life after years of being stage-shy. The crowd was small and cozy, and the

157

light was warm as the guitar hummed. I ignored my fear, because everything was perfect, and let myself be free and sang and sang . . .

I don't know whether Ronald Reagan is good or bad.

People who argue that nuclear war is bad annoy me because they assume that someone on earth thinks that nuclear war is good, and avoid the real issue, which is how to prevent nuclear war.

I don't understand people who hate camping. I hope that I never feel that business and politics are more real than a pine forest or an open plain.

Reality and perfection are in my mind synonymous. I think that the word is perfect. Even things which I hate are perfect because hatred is no less real an emotion than love. Famine is terrible, war is terrible, murder is terrible. But to say that nothing terrible should exist is denying everything this world contains. There cannot be wonderful without terrible. Pain is just as beautiful as joy, from an objective point of view.

The exciting thing for me is that I know that there is so much more for me to learn, and that everything I embrace as truth now is a very small part of what I will eventually be able to recognize.

The terrible thing is that I know when I die I will not know a millionth of the knowledge which all people on earth collectively hold. No matter how many days I sit and read, research, engulf information, I will never be exposed to everything. And right now I want to be exposed to everything.

COMMENTS:

Philosophical, poetic young lady. The introductory paragraph is a bit histrionic; the next several reveal some beautiful appreciations and recognitions; the third last is confusing. The last two are honest and genuine. I'd take her into my honors program. (MAH)

Absolutely wonderful. Insight, depth, expressive, clarity—all are part and parcel of this essay. Not only do we know the writer but we can understand her. P.S. Extremely well done! (JLM)

Jordana Simone Bernstein
College: Harvard University

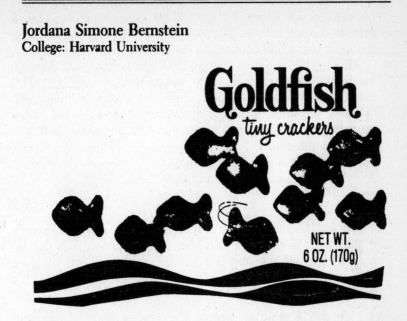

Goldfish
tiny crackers

NET WT.
6 OZ. (170g)

This one has the right idea. He knows where he wants to be, and he is determined to get there, even if it means swimming against the tide. He might be forced to push past those in his path, but he seems sensible enough to do it gently, without disturbing the flow. He may not be making the best move, but he feels it is right for him, and that is all that matters. One cannot be sure if he is turning toward something or away from it, but there is purpose in his stroke and he has a goal. One hopes he will achieve it; he probably will.

Independence of thought is marvelous. With an idea and a desire to fulfill it, the possibilities are infinite. To develop such an idea, one first answers the basic question, "What is it that you like to do?" The response is a personal one, and in order to reply accurately, there is the need for exploration.

I am pleased to have been offered numerous opportunities to explore many different areas. There have been clubs to join, organizations to belong to, activities to participate in, and experiences to share. My greatest difficulty seems to be that I am interested in too many things for a twenty-four-hour day. I have learned to set limits for myself by developing a sense of priorities. I can only try to move in a specific direction, aiming toward a goal while continuing my investigation along the way.

Although he is only a Pepperidge Farm goldfish, the depth of his message is greater than the paper he is printed on. This creature makes a subtle and important statement. His individuality separates him from the crowd. Success is not always measured by achievement; sometimes it is simply the ability to see things differently.

Perhaps that is why he is smiling.

COMMENTS:

Jordana has a cute idea and therein is its limitation. Certainly it shows initiative and a coherent style to present her deviant goldfish in such glowing terms. Alas, it also reflects the slick condensation of advertising, replete with audiovisual aids. Is the fish breathing a little too heavily perhaps? (SAB)

I like this. It is simply written but makes a powerful statement for independence that most students (and adults) can relate to. Using the *Goldfish* heading catches the reader's attention. (BPS)

Catherine L. Censor
College: Columbia College

LATIN ME THAT, ME TRINITY SCHOLARD!

"I shall burn the city." This motto appeared on the shield of Capaneus in *Seven Against Thebes* and it struck terror in the hearts of his enemies. I have taken that very phrase as my own motto not because I am planning to become a career arsonist, but because it is a reminder of the power of the individual. As Achilles could turn the tide of battle, as Hektor alone could defend a city, so can the individual, even in these quotidian days, reach the mythic heights.

My shield and sword, as of late, is a word processor. Nightly, the program loads, sounding like a thousand cockroaches tap dancing, as I rack my brains for a battle plan. The shimmering city of literature is begging to be torched! It is fortified with dry wood.

I believe that in many ways, the present age is a rather undistinguished one. For example, my favorite form of communication, writing, has suffered to the extent where the well-written letter is a rare find. But I have not despaired of my generation yet. I believe in the power of the individual and I believe that with a little guidance I might become a very powerful individual at that.

Me, in short: Since the age of five, I have been able to spout words like "quotidian" or "anthropocentric." I tried to read *Finnegans Wake* when I was eleven, and only in the midst of the second chapter did I admit that I was baffled. I am contemptuous and jealous of mathematicians as I have never been able to do long division. While working as a volunteer at the American Museum of Natural History, I suffered one of the most humiliating experiences of my life. I was assigned to the "Dino Cart," a portable sales unit replete with glow-in-the-dark dinosaur keychains and a cash register. The problem was that the cash register was not one of those marvels of technology that tell you how much change is owed the customer. I was stuck, horror of horrors, doing the computations in my head! I had the change all figured out for a dinosaur aficionado when he handed me two pennies. He had to count his change five times. From that moment on, I promised myself that I would send a copy of my first published story to that tourist with the spanking-new, glow-in-the-dark dinosaur keychain and case. I do not like to be thought of as mentally deficient.

I prefer the company of friends rather older than myself and stay up late into the night discussing matters of intellectual concern. I am, perhaps, a bit affected but never, I hope, to the extent of appearing ridiculous. I am not uncomfortable being alone for long periods of time and a little pleased to be perceived of as a bit "offbeat." I am consciously intellectual, sometimes pompous, but always distinctly me. I have lofty aspirations, but I feel I have the ability to achieve them. I have a prominent ego, a lively sense of humor, maturity, and a sense of style. I am a focused, eager, and happy person, and I can already smell smoke.

Ann Cox
College: Harvard University

I could tell you all about my wonderful achievements, slightly exaggerated of course, but I'd rather tell you what affects me, what I remember. The things like the way the six shadows of my tennis racket converged on the ball as it sat clearly marked in its yellow on the huge green court. And how the same ball was caught in the net by the back wall, like a fish. The way the herring plane in Maine swoops down on me all little on the long field. And the piece of hay stuck between my toes that stayed with me even as I went in to talk to my old aunt. How I promised to remember that and the time I was walking down the marble stairs of St. Ann's in my green knit skirt so I would know I existed then, that my past was not something simply planted in my brain. The way I've felt myself growing, almost physically, and listened to my growth settling into me, and welcomed it because it meant I was becoming more realistic about myself, so that not living in a world of illusions I could exist more in this world and feel all its happinesses and wonders which are greater than anything imagined because they are real—the most amazing thing of all.

The things that I love to feel and discover are the subtleties happening between people and events. How one person helplessly tries to make himself known to others, the way the others might ignore him, and the way he will stay with the others as friends because he's been saved from something he doesn't want to acknowledge anyway. The way masses or a nation of people will ignore some huge, very true situation, and then slowly discover it in a way that's as useless as if they'd never found it. The way I myself fit into everyone's patterns and the way my actions affect me, why they make me feel good or bad, and whether they really do. The things that are observed and given: trees, animals, ourselves, snow, and winds. Using my body to certain ends and to an end in itself: sexual, transportation, exploration, and to an immersion into an environment and discovering the physical realities of the world, as skiing does. Traveling, the feeling of "wanderlust" raging and satisfied, going wherever I wish to, encountering, dealing with, and enjoying new people, situations, and places.

And somewhere within this huge scheme of myself, learning fits in as a major part. Education brings all these parts of the world to me, and me to them, and I can work them and myself, as I use my own mind to deal with them, cast light on them, and encompass them. And so now I wish to present myself at one of the "great educational institutions" to gather, process, and give more.

COMMENT:

I liked the unsettling tone of the essay. The opening reminded me of Kenneth Koch's poetry—the images are startling and disconcerting. The essay walks a thin line, though, since it comes close to being so abstract and fuzzy that it loses its impact. The daring, almost free association saves it. I think, though, it's one of the weaker essays in this group. (PT)

Theodore C. Dros
College: Hamilton College

In his movie, *Zelig*, Woody Allen portrays a figure, Zelig, with a multiple personality. He changes his character and even his physical appearance to match the different situations he experiences. One minute he is waving to us from Hitler's entourage during a speech, the next, he is a cardinal in the Vatican, or up at bat for the New York Yankees. All of these experiences in his life are divorced from one another, each exists as an entirely separate entity, having no connection to his past or future. He is, in other words, the perfect chameleon, about whom we are left to wonder, "Who is the real Zelig?"

What I understand you to be asking me to address here is "who is the real Ted Dros?" As I began to answer that difficult question, I find myself needing "to do a Zelig" by relating to you some of the diverse environments in which I've been immersed over the last five or six years.

Growing up in a changing community during the sixth to eighth grades, I saw my grammar school, Our Lady of Refuge in Brooklyn, face a dramatic ethnic shift in enrollment. Over a few short years, the school population changed from being predominantly Caucasian to being almost totally black and Hispanic. I graduated as one of two "minority students" in the class, and I was treated as one. On the one hand, my teachers of my own race alienated me from my classmates by anticipating that I would perform "par excellence." On the other hand, my own desire to be accepted by my fellow students required me to hold back academically—to resist answering all the questions. There were definitely moments when I was tempted to get up and walk out on a system that was insensitive to the needs of someone who didn't conform to the majority, but I didn't. Instead, I withstood all of the unjust treatment that a minority typically has to endure. Having had the shoe on the other foot for that period of my life, however, I now more fully understand the injustice and resultant moral outrage that blacks and Hispanics must experience in our society-at-large.

In striking contrast, summertime has always provided me an opportunity to explore another side of life. During this time my family and I stay at my grandmother's summer beach house in Breezy Point, Queens. Consisting primarily of middle-class Irish families, this community has been a part of my life since birth and has served to put me in touch with my own ethnicity. At Breezy Point there is an Irish concern with ancestral lineage, a deep-rooted pride in family, and an interest in folk dance and music. My family, as are most in Breezy Point, is closely tied to an active religious life. Perhaps grounded in centuries of Irish oppression, the community is a hotbed of religious, social, and cultural bonding.

Finally, at the end of the summer four years ago, a totally new and unexplored environment, one that was chiefly academic, was first introduced into my life. At Regis striving for academic excellence was encouraged by all. It was quite a different situation than grammar school. Regis High School propelled me into another world—one that was more white middle- to upper-class and "preppy" than I had ever known. It gave me freedom through which I was able to pursue my interests with confidence, voice my opinions, exercise my right to be wrong, and accomplish my goals. As the result of being accepted for who I really was, I became more at ease with my world.

Given the three vastly different environments that I have just described in this self-descriptive essay, I imagine it's pretty easy for you to understand why I should think of myself as a Zelig-figure. There is, however, a striking difference between us: Zelig—chameleon that he is—totally adapts to his various environments and looks at each one as if it were an isolated set of circumstances. The effect of the diverse environments I have known on my perception has been dramatically different from that on his. I assimilate to the point of being comfortable with retaining my identity. As a matter of fact, when I move on from these learning experiences, I take a part of them with me: an idea, thought, feeling, emotion—a certain understanding.

This carryover from experience helps to explain why I still find it exciting to be teaching parish CCD classes at my old grammar school to Haitian, Jamaican, and Puerto Rican children. It also accounts for the enthusiasm I bring to the summer job I have held for three years at the Silver Gull Beach Club in the Rockaways. Here I cater to another cultural group—a Jewish community—of which I had no prior knowledge, but which I found myself drawn toward as a contrast to my Breezy Point Irish heritage.

While the answer to the question "who is Ted Dros?" may vary at any given moment according to my environment, I have, unlike the schizophrenic Zelig, a single, though evolving personality. While I value multiplicity of situations and diversity among people precisely because they prompt my personal growth, I do at most points know and like who I am. It's just that, building on my past, I also look forward to the person I will be tomorrow.

COMMENTS:

This student completes a difficult task with excellence. His initial analogy to Zelig arouses the reader's attention. He describes his varied experiences in a clear, concise form that flows naturally from one to another. I would have no difficulty accepting him for both his background and his description of it. (TG)

A well-written, clear account of Ted Dros, whom the reader knows quite well after reading it. Where many essay writers may have fallen into a rather tedious autobiographical format . . . "I was born . . . ," Ted has neatly woven Woody Allen's *Zelig* to create a thorough, interesting, and informative essay. (JWM)

Susan Glueck
College: Harvard University

I like ducks.

When most people think about typical duck-lovers, they envision "preppies" in lime-green pants, Sperry Topsiders, and flamingo pink shirts with little whales. Surely an affection for ducks is part of what makes preppies preppy. After all, it fits right in with old money. Ralph Lauren ads, the chateau in the Adirondacks, and the Orvis catalog.

And when most people think about ducks, they see chubby white barnyard Pekins with carrot-orange beaks or green-headed mallards in the park pond.

But I like ducks and am not a preppy by any stretch of the imagination. And when I think "ducks" I see waterfowl with long beaks or short beaks, tufts or tails, hoods or cowls, diving or dabbling. The world of waterfowl appreciation contains more than meets the casual eye.

I first began my love affair with the family *Anatidae* when I was around five years old. Ducks must have had a definite impact on me even then, as I nicknamed my older brother "Ducky." As I and my interest grew together, I travelled to water as often as possible. The zoo duck pond, the lake in a nearby park and any drainage ditch on long road trips all held the promise of quacking web-footers. One of my favorite activities during each summer spent in Michigan was (and still is) to paddle "downtown" to visit the mallard denizens of the marina in Round Lake.

Now as a duck aficionado my appreciation extends not only to mere duck-watching but also to drawing ducks, photographing ducks, writing about ducks. But never (good heavens!) eating them. For me, eating a duck would be like making ragout out of my best friend.

I most often draw ducks from memory, but have found it useful to refer to photographs in order to get that curve of the tail just right. I have also sculpted a duck in my seventh-grade art class (it sits complacently on my dresser) and am working on a whole felt aviary of mallards, pekins, scaup, mergansers, etc. I doubt, however, that I will ever become the famous artist of a Duck Stamp, for my fowl have a particular Thurberian look to them.

If you are wondering where I keep all my ducks, the answer is in a special folder marked "Ducks and Achievements." By now, the half filled with photographs, magazine and newspaper articles, and cartoons far outweighs the also voluminous pile of certificates, medals, etc., found under "Achievements." (Perhaps this reflects an interesting philosophical statement as well. Which should man prize more highly, his paltry accomplishments, which shall some day be forgotten, or the colorful endless lore of the duck, who floats on the ponds of Rome centuries after Caesar?)

Perhaps another reason I value ducks so highly is their memory-evoking capability. Often I can recall my extensive travels to the letter when I remember the ducks I saw there. The thought of Barrow's Goldeneyes (mother and chicks) swimming on the Vermilion Lakes is the perfect metaphor for Canada. I fondly reminisce about ancient Christian mosaics in Israel, not because of their depictions of holy men but for the ducks decorating the corners. And what better image for France than the duck? Nothing can bring back Mont Saint-Michel like my remembrance of standing ankle-deep in ocean mud during low tide, feeding my breakfast brioche to a bevy of green-winged teal I saw out my hotel window. But what best sums up the relationship I perceive between ducks and travel is what I heard a little French girl say to her mother, upon seeing the ducks at Fontainbleau: "Mais ou sont les autres canards? Ou sont les petits bébés canards?" Ducks obviously have a worldwide appeal for children of all ages and nationalities.

This is why I like ducks.

Don Hoffman
College: Amherst College

AN ESSAY

I am a product of hippies, he wrote, startled that he had begun with such an idea. It was an interesting way to begin, he pondered, though not totally accurate. He wasn't actually a *product* of hippies, but he had been given a brief, fleeting vision through their eyes. Yes . . . he and Joan Didion had walked through the place where the kissing never stopped, they had met Comrade Laski, they had taken courses at the Joan Baez School; his visions had caused him to redefine his beliefs. Was his outlook on his life his own, or had his ideas been passed on to him like genes? He sat outside on the Senior Patio and read her book, *Slouching Towards Bethlehem*; "space is a place" was written on his jeans in the spirit of Hippie Day. He believed he was a product of the ideas he encountered; shouldn't it be that way?

I am a product of everything, really. Just as he wrote, he noticed that he was finally doing it: writing those dreaded essays.

He once knew a friend who had visited the Temple of Essays. As he was being lowered down into the pit, he could hear the awful hiss of the essays below him, like snakes. "I hate snakes," he though, helplessly. What did they want? The meaning of life on paper. He could give them the fundamental theorem of calculus, the definition of Newtonian relativity, perhaps the three qualities of good writing, but only if he referred to his notes from September.

He had a great idea for an essay, but it passed like a gray freight train on the tracks near the river, where trains were no longer that frequent. Another idea came, then a multitude of others, pouring down on the paper as if falling from the waterfall in North Carolina named Silver Run. Some were tears, perhaps, bits of the soul. When he looked at the paper, he saw that the ideas had soaked it and made it soggy and impossible to read.

Then, there was a knock at the door. He opened it with trepidation, fearing a younger brother or perhaps another terror not so bad as that. Standing there was an original idea for an essay, naked and somewhat unformed. He wrestled with it, questioning it until he became a part of it. His life was merely an extension of this wonderful yet terrible idea, swirling like a hurricane. In his humanities class at school he was studying World War I, but he often felt like *he* was the one in the trenches. He was called daily to charge some great unseen idea. He used his pen as the sword, often finding it an unsuitable weapon. He never knew who won his war, but he knew by his grades that he had won at least a few important battles.

Besides fighting ideas, he was fighting to establish himself. He was fighting against being seen as impersonal; he was fighting against impersonal things. He loved dwelling on his own personal ideas, experiences, emotions. He had fought a grand battle with standardized tests. Could it be that this one important battle would change his life?

I don't think standardized tests deal with ideas, he realized. He *did* have aptitudes, but one for lapsing into extremes. But he enjoyed this because he often learned more because of it. Whether he explored Brighton or Bethlehem, he did so with both joy and fear. He loved ideas as well, writing English papers when the ideas flowed freely from him. Then, he actually believed in what he wrote, hearing the words, like foreign voices. He realized that ideas were not the only things that could possess him. Music controlled him too, signing him up for the church and school choirs, making him audition for musicals, driving him to create songs on the piano.

Other things control me too, he continued. He loved running, but often felt that he temporarily relinquished control of himself when he ran, as when he wrote English papers. When he ran, he sometimes felt that he would not be able to finish the race, he would have to stop and rest. He often wondered why he ran, as it was so difficult. The words of the coach, however, had given him a vision, an idea, to commit himself to the run: As the run came to an end, he always felt refreshed. He would be ready for tomorrow, he promised, he would get out there and run hard again, challenge himself, sometimes not knowing why but running hard just the same.

I am controlled by what I do, he rewrote.

COMMENT:

The author is controlled by metaphors and similes rather than having control over them. The ideas are complex and the writer is clearly intelligent. But, as he tries to show his complexity as a person, he loses control of the essay. The result is diminished by overabundance. (PLF)

Josh Jacobs
College: Amherst College

Some people, I am quite sure, go through all of high school without a single moment of social hesitance or exclusion. I would imagine that many cheerleaders and football players fit this mold—at least, that's what I've always heard. At any rate, I certainly have not had a maintenance-free high school social life; however, aside from the Whipped-Puppy Crush, which most adolescent males suffer at least once, I have had only one major watershed in these four years, a time when I realized that the past was ending, and that the future could go anywhere. This was when my best friend of four years, who I will refer to as The Philistine (or TP, for short), totally severed relations with me in the first weeks of my junior year.

An unsigned *New Yorker* editorial once described a true crisis as one in which ". . . for a measurable, anguished period . . . nothing happens. Truly nothing. . . . At a false turning point, we nearly always know, within limits, what will happen next; at a true turning point, we not only know nothing, we know that nobody knows. Truly nobody." As in this quote, I had several weeks in which I had no idea what to do. I had always been aware of the fact that TP was better-looking than I, and more confident as well. The fact that TP picked up a steady girlfriend mid-way through my time in Coventry brought me to the conclusion that I had become too great a burden on him, that my function as an amusing second banana had ended. I was becoming aware of the fact that there had always been a certain coolness about TP, one which I had not been exposed to being his friend. At times, I thought TP would come to me and apologize, and that all would be sweetness and light once more; I came to realize, however, that I could never accept such an apology in the unlikely event that it were to be proffered. Once revealed, a person's true feelings are nearly impossible to plow under again.

It was during this bitter time that I first became friendly with my current group of closest friends. I believe that I was attracted to them because, not to demean their maturity or complexity, I sensed that there was something about them that was more willing to care, and much less cynical and begrudging than TP was. It was hard to say why they were attracted to me; I do not remember trying particularly hard to impress them with my wit or intelligence, perhaps because I did not realize completely that I was growing closer to these people. It may be that my subconscious mind was, in a subliminal way, going all-out, realizing that this was a golden opportunity to make a transition from knowing and trusting just one person to having several confidantes.

It is with this group that I have spent the happiest months of my life. To be loved is the most joyful, most uplifting emotional state; giving of one's own love is a close second place, however, and with these friends I have had both. I have become more outgoing and spontaneous, and quite a bit sillier—in short, I feel better about being myself. Reflecting on the friendship that TP and I once had, I can say that the saddest lesson that I learned from my transitory semester in high school is that the best things in life are often the hardest to preserve, the hardest to hold on to; in the words of Robert Frost, "Nothing gold can stay."

COMMENTS:

My concern is that the essay appears to tell more about "TP" than about Josh Jacobs! I think that the topic of rejection is an interesting one. However, it would have been far better for me to know *specifically* how "JJ" has ". . . become more outgoing and spontaneous . . . sillier." The final paragraph is weakened by the use of generalizations. While candid about his relationships, Josh may be too confident about what he perceives as the reasons for the demise of his friendship. (AAF)

In my opinion, this is a very good essay. The organization and sentence structure are first-rate, the vocabulary provocative and appropriate, and the literary allusions are apt and unobtrusive. The writer gives us a lot of insight into the kind of person he is without making himself seem unduly boastful. It is an effective bit of writing. (RCM)

Joseph Libson
College: Princeton University

MY LIFE

Chapter One: I become a truant

The best thing that I ever did for myself was skip nine days of school in a row in the eighth grade. Actually the benedictions did not arise so much from the truancy as from the apprehension. This does not mean that I had been an axe murderer for the previous sections of my life, but rather that an unusual circumstance led to a great improvement in almost every aspect of my life. I was getting mediocre grades (i.e., B's and C's) at a mediocre school. I was not taking drugs or doing anything particularly nasty, but I was being incredibly lazy. This sudden burst of lethargy that led to the nine-day truancy overcame the activation barrier that had prevented my parents from taking retaliatory measures in response to all of the smaller things that I had done. Their response was draconian; first they separated me and my brother (we are exponentially more troublesome when together). In addition to deciding to send me to another school to separate me and my brother, my parents also decided that the punishment should extend into the summer since the deed had been done late in April and the schools punishment of nine Saturday detentions (yes, like the ones in *The Breakfast Club*) and disciplinary probation seemed insufficient. This planting season sentence consisted of my taking summer courses. Thus, it came to pass that I took algebra II before ninth grade.

When I arrived at Walnut Hills, which is the best academic public school in the city, I knew no one. This temporary exile resulted in a great discovery. Since I had no one to talk to during class, I decided that I would listen to see if the teacher was saying anything interesting. Lo and behold, knowledge flowed into and through me as excellent grades flowed out. At the tender age of thirteen, I had discovered that if I listened, I would understand. I had four straight-A quarters at Walnut Hills and transferred to St. Xavier, an even finer institution. It was closer to home and besides that my parents had heard that it was a "tough" no-nonsense school (good for discipline problems). As an additional plus, due to variances between the curricula of Walnut Hills and St. Xavier, I was able to become two years advanced in mathematics. Thus I was taking BC Calculus during my junior year at St. Xavier. My innovative listening theory still held at St. Xavier although more effort had to be put in to get the same grades simply because St. Xavier was a more difficult school.

Skipping nine days of school made me a better person, there is no doubt about it. Not only did my academics improve, but my devotion to athletics was enhanced to that of a religious fanatic and my sense of morals was even improved. I changed from a selfish rather unfriendly and sarcastic person into a more giving and open (but still sarcastic) individual. But, I was lucky; I got caught.

COMMENT:

The truant manages to show the reader, in very few words, just how much perspective he has on his past experiences. His focus on "getting caught" highlights his obvious self-awareness because it is so "unadolescent" of him to see his "getting caught" and being "punished" as a catalyst to his own intellectual and personal growth of which he is so clearly proud. This anecdote had a strong impact on me because it rings true and because Joe's tone is very sincere. (AST)

Heather L. Nadelman
College: Yale University

"Coffee or tea?"

A simple enough question, a question that seemingly requires an absentminded, automatic reply. Clearly, in this world one is either a coffee or a tea drinker. I, however, am an exception to this rule; I constantly vacillate between coffee and tea. My enjoyment of both drinks does not stem merely from flexible tastebuds, nor does it originate in a desire to be as little trouble as possible by drinking whatever is available. Rather, this ambivalence depicts two distinct sides of my personality.

Coffee is lively, exuberant, and extroverted: a wild, wet dog show, complete with pouring rain, whipping winds, and a dog who simply will not behave. The ring has become a sea of oozing mud, turning the dog you so perfectly groomed last night into a mud-splattered, bedraggled horror who resembles an alley cat more than a purebred show dog with a pedigree going back to the *Mayflower*. Animals who never before had shown signs of unstable temperament suddenly decide to be terrified of the wind's flapping their handlers' yellow rain slickers. All dogs are quick to take advantage of the fact that their handlers, with fingers numbed from cold and eyes half-blinded from rain, have very little control over them. On such a day, a steaming cup of well-brewed hot coffee is one's only salvation; only coffee can transform such misery into a memory that will be laughably, almost fondly, recalled.

Tea is sedate, thoughtful, and introverted: a cold November afternoon with a friendly fire crackling in the background. One sits in an overstuffed armchair with an open copy of *Wuthering Heights*, reading, dreaming, and listening to music that plays softly from the stereo. The novel and music flow into each other, transporting the room to a time that perhaps was, perhaps never was, or perhaps always is. The world's worries are locked outside, flung to the chilly winds; inside, all is peaceful and relaxed. On such an afternoon, one feels able to solve every riddle that the greatest minds have pondered. Yet oddly, on such afternoons one never attempts solutions. So near the point of understanding, one allows all answers to escape; if the mysteries of life were solved, much of the pure pleasure of thinking would be lost forever. At such moments of partial meditation it is tea, the world's most civilized drink, that is one's only conceivable companion.

Although often contradictory, my need for coffee and my need for tea balance each other nicely. The freneticism of the world of dog shows is as important as the quiet reflection of a peaceful afternoon. Perhaps I will originate a new personality classification, the "coffeetean," roughly equivalent to an introverted-extrovert or extroverted-introvert. Unlike the simple lives of people wholly shy or wholly exuberant, the life of a coffeetean, if a bit complicated, cannot fail to be varied and exciting.

Those who drink coffee, tea, and hot chocolate, however, are far too schizophrenic for their own good.

COMMENTS:

An interesting, relatively original, although somewhat contrived way of presenting two sides of her personality. The purpose of the essay is a good one—to attempt to give a clearer picture of how she sees herself. (JWM)

A rather abstract evaluation of a very simple idea. The vocabulary appears to be forced at times, possibly in an attempt to impress the reader. The well-chosen analogies, however, reveal a very imaginative student who expresses her ideas with both brevity and clarity. (TG)

Christopher C. Roberts
College: Yale University

I am not the kind of "people person" who requires great numbers of friends and people around him to be happy. I am independent, and am fascinated with people even more in the sense of wanting to learn from them and serve them. I do not even need people with me to learn from them. I frequently consider persons and their philosophies when I am alone.

This fascination became strongest about a year ago, and since then I can see how many of the people I have met have influenced me. For example, in the summer of 1985, I worked as a dishwasher/stockboy with a man named Tony Sumo. Tony was from a small village in Africa, and had been the secretary to the president of Liberia. When his country had a revolution, he fled to the United States, went to college, and took the same job I held as a middle-class high school student. Tony became a Christian along the route, and his world view fascinated me. Tony impressed me with how difficult it was to understand values and methods of reasoning drawn upon experiences alien to my own, but how those values and methods of reasoning could be none-theless valid.

Other individuals and groups of people have made similar impressions upon me. There is my father's friend who went to Yale, spent some time as a teacher and in the Peace Corps in India, and is now active in state politics. To me, he is an enlightening, and sometimes disturbing, blend of sixties' radical and smooth law school graduate politician. My supervisor last summer, when I worked as a volunteer in the Rocky Moun-tains, lives on an island in Puget Sound. On a minimum of income, he is building his house, and along with his wife, making his clothes and other necessities. From his island home he has sailed all over the Pacific in a boat he built himself. His lifestyle forces me to reflect on my own—how many of society's conventions must I accept? any? a few? I have a Soviet friend I met in Leningrad who does not subscribe blindly to all the Party propaganda nor to the American version of the news. Talking with her gave me yet another perspective on my own society's convictions and values. Another friend is a prison convict whom I met while I was a volunteer construction worker for a slum rehabilitation project downtown. He is not stupid, but he is simple. He reminds me of how lucky I am, but he also reminds me of the good and simple parts of life that I sometimes pass over. The lesson I draw from all of these people, though, does not concern the relative merits of each persons' way of life and philosophy, although that is a part of it, but rather that there are many possible, valid, and understandable ways of viewing the world.

Groups of people fascinate me as well as individuals. Leading a group forces me to examine my own motivations and strengths. I often ask myself, what makes this group of people special, and why are they worth belonging to? While working on political problems, it is necessary to examine groups of society. If I am to deliver a speech on teenage pregnancy, I need to know the psychology of high school dropouts, single-parent homes, and low-income families. If I am to sway an opponent of nuclear arms control, I need to understand the fears of people and the facts of weapons. I find when people are not causing me to work and reflect within my own mind, I am using my mind to work with them.

Over the last few years, I have developed the habits of personal reflection and discipline. I do not know whether it is other people or myself who should take the credit for this, but I do know that other people regularly educate me. Sometimes it is someone I do not know educating me through a book, or through something he or she has done that is in the newspapers. Sometimes I am enjoying a canoe trip or a mountain climb more because of the presence or memory of a friend. Sometimes people educate me directly, by conversation or letter. It is my personal reflections, so often catalyzed by other people, which change me. I am an extrovert, but a thoughtful and philosophical extrovert. People can be my friends, teammates, coworkers, and supervisors, but they are always my teachers.

COMMENTS:

This is basically a good essay. Although it is written in an easy, conversational style, which is appealing, it is sometimes grammatically awkward. The numerous examples back up the theme in the first paragraph and provide the reader with a great deal of information about the student's activities and associations which may not appear elsewhere in the application. The fourth paragraph is poorly written and does not hang together very well. It should have been edited and/or revised in order to fit in more easily with the total essay. (NA)

There is something about this essay that does not ring true. When the writer is talking about Tony, he is effective. Throughout most of the essay, however, he relies so heavily on the first person singular that the piece becomes tedious and self-serving. (TH)

Phillip Rodgers
College: Columbis College

Demosthenes, Moses, Winston Churchill, and Somerset Maugham. You're probably wondering what possible link these great men of years past could have to this piece about Phil Rodgers. Furthermore, you're probably thinking that they have no apparent relation to each other. One was an orator, one a biblical figure, one a statesman, and still another an author. But a little-known fact is that all of these men were stutterers. Add me to the list.

To fulfill your clinical curiosity, I'm classified as a secondary stutterer, which means that I was not born with the malady. At age eight, for some not yet diagnosed reason, I simply began speaking dysfluently. A quick mathematical operation tells one that I've been stuttering for nine years. My family seems to prefer to think of it as that I was fluent for eight.

But sometimes I wish that I didn't have the memories of my period of fluent speech. My mother, whom I love dearly and upon whom I place no blame for my problem, always speaks of me when the subject of children arises. She talks of how bright and intelligent I was, and how I loved to talk and be inquisitive. My big claim to fame was my relative eloquence at an early age. This is why I sometimes wish that I had been born a stutterer. My relatives, my parents, and most importantly, I, know what it was like for me to speak fluently. This knowledge imposes a feeling of guilt along with the other negative feelings associated with my speech problem. Guilt for not giving my parents the perfect son. Guilt for not being what I could have been. Guilt for not being a whole person.

But the guilt is only part of it. The more dominant feeling is frustration. Frustration perhaps about what I'm not to my family, but more importantly about what I'm not to myself. I want nothing more in this world than to make my family, and myself, proud of me. I want to make a contribution to somebody or something that will make a difference. But when the situation is such that I encounter an opportunity to make a contribution that may be hindered by my stuttering, my initial response is to shy away. And if the hindrance will burden others, I back off completely. As far as I see it, the problem is mine and I have no right to impose upon others to any greater extent than that which is necessary in verbal communication. As a result, I don't experience all that life has to offer. Frustration.

This is not to say that I've withdrawn from society. I truly believe the old maxim that whatever can be conceived and believed can be achieved. And if I attain nothing else in my life, this is what I want to do. Perhaps this sounds like a rather trivial goal, but what I desire most is to be fluent. I want nothing more than to express my feelings, thoughts, opinions without the ugliness of my stuttering in the foreground. But if I can't make my contribution to the world fluently, then I'll have to do it as I am.

However, contributing can get painful. Every time I open my mouth I take the risk of being jeered, laughed at, labelled "retarded," and so forth. And the hurt that I've experienced has stayed with me. All of the jokes, the insults, and the feelings of inferiority rarely expressed remain in my memory as clearly as yesterday. And I'm glad they do. They give me the strength to cope with what to me is a serious shortcoming. When I'm up against a situation in which I might be vulnerable, all I need do is recall the pain and almost desperate loneliness, and somehow I draw strength from it. The strength that I need to achieve all that I want to achieve. The strength to survive.

I recall a drawing I did in sixth grade. I composed it after being physically and emotionally humiliated in a brawl by three older boys who said that they didn't want a "retard" in their school. The drawing was a tear-stained image of a butterfly in a cage. That's a metaphor for who I am. I am a person wanting to share so much with the world, but encircled by a barrier stronger than that of any steel. I am a person wanting to express every thought, every emotion, but stymied by a force that is out of my realm of control. I am a person wanting to be able to speak without fear of ridicule or ostracization, but restrained by a weight greater than that of any physical burden. I am a person wanting to be freed from a perennial hindrance. I am a butterfly who has broken through his socio-erected limitations, but not his own intrinsic weakness.

COMMENT:

My reaction to this essay is one of sympathy for the writer, as much for what he appears to have endured from his family's reaction to his stuttering as for the suffering he has endured as a result of the stuttering itself. His latent handicap seems to have all but engulfed his consciousness to the point where everything in his life is measured in terms of what he cannot do, rather than what he can do. I found myself wanting to say, "It's not your fault *AND* I really don't hold it against you." Somehow I don't think saying anything would help. (AST)

Sara G. Silver
College: Columbia University

It was a beautiful day and my mindcleaning was proceeding nicely. I generally despise any sort of cleaning and avoid it whenever possible, but mindcleaning is different; it's much too important and delicate a job to delay. And it was doubly important that day, for I was debating starting my life anew in New York and I needed to rid my mind of old prejudices to make room for fresh ideas. So I ascended the stairs armed with garbage bag and duster, opened the door to my mind, and went in. Now, everyone has their own particular taste and everyone arranges their mind differently. In mine, all the rooms are arranged on different levels according to category around a big winding staircase done in red velvet plush, and it was to the first level of this staircase that I was ascending on that bright, clear day. Everything on the first level is memories of some type. They are easy to clean because there is nothing to throw away. True, I sometimes push a bad one behind the shelf or sweep it under the rug, but most memories take root too deeply and quickly to be disposed of, although I do misplace quite a few small ones between cleanings. So I just dusted them all off, arranged them neatly in rows, and proceeded onward. On my way up I wrote a reminder to myself to add on a new wing, as the existing rooms were becoming quite crowded, and if there is one thing I can't stand in a room, it's clutter.

The second level is for talents and impulses. Many people think that these are things which come spontaneously and therefore just let them wander freely, but I find it much easier to have them categorized. For instance, how many times have you missed a train because the impulse that should have warned you to arrive at the station earlier was nowhere to be found? And if someone should ask you to show off your singing talent, what if that talent is hiding in a corner and refuses to reveal itself? That's why I categorize mine. Upon going through them, I found a misplaced unfinished thought and carried it up to the third level with me.

The third level is a bit different. It has only two rooms: Miscellaneous, and the Day Room. After I placed the thought safely in Miscellaneous, it was the latter room to which I turned my attention. The Day Room is where all the daily traffic collects to be sorted out each night: with whom I met that day, what each person said, and everything else that transpires. After having attended to this daily task, I sent everything to where it is supposed to be stored via a special elevator I had installed for the purpose and, hopping a ride myself, arrived at the fifth floor. On this level I don't dare to enter the rooms unless there is a pressing emergency, but just peek through the little glass windows to ascertain the working level, for here is the crux of my brainpower—the delicate processing and reasoning machines. I possess only the latest models but I am a terrible novice around such machinery. So with resolutions to gain more experience and then tinker, I just checked a readout or two and went on.

The last level, my favorite, is my knowledge level but I prefer to call it my library. This is also a most important level, although not quite as delicate as the logic machines below. Here, every little thing I learn is recorded and kept safe. After dusting all the shelves, I leafed briefly through a few of the latest volumes to be sure that yesterday's history lectures had been duly recorded. I then hefted my garbage bag under one arm, my duster under the other, and started back down. But as I turned to leave, a door at one end of the library caught my eye. Strangely, I'd never seen it before. I put down my bundle and strode forward to take a closer look. As I opened the deceptively shabby door, a burst of light and color streamed out! Curiously I entered the room—and stopped short, unable to believe my eyes. For beyond the dusky, stately, library lay a wonderful room, a room filled with hope and joy of every color, with sunshine playing gaily over it all. Across the gleaming floorboards I spotted an evanescent figure dressed in red, gold, and white sequins beckoning to me and sparkling until I was nearly blinded. But before I could recover from my surprise enough to wave back, the entire room disappeared and I was left standing in the shadowy library once more.

Bewildered, I picked up my load and descended the stairs, still deep in thought as I left my mind and shut the last door, my task completed. I was filled with a deep fierce longing, for in the one glimpse into that room I had felt more love and color than I had ever dreamed existed within me, and I knew the room's contents were the reason. From then on, I yearned for another glimpse of what I could become. Not until my plane was circling over New York City in the ever-deepening sunset and the city's lights began to twinkle on did I fully understand what that one secret room contained. And it was with hope and relief blossoming anew that I opened the room forever, a small secret smile lingering on my lips.

COMMENTS:

An interesting idea for a personal, revealing essay. It starts off slowly, and seems too "cute" to be effective, but the ending saves it and leaves the reader with an overall impression of a successful piece of writing. (HDT)

This is a wonderful essay with a few basic grammatical flaws. The progression is clear, and the imagination wonderful. (PLF)

Dawn N. Skwersky
College: Mount Holyoke

TELL US ABOUT YOURSELF

Q: What is so great about being deaf?
A: Hey, I can't believe someone finally asked me that!
  Ok, here's a list:

—If someone is singing off key I can turn them off with a switch.
—Airplanes aren't so loud.
—In the morning when my dog wakes everyone up with his barking—I stay asleep.
—People can yell in my ears.
—Music sounds great without my aids because I have low frequency hearing, which is what most music is.
—Nothing is too loud. If, in a rare instant, something is too loud, I can switch the noise off.
—I learned to read lips; I usually have face-to-face contact with people when I talk.
—I developed a predilection for watching subtitled movies and close-captioned TV shows.
—I am a lifer at a school for the hearing.
—Um . . .

Q: WHOA! A school for the HEARING? How did you end up there?
A: My parents placed me in the school. The funny thing is that I never thought I was any different. My parents raised me as if I were a hearing kid.
Q: Wasn't it tough?
A: Yeah, especially when I got older, the guys think I like them because I'm always looking at them, but that's how I read lips.
Q: Hey, but that's still a good excuse to use to stare at guys anyway.
A: Yeah.

Q: How did you take notes in class?
A: That was tough, but I was able to handle that. You see, my success in taking notes depended on

  a) my lip reading skills
  b) the professor's voice and enunciation skills
  c) my position in the classroom
  d) all of the above

However, if the teacher was too hard for me to understand (enunciatively) then usually a friend of mine took notes for me.
Q: Did you take any foreign languages?
A: Why do you ask?
Q: I was wondering if you could lip read in other languages.
A: As a matter of fact, I've taken French for five years. In the third year the classes were conducted *tout en français*. It was hard at first, but I was able to adapt to this situation. I guess I have a gift in lip reading languages.
Q: That's awesome. What is bad about being deaf?
A:

  —Phone conversations are difficult. Not too many people have TTY's (Teletypewriters) or TDD's (Telecommunications Device for the Deaf).
  —I can't hear everything around me. For example, it is hard for me to keep up with everything that is said in a social discussion, unless I can see everyone so I can lip read what is being said.
  —People usually need to repeat things for me.
  —I hate to do the dishes.

Q: What a moment! Dishes are irrelevant!
A: That's true, but I said that because doing the dishes bugs me and there is one thing that really bugs me about being deaf.
Q: What is that?
A: I don't like it when people turn their backs to me because they think I may be dull or because they hate repetitions. How can a person judge me who doesn't know me? As for repetitions, the more I talk to a person the fewer repetitions there are. In any case, I've learned through experience that those people who don't take their time when they talk to me aren't true friends.

Q: One last question, is there anything you really want to do in life that you just can't keep secret any longer?
A: Yes, there is.
Q: Ok! let me hear—no, on the other hand, let me lip read it!
A: I WANT TO SPEND MY COLLEGE YEARS AT MOUNT HOLYOKE!

COMMENT:

Let's forgive the ending. It shows a nice sense of humor and much maturity and self-awareness. The writer exhibits good control. (JMcC)

Julia Marie Smith
College: Bowdoin College

'Orphan' best describes my outward appearance at the beginning of my ninth-grade year at Annie Wright. My plain white blouse was more frequently than not untucked; my Campbell plaid skirt hung randomly from nonexistent hips; and my yellow class-tie, which kept unknotting by itself, gave my face a distinctly hepatitic cast. To complete the picture of a lost child, my navy blue socks resisted all efforts to remain below my knees, preferring to bunch down over scrawny ankle bones. This was Julia Smith, new student, adrift in the awful experience of her first school uniform. Not only did I learn to manage my uniform as I grew into it and myself, but I found that this seemingly dreadful mandatory outfit was to become a catalyst for individuality, mine and that of my fellow students. Just as in science sulfuric acid brings about the conversion of butane to isobutane, a school uniform stimulates the development of a set of characteristics which make a specific person unique among others without contributing to that uniqueness. Because everyone looks alike on the outside, uniforms force the emergence of distinct inner qualities. Individuality, thus, can not be and is not expressed by a superficial style of dress; people at Annie Wright become themselves just because they don't have to, and because they don't want to reflect the mundane nature of our required attire.

I have worn my Campbell plaid skirt for four years and its effect on me will remain with me for the rest of my life. My uniform has caused me to grow into myself as I grew into it, and has caused me to discover my quirks, my druthers, my strengths, and my weaknesses. I am a perfectionist, and yet, if I had those druthers, I would rather spend a lot of time outside enjoying nature or reading a book. I have great determination and perseverance, and yet I am still shy in new situations.

As one member of a school which includes some three hundred students dressed alike according to size, I can attest to my independence from the mob. I have learned to look beyond the uniform in others, eager to search out their special qualities. Pleated polyester in blue and green has enabled me to ignore the outward and superficial appearances of people and has allowed me to treasure their differences. The students at Annie Wright may look like lemmngs, but they do not behave like them.

My uniform now fits me, and I no longer look like a neglected orphan. My skin has gradually accustomed itself to the color yellow; the hours spent ironing the rumples the washing machine inflicted on countless pleats and my struggles with recalcitrant socks have been worthwhile. I have accepted my uniform as I have grown beyond the need for a catalyst for individuality. I am Julia Smith, a distinct person, about to begin the next stage of my life adventures.

COMMENT:

The first paragraph is interesting, but the topic doesn't milk well. The essay is cliché-ridden. (JMcC)

Dimitri Steinberg
College: Princeton University

"It is a truth universally acknowledged" that things which come hardest taste sweetest and thus make all the difference. At the beginning of tenth grade, I was, in all honesty, a porker: not obese, perhaps, but definitely overweight. I was also not as popular as I would have wished. I doubt that there was a direct correlation, but I'm sure that my self-esteem was affected by this weighty problem. Although I knew that one's essential substance is more important that superficial show, I could not deny that I was showing more substance, physically, than was desirable. I had carried this burden, on shoulders and hips, since I was eight. In short, at eight, I ate. After several fruitless (but cake-filled) attempts at dieting, I found myself thirty pounds on the wrong side of 140 at age fifteen. I still vividly recall my sincere desire to lose weight, my great love of food, and my frustration.

I needed an incentive to diet. As many previous attempts to shed pounds had gone awry (along with pastrami), a diet seemed a doomed and discredited project. Nevertheless, my parents wisely proposed that all three of us go on a diet and by four weeks the one who had lost the most would be paid $10.00 per pound for each pound the others failed to match. I accepted the challenge. A fierce battle of weights ensued. My chief weapon in this struggle was the 250 callorie [sic] Dannon Light strawberry yoghurt. That, and a glass of orange juice was all I consumed until dinner each day. The three S's became my deadliest enemies: starch, snacks and seconds were banished from sight and stomach. The possibility of financial renumeration on one hand or monetary loss on the other overcame my urge to rush the refrigerator. At the weigh-in four weeks later, the scale shoed [sic] me minus 13, my mother minus 5, and my father minus 8. I thus extracted a poundage of $130.00 and at the end of the contest I felt as if a huge weight had been shifted from my shoulders to my wallet. What happened afterwards was even more palatable. I had so conditioned my appetite to a glass of orange juice, a cup of yoghurt, and a small dinner that I maintained those eating habits for the rest of the year and thus continued to lose weight until I tipped in at a truly healthy number. I felt better about myself during the second, stabilized phase because I was deriving my pleasure from results gained without ploys or programs.

Before this success, I had often felt myself to be an outsider, looking enviably upon one clique or another. This situated changed quite dramatically. Over the next two years I made many new friends. Just as importantly, I stopped viewing those who weren't my real friends as somehow unapproachable. The inner clique that exists in all high schools and which most everyone aspires to be part of now seemed unappetizing because, having made my own friends, I no longer craved to sit at their table. Losing weight and keeping it off was an accomplishment that allowed me to feel more self-confident. As a result, I was better able to deal with my peers. I got more out of the last two years in and out of school than from all the ones before. The ability to have the discipline to overcome this obstacle has meant a lot to me, not only because of the immediate benefits, but also because of the evidence it gave me about my internal fortitude.

COMMENTS:

This essay shows an excellent writing skill and a good analysis of a marvelous undertaking with positive results to the body and psyche. However, its introspective content suggests a selfish person. (PLF)

Content/idea for the essay is a good one—Misspellings detract from it as do all the cute puns—Better to stick to the facts and simply tell the tale—The merit lies in the truth, not in the style. (HDT)

Jo-Ellen Truelove
College: Columbia College

From somewhere deep inside the earth's surface, analogies are produced. They seep through the molten lava and the rocks and the soil. They leak into the air and are spirited about like autumn leaves. Eventually, they are seized by English teachers, or solitary philosophers, or those persons who write the verbal section of the SAT, or by people like me: college applicants who, by the light of a fluorescent lamp, hope to structure a profound essay on a comparison. On such analogy has settled upon my own desk, just between the diet Pepsi can and my lint brush.

I am malleable. I have a tendency to adopt the ideas of others. My philosophy varies with every new author that I read. When I emerged from the theater after seeing *Chariots of Fire*, I was determined to become a sprinter, and ran down the sidewalk in slow motion. After I read Sherlock Holmes, I began studying people while I rode the subway. I tried to uncover bits of their lives by studying their shirt sleeves.

However, like a blob of Play-Doh, I always return to my can with the air-tight lid. Once I ease back into my natural cylindrical shape, I experience my own bursts of creativity. From one such spurt came forth my plan to keep pies fresh in diners. [I believe that if the rotating dessert cases in diners were spun at the speed of light, the pies inside would (in accordance with the Theory of Relativity) actually grow younger as the patrons outside aged normally.] But once I encounter a fresh perspective, I am molded once more.

There are certainly advantages to having an easily sculpted mind. Concepts are more readily understood when they are fully embraced and analyzed. I am also more receptive to new ideas and experiences than many people. In fact, the only real disadvantage is the lack of strong core of self-consciousness. I do not want to go through life with my self-definition being a hodge-podge of outside influences. What to do?

Will Jo-Ellen forever be an impressionable lump? To answer this question, please permit me to stretch my analogy a bit further. When one shapes a Play-Doh masterpiece (a breathtaking likeness of Carmen Miranda, for example) one leaves it on one's bedpost to become more permanent. One might add another fruit to Carmen's hat now and again, but basically, it is set.

At Columbia, I hope to shape myself into a masterpiece that will transcend my humble Play-Doh origins. I want to take advantage of all that the classes, faculty, students, and the City have to offer. Using the insights that I will have collected, my own interpretation of a variety of views, the whole of what I will have gathered from the humanities, and all that I have lived, I will shape myself. And there I will sit proudly on my bedpost—a masterpiece created by the joint efforts of Jo-Ellen Truelove and Columbia College.

In conclusion, I would like to note that some dissimilarities do exist between myself and a can of Play-Doh. So saying, I release my analogy. I send it off, so that it may be used again, to the Analogy Recycling Plant (located in a brownstone just outside of Jersey City).

COMMENTS:

This essay teeters back and forth between being cleverly outrageous and self-consciously cute. Unfortunately, it seems to me that the final paragraph falls into the latter category. There are, on the other hand, some original concepts that are fresh and informative—for instance, the idea for keeping pies fresh in diners and the notion of sticking Carmen Miranda on the bedpost. Technically, the writing is fine. Furthermore, reading the essay gives a clear idea of how the writer views herself in some very important regards. So, on balance, it is a fairly good effort; I just wish she had stopped one paragraph sooner. (RCM)

Shows creativity, imagination, ability. She skillfully carries through her comparison in an engaging light-hearted fashion. I enjoyed it, along with her flashes of humor? Weakness? I thought the essay was a trifle self-conscious—a "quality" she says she lacks. (AAF)

David C. Weymouth
College: University of North Carolina-Chapel Hill

Four-thirty A.M. and the sun was just a sliver of golden promise far to the East. As that sun rose, I began the first day of my summer job. In the fall I would start my first year at St. Paul's, but it was during that summer that I was able to undergo some great changes as a human being. To start with, I was entering the world of lobstering, Maine's oldest and most famous industry. I soon learned there was much more to lobster and lobstering than melted butter and brightly painted buoys. I was aboard a boat ten to twelve hours a day, six days a week, and the work was really hard. This was one thing I learned.

"Sternman" was my official title, a designation which enabled me to do most of the work while the captain (also the owner) would navigate his boat from buoy to buoy. Aside from a ten-minute lunch break, we worked nonstop hauling traps aboard, emptying them of their catch, baiting them, and finally, resetting them. The meaning of "exhaustion" was one more lesson of the summer.

Still, it was not the physical labor that provoked the major change in me. I liked physical labor and was proud of my ability to accomplish so much of it. Rather, it was my introduction to my fellow workers that changed me. Many, if not most of these people, lacked high school diplomas. Surely none had, or would ever receive, a diploma like the one I will earn in June. This is what I discovered that summer; this is what I hauled up in my own personal, metaphorical, lobster trap—the joy of meeting people who, for me, had never before existed.

It was a good joy to experience, and it was a good experience with which to start St. Paul's School. Already, I was coming to St. Paul's much changed from the person who had applied for admission the year before.

Prior to my arrival on the grounds I had been somewhat one-dimensional. Athletically, I was a hockey player, and a hockey player only. I had played other sports, but only rarely and halfheartedly, and only because ice was not available year round. When I came to St. Paul's, I couldn't go out for hockey in the fall. Consequently, I went out for cross-country, figuring, of course, that all the running made it the best sport with which to get in shape for the hockey season. The track on which the cross-country team ran encircled the gridiron, and after several days of running around . . . and around . . . and around it, longingly watching the football practices, I decided I would go out for a different sport and see if my hockey experiences would help me in getting on a football uniform. Since I had never played the game before, getting into my pads was only the first of many lessons I had to learn.

Because the team already had an excess of running backs, or perhaps the coach had seen me running daily on the track and not been as impressed with my speed as I was, I became a lineman. At that time I weighed only 160 pounds, and I can best and with least embarrassment describe the first couple of weeks as . . . "The Time I Learned to Protect My Body." I found myself going up against a defensive lineman referred to only as Hambone. He had slimmed down to a mere 220 pounds over the summer, he rarely shaved, often drooled, and never spoke. Needless to say I picked myself up off my backside more than once during those first few weeks. But I did improve. That year, I played junior varsity. Last year I started on the varsity and was elected to the Second All-League Team. This year I was co-captain of the team and was elected to the First All-League Team.

I still play hockey, and love it, too. But I no longer feel one-dimensional as an athlete.

Academically, I had also arrived at St. Paul's somewhat one-dimensional. I had taken a very ordinary program of math, science, English, and Spanish as my foreign language. Upon coming to St. Paul's, and inspired, perhaps, by too much lobster, I was temporarily insane and dropped Spanish in favor of taking Chinese, which was being offered for the first time.

I must admit that, especially at the beginning, the language was very difficult for me. It was completely different from anything I had studied or spoken before, and, while being new and exciting, it required some major adjustments in study habits. Since first or second grade, my teachers have not only complained, but have yelled and screamed about my handwriting. If one can't master 26 English letters, imagine trying to learn several thousand Chinese characters. If I could barely write my name in English legibly, what was I supposed to with my name in Chinese?

Well, I am now three years into Chinese. I am cofounder and president of the Chinese Society, which meets regularly to discuss China and to learn about its culture and customs. One-dimensional no more, I have discovered a subject that has truly captivated me and which I will continue to pursue.

In June the sun will set for me at St. Paul's School, and though I will miss the place, I will not regret leaving it. St. Paul's has made me want to go on. It has provided me with an atmosphere of opportunity. Equally, I have taken full advantage of that opportunity, and I hunger for more.

It is the appetite for new experiences, even more than football or Chinese, for which I am grateful. I am looking forward to more sunrises in my life.

Joanne B. Wilkinson
College: Brown University

HANDS

My father has always said that I have "brain surgeon hands," probably because they're rather large with fingers so long and thin that my school ring has to be held on with masking tape. Those who knew less about my ambitions tend to call them "basketball player hands." Of course, there is always that small minority that persists in calling them "ballet hands." (Although I danced for nine years, I no longer harbor dreams of Nutcrackers and Swan Lakes.) Under it all, I am primarily a writer; writing has allowed me to express my thoughts and ideas in every discipline, and in the words of Carl Van Vechten, "An author doesn't write with his mind, he writes with his hands."

Often, when I have a free moment, I find myself looking bemusedly at these hands of mine, and reflecting on the many things they have done. When I was a child, these hands curled themselves around a crayon to scrawl my first letters; they clutched at the handles of a bicycle, refusing to trust my training wheels; they arched delicately over my head in pirouettes and slid, wriggling, into softball gloves. Later, they held a pen ready to express all the ideas and questions and answers that bloomed in my mind. These hands once plunged deep into the pinafore pockets of my candy-striping uniform, emerging to write messages and lab orders, punch telephone numbers, steady syringes—all with growing ease and authority. They went with me when I babysat to earn pocket money and volunteered in my pediatrician's office, and they touched feverish foreheads and held smaller hands, trying to comfort and cheer.

They graduated to a white lab coat's pockets and learned to inject mice and create charts for lab data. They supported my chin during late-night studies. They hoisted my increasingly heavy knapsack to my shoulders and toted it back and forth to literary editing sessions, Spanish dinners, and council meetings. They donned white gloves to ring handbells with the Lambrequins, and twisted nervously behind my back while I performed; they adjusted colored lights for school performances and learned to pluck a microphone from its stand with apparent ease. They dissected pigs and worms and cows, and thought they would never be rid of the smell of formaldehyde, but they survived. They have endured mouse bites, chlorinated water, chemical spills, and poison ivy; when they needed to retreat, there was always a plush teddy bear to cuddle.

Someday, these hands will grip forceps and retractors, tense and slick; they will rake through my hair with fatigue as I sit in library carrels studying graphs and figures. Someday soon, they will hold a daisy-adorned diploma from Lincoln School, and they will hold again, as they have in the past, trophies and book awards and certificates. I have confidence that they will become the hands of an M.D., with the power to heal and comfort solemnly implicit, and I have every hope that these hands will someday, thrilled and proud, touch the opened Van Wickle Gates as they enter.

COMMENTS:

Excellent, creative, original, and beautifully written! This is a student I would like to meet and know. She has a wonderful facility with words, the perfect ones to describe her thoughts. (NA)

For clarity, this essay has to be considered as one of the best. The individual is described to a "T." The reader is able to understand the maturation of the writer, see the ambition, and gain a good grasp of the strength of character. (JLM)

An excellent essay. Great image carried through in multiple instances with interesting and varied use of words and ideas that express not only her activities and goal but her philosophy of life and values. (MAH)

Compliments on taking on the risk of a difficult extended metaphor. It is consistently done, even if it becomes slightly tiresome. The playful self-deprecation of the first several paragraphs is entertaining. (TH)

ESSAYS ON
SPORTS AND ACTIVITIES

Shelley Ledray Bornkamp
College: Washington State University

EVERY LITTLE GIRL'S DREAM

Every little girl's dream is to become a dancer. It was my dream as well.

At the age of seven I entered the dance world, and attended beginning ballet class every Saturday morning for one brief hour at Susan Cooper's School of the Dance in Mt. Vernon for little dancers. I remember how I felt at my first lesson, excited and scared, with visions of myself in the distant future as a prima ballerina in a glorious, spangled pink tutu. I continued to dance, advancing slowly by levels each year, adding then multiplying the hours that I invested at the barre. By age ten, I was dancing six hours a week, while my peers back at school were playing basketball and discussing boys. At lunch, everyone talked about what happened at practice and whether the cool boy in the math class would come to the birthday party. I lived and breathed ballet; their interests and mine no longer converged. As I increased my hours spent in the studio, my feeling of being an outcast increased proportionally.

Dancing was not a hobby to me, it became what I lived for. I did not care that I had little in common with my classmates; I enjoyed my isolation because the feeling that I had at my first ballet class was still inside me. I was going to be a professional dancer, and I would do anything to achieve that goal. That tutu changed to sweaty rehearsal clothes, leg warmers, and tattered toe shoes. Ballet lessons four times a week. The basement room in my parent's house became my practice room and the Ping-Pong table was a substitute barre. In addition to my winter work, I attended intensive summer dance camps for three years, concentrated dance training taught by professional dancers from all over the world. These summer programs not only improved my dancing skills, but also they gave me a sense of self-discipline and independence that has stayed with me to the present.

199

The climax of my dancing career was my acceptance to the Pacific Northwest Ballet Summer School in 1983. I was thirteen with braces and stars in my eyes. I can still remember the day I auditioned, the first time that I had been surrounded by serious competition. I thought that there was no chance of me being accepted. When the letter of acceptance came in the mail, I was shocked, amazed, and very pleased because I was accepted to the "elite" ballet school in Washington State. My success gave me the incentive to work even harder at my hometown ballet school; I knew I had to push myself in order for me to be able to compete with the other dancers.

The day finally arrived for me to go to Seattle where I would begin the six best weeks of my life. I learned new skills, a fierce independence, and continuous discipline. My urge to be a ballerina grew stronger and stronger. At the end of the six weeks, students were evaluated on their performances and a select few were offered the chance to continue through the year. I was so proud to be chosen. The decision was not hard, although I realized that I had to leave home, parents, and friends for a time. I knew that was the price I was going to pay if I really wanted to dance.

I moved to my new home with Debra Hadly, one of the principal ballerinas in the company. I began my new regime: three hours a day, six days a week, at the same time attending a demanding all-girls Catholic School, Holy Name Academy. It was a special year, not only for me but also for the Pacific Northwest Ballet, because the company worked feverishly to produce the world premiere performance of Maurice Sendak's *The Nutcracker Suite*, a re-creation of story, costumes, scenery, sets, and choreography. Without much confidence I attended the auditions, hoping for a part, any part. My wish was granted with two fairly demanding roles: part of the Calvary and a Scrim Mouse. I was ecstatic! Even though I would have to spend every weekend in Seattle for rehearsals, I did not care. I lived and breathed the exciting world of professional ballet. Opening night was sheer magic. Exhausted but delirious with accomplishment, I did my homework in backstage corners in between rehearsals.

Unfortunately, the *Nutcracker* also marked the beginning of my failure as a dancer. I began to worry more about my competition than about my self-improvement. My body began to take the shape of a normal teenager rather than that of a dancer. I found that I really missed being connected with my mother, a crucial part of a young teenage girls's life. By mid-April I was depressed; I had put on fifteen pounds and dancing no longer made me happy. It was time for me to do some serious evaluating of my situation. I met with the head of the Ballet School and with my mother many times, and I finally concluded that it was time to give up dance. This was the hardest decision of my life. It led to a good year of finding a "new" Shelley. I felt that someone had taken away the past fourteen years of my life and I had to start all over. It was an extremely hard time for me, but with the encouraging support of my mother and close friends, I pulled out of it, I worked hard to become a normal teenaged girl. I learned to like football games, parties, cheerleading, friends, and good times. I also learned to like myself once more.

When I look back at what I had to go through and what I gave up to become a dancer and then at my decision to leave the world of ballet, I wonder how I made it through my fifteenth year. I have come out of that black period of my life with a great many personal strengths. I have talents other than dancing; I am a strong, independent, and caring person. I have met with depression and have turned my failure into success. Somewhere in the back corner of my head lives a pink tutu, but my years as a dancer are behind me and I am ready to take on new challenges.

COMMENTS:

Well-organized and generally well-written essay about a very important part of the writer's life. The subsequent emotional conflict it created for her and the traumatic decision she had to make reveals her strength of character and her eagerness to look forward. I think the same story could have been told in fewer words, however, and perhaps this is its only weakness. (NA)

Shelley relates a profoundly significant personal story, some-what tragic given the way she portrays her long journey into dance, and then the way it became so suddenly rerouted. I feel that I'd like to hear more about the outcome, having heard so much about the lead-in. She pokes a lot into the last two paragraphs and well, but less profoundly. However, it is an excellent essay and very interesting tale. (MAH)

A decent, well-done, but workmanlike essay, it is ultimately dull. She would have done better to describe the dancing and its impact than to recount in lockstep chronology her autobiography in dance. This is straight history without images. (TH)

The "decision" essay is often very predictable. This one is no exception. While the outcome was not in doubt, Shelley is able to portray a dedicated dancer, and we get a good picture of Shelley's personality. The dedication is evident as in the pain of the decision, but also is the knowledge that it was the correct one. (JLM)

Charles D. Haley
College: Princeton University

I remember reading Tom Boswell in the *Post* and being mesmerized by Roger Angell's view of the '75 Series. The singular love of sport has been with me always. Never grasping the attraction entirely, I learned first the rules and the names and graduated to nuances. As I learned more, an understanding of sorts crept into the box scores.

I suppose the principle is like that of models, where miniaturization allows close scrutiny of small parts. A sport offers all the bitterness and affection of life without the responsibility of actual relationships. Sitting in a freezing aluminum chair in RFK Stadium, I feel momentary warmth from an effigy of a Cowboy, clad in the same silver as the athletes on the field. The burning is fun in its mock hatred; it is decidedly more enjoyable than the Carters burning all over Tehran. Often one can shrug off all failure. Before the separation of the American League into divisions, my father would lament the second-division finishes of the Washington Senators. Terribly inept, the Nats would stumble through the season and leave behind their distinctive mark. Men like Carlos Paula would lope toward first base, straining for a shoestringer, only to hear the ball nick the fence for a triple far behind him in right field. My dad would wring his hands; but by the time the team slunk off to Minneapolis and a pennant, he was sighing over fifth place and gloating over fourth. How different from a business venture, where losses are met with gray hair and depression.

The joy in sports is not only in harmless failure; it is in the condensed ironies that can be viewed day to day. There are things in life that haunt us, small repeating glitches and large flaws. The same is true for many teams. Some men have more friends than they want, but never get a date. The Boston Red Sox have a plethora of spray hitters but consistently lack starting pitching. They bring up a minor league player, Wade Boggs, and he wins two batting titles. But they can't find a good pitcher. On the rare occasion that a date is discovered, how often will it turn out a brief affair? The Red Sox have the same problem: In '67 Jim Lonborg won twenty and broke his leg; in '78 Dennis Eckersley won twenty-two and his arm fell apart. The nagging problems are there in every team and everyone. The strange thing is that these small faults seem so easily corrected but rarely are. I am a Red Sox fan; and whenever I find myself repeating old hang-ups, I think of Mark Fidrych, shooting star of the seventies Sox. I smile and know I'll make the same mistakes again: Fidrych talked to baseballs. Now he has a pig farm.

A love of sport is a way to stir oneself through emotion—joy and humiliation and all else—in sets, quarters, or minutes. I love the escapism, the generation of stunning feeling that dissipates minutes after the fact. I revel in pre-game promises of championship, little bravado of airy summits comforting in its non-worth. I smile at grown men arguing over the amount of pine tar on a bat—and at myself for equally silly complaints. All 280 pounds of Jeff Ruland make me chuckle when he glides in, smoother that I could ever be, for a lay-up. And I am blindingly happy with green elbows streaking downfield for a tackle. Because real life has too few ways to act idiotic as it is, I need all the sports I can get. I love every season like Jim Rice loves a low fastball.

COMMENT

The success of this essay lies in the rich detail and perceptive observations which fill this interesting analogy between life and sports. Most "sports and life" comparisons are unimaginative attempts to write about a subject the writer thinks he knows a lot about; this writer does know a lot about sports and the connections he draws between the two worlds are provocative and insightful. Sports are not just an escape from life for this writer; they are a microcosm of the larger reality, and as such, are more easily understood and enjoyed. (AST)

Joseph Libson
College: Princeton University

At the risk of transforming this application into a tract on the wonders of wrestling, I nonetheless wish to discuss my recent vacation through hell. Hell, by the way, is not located under the earth. No, the current residence of Satan is Edinboro, Pennsylvania. Hell opens for two weeks every summer and the operators slap on the snappy title "J. Robinson's Intensive Wrestling Camp." The daily routine for this camp is so rigorous that graduation with honors consists of receiving a black shirt with the daily schedule inscribed on the back in mute testament to the existence of this habitation of fallen angels. Each camp session the dropout/casualty rate varies from 25 to 50% (even with an avowed policy of no refunds). I cannot describe the total impact of this place but I can sure as J. Robinson's Intensive Wrestling Camp try.

We wake at 6 A.M. every morning. If your group is lucky you lift weights, if not you run. This exercise is not a typical long-distance endurance run, but rather sadistic combinations of endurance and sprint running. One section, deceptively called the 'Buddy Carry,' involved running with a partner about my size. The instructor ran us down a long country road about three miles from camp. At his signal, I carried my partner on my back at as fast a pace as I could muster. At the halfway mark we switched and he carried me. The indescribable pain that accompanied this operation almost broke me. But, of course, the "almost" is what the camp is all about. The run lasted an hour and a half. We showered, ate breakfast, and crawled back to our rooms to catch a nap before Technique Session. Technique Session is a two-hour "easy" practice that is as difficult as normal wrestling practice at most schools. After the first session I was convinced that I didn't want to see the "hard" practice. I was right. Hard practice is live wrestling for two hours. I have never been so tired as after a hard practice. But, it made the technique sessions seem really easy. I never got used to hard practice. Every day panic would creep into my thoughts. "This is never going to end. I can't keep this up any longer." Invariably I survived the practice and staggered to shower and dinner, after which came the fourth session. This was almost a repeat of the morning session in difficulty but is preceded by a motivational talk, during which most of us practiced sleeping standing up. Days passed until finally, on the schedule board, in the section devoted to the Hard Practice drills, appear the words

RED FLAG DAY

Curious, how such innocuous words could inspire such terror. The rumors of Red Flag Day had been circulating throughout the camp since day two. When it finally arrived, dread filled every wrestler's heart. One hour and forty minutes of non-stop wrestling was assigned, with no breaks or instruction periods where a wrestler might catch his breath. If regular hard practice was difficult, this was surely impossible. But, we did it, most of us, and we did it twice. On the last day, before the end of the camp session we had another Red Flag Day; this one was two hours long. To graduate with honors a wrestler had to have 500 points. Everyone in camp started with 800 points, which could be lost through bad room checks, discipline problems, or not working hard enough during practice. Two minuses and one plus were awarded during every practice. I have never worked so hard for anything as the one plus I received in one practice during that hellish two weeks. The last exercise of the camp was a twelve-mile run. It was unbelievably easy, for we all knew that after the run IT WAS ALL OVER AND WE COULD GO HOME.

In spite of my sarcasm, it is probably obvious that the camp was one of the greatest experiences in my life. It taught me that there are very few limits to what achievement a person can attain. Having the coach yell, "Sprint dammit!" when all that you desperately desire to do is fall down and sleep right there not only conditions your body, it also disciplines your mind. This mental strength has enabled me to work harder at anything that I try. One cannot endure an experience like that camp and not be the better for it. I am no exception.

COMMENT:
This essay is good because, although the experience occurred at a wrestling camp, the writer avoids the trap of letting wrestling become the focus of the essay, but just barely. What this piece does do is show that the writer can endure physical hardship and pain without quitting, over a relatively long period of time. In that sense the scope of this essay is a bit one-dimensional. (AST)

Gregory Lippman
College: Princeton University

There is a certain smell when you walk into a gymnasium, a hermetic, airless kind of smell. A smell of leather, of shellacked parquet floors, of old sweat. I like that smell.

Basketball has always been for me a lot more than simply a release at the end of the day or just another of the seasonal sports. The intensity, the speed, the sudden drama inherent to basketball is matched by few other games. I love basketball not because I am especially good at it; on the contrary, I fit perfectly the stereotype of the "preppie" player: no speed, no leaping ability, no quickness. I have a decent outside shot, and that has carried me to the varsity level at a high school with an unremarkable basketball tradition.

But basketball has that ineffable quality about it, that certain thing which I find it hard to pin down but which keeps me coming back to the court day after day. Maybe it's the power and the dexterity all wrapped up into one, or perhaps that feeling of fluidity and constant motion as the ball flits from player to player in a kind of schoolyard ballet. And ballet is not an inappropriate word here, because basketball is the most graceful of all competitive sports. I know of no sight more graceful than a man, weaving and bobbing through defenders, to suddenly, forcefully, move toward the basket, arm outstretched, and lay the ball gently in the hoop.

But those are just the surface attractions. The real allure of the game comes for me in other ways. It comes in that tight pull of pride when you and a teammate combine a bit of passing fancy to set up an easy score, slapping five gently as you run back downcourt to set up on defense. It comes from the eye contact across the court, to know instinctively and instantly what your teammate is going to do. When that unspoken communication exists, the game suddenly becomes easy. The joining of wills, the confluence of desire between myself and my teammates is the most satisfying part of basketball. In all the other sports I have played, nowhere in the sense of team so immediate and blunt. The absence of it is felt just as strongly as its presence. And when it, that indescribable it, is there, the rush of emotion is unmatchable. Teamwork can be talked about, diagrammed, planned out ad infinitum, but it never comes that way. But that slap on the hand and that look across a crowded court, that's where it comes from and that's where I go looking for it every time I step on to the court.

COMMENT:

It isn't terribly unlike the hundreds of "sports essays" a committee is prone to receive, but in its own way, this one is fresh and interesting. The writer avoids cliché and, particularly with its use of the term "schoolyard ballet," expresses his feelings toward the game in creative, original fashion. The essay is concise, and well organized. It combines some measure of formality with an equal measure of informality—making the piece entirely appropriate for a college essay, but also highly readable. Not profound, but nonetheless effective. (RJO)

John C. Martin
College: Yale University

WHAT ACTIVITY OR INTEREST HAS MEANT THE MOST TO YOU? WHY?

I have never been able to convince my nine-year-old sister to change television channels. As a fourth-year debater, supposedly gifted in the arts of persuasion, this knowledge should be disturbing to me. Yet, for some strange reason, it isn't. While I've tried very hard to discover the reason for my relaxed attitude toward this problem, until very recently I couldn't find a solid answer. At first I thought my attitude might indicate a lack of the "killer instinct" that is necessary to any good high school debater, for my interest in Lincoln-Douglas debate has never been limited to the numbers in my won and loss columns. Yet, I would be the first to admit that I have found victory to be thrilling and defeat to be agonizing. Furthermore, when the issue at hand deals not with the propositions of great value found in "Philosophies of Hate Should Be Suppressed for the Good of Society" but rather with the more mundane concerns presented in "*Dallas* Reruns Should be Suppressed in Favor of *Monday Night Football*," a lack of enthusiasm might well be expected.

Perhaps my problems with my sister arise from a lack of logical argument, for part of my enjoyment of debate stems from my passion for rational discussions of the political and moral philosophies of such giants as Immanuel Kant and John

Stuart Mill. In contrast to this, my arguments with my sister are anything but logical, calling on "family rules" that are often invented on the spot and are, more often than not, unfairly biased toward the inventing party. Fortunately, while debate is theoretically based on rational argument, it has also provided me with experience in dealing with such irrationality. Take, for instance, the resolution "It is Better to be a Dissatisfied Socrates than a Satisfied Pig" in which many debaters ignored all possibility of metaphor and argued the value of a somewhat unhappy, and very dead Greek philosopher versus that of a happy, well-fed quadruped rolling in the mud. Other example lie in the hypotheticals in which Mr. T goes back in time to defeat Socrates in a boxing match, thus proving that "Conflict Limits Humanity," or in debates where crucial arguments rest on quotes from "The Saurus" or "Ibid." With rational argument thus eliminated as a possibility, it seemed as if my quest for an explanation might be utterly fruitless.

As is the case with most debaters, I had failed to find a reason for my lack of disappointment because I had forgotten something elemental. In this case, I had forgotten what was, in many ways, the most important difference between Lincoln-Douglas debate and arguments over television rights. As a Lincoln-Douglas debater, I am constantly reminded of the fact that I am a member of a team. The process of developing arguments is such that it cannot possibly be done by one person alone. Brainstorming sessions and constant informal arguing are a necessary precondition to the proper preparation of a resolution. It is here where I have played my most important and most enjoyable role. While my personal won/loss record may not be as fantastic as those racked up by many of my fellow debaters, the record of those team arguments that I have played a critical part in developing is a source of great personal pride. While it is always satisfying to know that I have done well myself, perhaps my most satisfying moments as a member of the Hearn (Regis' pet name for its speech and debate society) have been those in which I have seen a fellow Hearn member who had turned to me for help in debate use my help to go on and win a state championship or other major award. While I may be personally hurt by debate decisions that didn't go my way, the satisfaction of being a crucial part of a winning team more than makes up for such disappointments. Thus, it was no surprise that I was not terribly upset by losing battles over television control with my youngest sister. After all, I have two other sisters, and, as a team, we're unstoppable.

COMMENTS:

Although this essay is well written and cleverly presented and, at the same time, does give the reader some insight into this young man's thoughts and feelings, I feel he spends an inordinate amount of time describing a couple of personal interests or views. (TG)

A very readable approach to what could have been a dull subject. The last paragraph is especially good because Martin finally emerges from behind debate topics and even hints at a little sense of humor. (JWM)

Kimberly I. McCarthy
College: Brown University

"Here she comes again. Just like always—running in, breathless, a stack of books in her arms. She throws the books on top of me and glides onto my bench, screeching to a stop in its center. Then she gently lays her hands in position on my keys, and sighs. 'I really shouldn't be here,' she tells me, 'I have chem to study, and a creative writing paper, and eighty lines of Latin, and a watercolor, and . . .' She begins to play. It's my favorite, the Moonlight Sonata. It always reminds me of her—gentle and loving yet deeply passionate. Her fingers press tenderly at first as if my keys were ivory eggshells and ebon velvet. Then she is swept up in the tide of her own emotions and begins to play louder, stronger, faster, her fingers working furiously, faster and faster and then over. She caresses my keyboard, eyes closed, then gasps. 'Oh, God! It's 3:15! I'm going to be late to karate!'

She jumps up and runs out the door without so much as a glance over her shoulder—but that's all right. She'll be here tomorrow. Maybe not at the same time, maybe with different books. But she'll be here. She told me—no matter how hard the courses get, no matter how smothering the work, no matter how little time, she could never give me up. It's wonderful to be loved."

COMMENTS:

Enchanting essay which reveals the writer's flair. It says a great deal about the student in very few, simply stated, and carefully chosen phrases. Wish there were more essays like this one to read. It demonstrates that "less" can be excellent. (NA)

I like the brevity; the whimsy; and it's a good glimpse of who this person is and what her interests and commitments are. (MAH)

This piece is beautiful. There is a wonderful expression to it, and yet it is short and to the point. One gets a good picture of the girl and her emotions. (JLM)

Mitch S. Neuger
College: Yale University

CYCLING

I came home from school, inhaled two bagels and a glass of orange juice, squirmed into a new pair of black Lycra chamois-lined cycling shorts, pumped up my tires, and carried my bike down the front steps to the driveway. Some days I rode south, up a hill, across a street and onto the bike path. Or north, past the polo field, along the river. I sang to myself, watched the odometer, and daydreamed, looking up occasionally at the trees whose leaves were just losing their summer green. In an hour and a half I returned home and recorded my distance and average speed on a homemade chart on my wall.

I began this routine in September of my junior year, a week after returning from my summer job as a bicycle mechanic in Massachusetts. I was training, preparing myself for an organized ten-week cross-country bike trip that was eight months away.

Miles accumulated: fifty . . . one hundred . . . two hundred fifty . . . six hundred. When the oak trees hung on to their very last leaves, I pedaled inside on a stationary bicycle and joined the weight-lifting club at school. Six days a week I exercised until one day in December I lost all feeling in my big toe. The numbness persisted; I loosened my toe straps; I stopped exercising; I called my pediatrician, a sports physiologist, and a neurosurgeon; I wrote to *Bicycling* magazine. A new pair of cycling shoes solved the problem. On a mild day in February, I took my new shoes for a ride in the park. I returned shortly with a flat tire and deflated spirits.

Miles paid off in more pain and frustration. In April I developed Osgood-Schlatter's disease, a tendonitis of the knees. Again I consulted unconcerned doctors and gym teachers, read health encyclopedias and *Prevention* magazine, rested, stretched, and took vitamins. Suddenly it was spring. In just two months I would be riding "seventy to one hundred miles a day" on a bicycle loaded with fifty pounds of clothing, food, and camping gear.

I told none of my classmates what I was doing. I was afraid of impressing them with my ambitious plans and then not following through because of knee trouble or illness. And would anyone believe that I, a scrawny kid, a failed soccer player, was gong to pedal my bike four thousand three hundred miles? I scarcely believed it myself; I was sure that some injury, some accident, would render months of training useless.

As the dogwoods bloomed, my enthusiasm wilted. The road was so familiar, progress was barely noticeable, and I had run out of daydreams. My new bicycle, which had arrived completely unassembled in three boxes, made a new noise every day. One day an older cyclist caught up to me; he wanted to coast and chat. I told him after a while that I was training to ride across America. "That'll take some serious riding," he said with a laugh. The bike tour brochure gave two prerequisites for this trip: "You must be in *great* shape" and "You must *love* to bicycle!" When I had first read about the trip over a year before, I believed I could do it. But now I wondered if I were meeting some personal challenge or just inflicting punishment upon myself.

And then one magic day in gym class, I was trying desperately to do a handstand when my teacher said, "Hey, your legs are getting bigger, you been working out or something?" On the road that afternoon, I met a young couple who was riding from California to Maine. They told me that the TransAmerica Trails, which I would be riding, were wonderful. Every hill I climbed on the way home that day was an Appalachian pass; every headwind was a Colorado breeze. I rode up my driveway exhausted, but restless and excited.

During the first week of summer, I began to pack—among other things, a flashlight, five new tee-shirts, and my cycling shorts, now tattered, the chamois dry and cracked. I disappeared every morning with my bike and a snack and reappeared late afternoon, sweaty and mosquito-bitten. I constantly wondered about the other kids who signed up for the trip, if they were somehow more prepared and confident.

On the morning before my trip, my thigh muscle tightened up. My doctor was on vacation; the library was closed; I decided that I'd be back home within the week. But by midnight, my bicycle was sealed in a cardboard box along with an empty journal and a bottle of vitamins. I lay on my bed, exhausted but not sleepy, thinking about tomorrow as I had for many months past.

COMMENT:

The "cyclist" in this essay presents us with a picture of himself that is rich in the details of his physical and emotional struggle to meet his commitment to the summer trip. In the process his qualities of determination (sticking it out to the end), resourcefulness (building his own bike), and "heart" are made completely apparent to the reader in subtle but powerful ways. This essay was written by a keen observer of the world he lives in, and a person whose self-awareness is very high. (AST)

Christine Richardson
College: Princeton University

My dance lessons began in the seventh grade. It was not watching a performance at the Kennedy Center that prompted me to beg for the lessons; instead it was watching a friend's ballet class one evening that sparked my enthusiasm. I wanted to fly through the air with pink, satin pointe shoes on my feet.

When doing my homework, I often look at a poster that hangs on the wall across the room from my desk. Six pairs of dance shoes line the bottom of the gray poster and in the middle, written in large white letters, reads, "Dance is the only art wherein we ourselves are the stuff of which it is made."

I believe in that quote. In dance there are no formulas like those in my physics book, formulas that always work. Dance is not the pointe shoes, or the jazz shoes, or the steps; it comes from within the dancer. It is her style, her interpretation that makes a dancer unique.

I now take ballet, jazz, and tap lessons, and each type of dance has many similar steps; but the steps are merely the technique; dance is the overall result of style. I can do a jeté, and depending on my execution, the music, or my mood, I can look like a sea nymph or a sports car. Shakespeare said, "All the world is a stage . . . ," but when I perform, the stage becomes all the world. The costumes, makeup, lights, and choreography draw the audience's attention to the dancer; for three or thirty minutes, the dance is the entire world. There is only one chance to do the steps I want to. I know that I have no second opportunity.

Dance is also discipline. Serious dancing means having to make all my muscles work while looking poised and graceful. Dancing can be exhausting and frustrating as sweat drips and muscles cramp. However, at other times, I actually feel the sensation of flying, flying through the air with the pink satin pointe shoes or the black leather jazz shoes. Dance, to me, is flying without wings.

COMMENT:

The author does not tell—but shows—her love for dance. She is wise to avoid using the essay to list her accomplishments in dance, and instead illustrates for us how she feels about it. In this way, we gain some insight into her personality, as opposed to receiving a list of accomplishments. The essay is concise, thoughtful, and entertaining. Well done.

Keith M. Rosenbloom
College: Yale University

One of the most unappreciated and unrecognized benefits of playing football is the post-game bath. Certainly the age-old tradition of showering after practice is plenty of fun (after all, the lack of stalls does allow for communal singing and, after particularly hard days, unified complaining), but there is nothing like the soft, gelatinous biosphere created by a warm bath.

As a comparatively slow quarterback on a team with a comparatively poor line, when I drop back to pass I usually get hit (either before or after I throw the ball). As a result, after most Saturdays, occasionally Friday nights, my body begins to tingle in anticipation of "the act": stepping into the bathtub.

Once in the tub I find myself with a therapeutic dilemma:

which part of my body to douse, and which part to leave susceptible to the elements. The cause of my dilemma is the length, or rather the lack of length, of my bathtub. It usually comes down to whether my upper body should be horizontally— forcing my knees to bend acutely—or whether it should sit up vertically, treating knees to an aquatic ecstasy. It is a Yin Yang situation, but at least I eventually get the full therapeutic and esthetic value from the bath.

The warm water hugs my torso, comforting it; while at the other end my toes appear to have shrunk, having diminished in the obscurity of the liquid covering. But that's only the short of it: pun intended. When my toes move, little streams of water shoot out all around. Hair all over my body reacts to this and other movements by slowly waving like Caribbean coral. Yes indeed, it's my little water wonderland!

In my aquatic sanctuary any of my aches, bruises, and malevolent thoughts dissipate. There is no need to hide my face in ignominy, or give the mandatory "high-five" after a score, or listen to opposing down linemen miraculously say something intelligible like "I'm comin' afta yous." None of those distractions in my bath, just me splashing contentedly.

Dani Ruran
College: Amherst College

Rose was a physically unattractive and overweight elderly spinster. She lived with her sister in a little white house, where she often gave music lessons to young violinists. The zenith of her day was when she sat in her living room on her black piano bench, leaned over the violin in her lap, and instructed a child on the essence of bowing and fingering.

I was six years old when I first met Rose, and I had just moved to West Hartford. I had begun playing the violin several months prior to our move and was very concerned about changing teachers. My first instructor was young, beautiful, kind, and patient. She was impressed by my love of music and with my willingness to practice; I had looked forward to our weekly lessons.

My mother searched for a replacement for June. She was told that Rose Kleman was the best teacher of violin for young children and made an appointment for me to meet her.

Rose arranged to interview me at her home. I took one look at this new and very different-looking teacher and promptly forgot all the music I had learned. I could not play a single note. But, she began to talk to me about music, asked me to call her "Rose," and brought me into one of the most heart-warming and productive relationships of my life.

As the weeks passed and we became better acquainted, Rose added dimension to the life of my family. With both sets of grandparents living too far away for frequent contact, she became another grandmother to my sisters and me and another mother to my parents.

The experience she gained through working with so many young children enabled her to give me guidelines for life while she helped me to develop as a violinist. She told me that I was "almost grown up now" and that I was to carry my own violin up the steps to her fourth-floor studio. When I had difficulty facing a performance, she would say, "You will do it," and I did. She taught me how to budget my time and how to balance my daily activities. Because of her rare dedication and true caring, she often gave me lessons at her home, for which she did not charge.

One Yom Kippur, the concertmaster of the Hartford Symphony (who would soon become my teacher) played Max Bruch's *Kol Nidre* in our synagogue. I remember sitting near Rose and looking up at her face in sheer delight, sharing two common joys with her—the spiritual mysteries of religious and musical fulfillment.

During the week of my tenth birthday, my family visited relatives in Philadelphia. On our third day there, we were awakened in the early morning by a telephone call. I saw my mother's eyes redden as she held the phone to her ear. When she hung up, she broke the news slowly. Rose had died unexpectedly. Soon, my whole family was in tears. I remember the distraught look on my little sister's face and the puzzled look on my cousin's as he peeked through the open door, trying to find out what had happened.

I vowed to remember Rose, her teachings and her kindness. I began taking lessons with my new teacher, the concertmaster, and I continue to work hard at the violin. Whenever I enter a competition, I think of Rose before playing my first note. I hear her saying, "You will do it," and I do. And silently, I dedicate my performance to her.

I would like to spend another evening with Rose. I would like to see the joy on her face as she learned that she had helped me to grow, both musically and personally, and heard how I was continuing what she had begun.

COMMENT:

Obviously, this is written with sincere, heartfelt emotion, but although it reveals that the writer is sensitive and musically inclined, we don't learn much about the writer herein. (Perhaps that was not specifically the purpose of this essay question). At any rate, it is a highly personalized response, and a description of a unique relationship. I do wish the writer had employed additional specific instances of anecdotes that would have further illustrated what this lovely person Rose was like. The one example of the concert at the synagogue is effective—but seems isolated in the essay. I'd call this a B+ essay that with one or two more specific recollections could become an "A." (RJO)

Peter Urkowitz
College: University of Chicago

I wanted to draw in the rain. It was not really rain, just a lot of people in raincoats trying to make each other believe that they were hiding from the sky for a reason. Well, maybe it was a bit wet, but no one seemed to notice that there were many more people on the streets than there would have been had it really been raining. Real rain would drown out the city with noise, wash pigeons into drains, sweep cats straight into the river, tip over garbage cans and float the trash away, and leave red marks wherever raindrops hit bare skin. This barely had distinguishable drops; there seemed a strange continuity to this rain, as if it were an extraordinarily dense mist, or a very airy river that was flowing out of the sky and oozing onto the ground rather than, as real rain would have done, attacking the ground like a machine gun.

It wasn't even dark. When I came out of the school building I had to blink my eyes, to let them adjust, in exactly the same way that I had almost every day since school had begun. I had my umbrella open, of course. Everybody had their umbrellas open. Everybody was wearing a raincoat, too. Everybody was hunched forward, shoulders tensed. None of them cast a shadow, but that was their own fault. Of course, I had no shadow either. Was I afraid of embarrassment?

Yet this light, from a sun ineffectively hidden by translucent clouds, was interesting in a way. When figures are equally lit from all directions, they become weird creatures, gray and colorless without becoming less lively. It was the illusion of rain that made them less lively. I thought about how I could draw objects without shading, how to describe contours on a uniformly gray mass.

Looking up, I was distracted by the view down the street. If drawing objects without details seemed hard, how much harder would infinite details be? As I looked down the street, and the facades of buildings formed unreproduceable angels toward the horizon, and the windows were placed in patterns so complex that it would take days to sort them out, and every iron railing on the steps was a work of art, I felt like crying.

I was quiet. Around me the city was unhurried but loud, except at moments when it grew silent and rushed past me. I felt the urge to paint the whole scene with one explosive stroke of a brush. It was clear before me, a true vision calling me out to be expressed, by the sudden release of boundless energy this vision could be communicated to the world. I didn't move. The energy was there, perhaps, but only if it were controlled and manipulated could this vision, if it were such, be expressed. That was the root of real power. The people I know who are powerful intellects all have this ability: to sustain their energy over extended periods, directing it to their purpose.

Only at rare moments do I feel intellectually powerful enough to sustain an artistic vision over the time that it takes to actually execute a drawing. Only when the execution itself requires a further insight can I remain in the state of excitement that the original idea provokes. As I improve in skill I find that this further insight happens more and more often, for I am more able to approach each line, each brush stroke, with renewed spontaneity.

In writing, this spontaneity is easier to achieve, for it is more obviously necessary. Because any piece of writing is broken up into paragraphs and sentences, and by the progression of an action or an idea, it is impossible to conceptualize the entirety of a piece before it is physically written. At the very least, word and syntax choices must be made as they arise. At best, a work grows in the writing to be better than its conception. And because each word presents a new challenge, I often feel the excitement which prompts me to begin drawing only after I begin writing. As I write I build momentum and confidence, until I reach a peak of concentration. All barriers to achievement seem to melt before me, and words and ideas come forth.

It is at these moments that I feel intellectually and artistically powerful: subtle and sophisticated, exercising immense control over a boundless force.

COMMENT:

This is a stunning piece for several reasons. First, the opening encloses the reader in a world where there are no points of reference. This world of shadowless rain and misty sun, of raincoats and tears and of questions and explanations, is evocative and disorienting, but gripping. Second, had he ended with the usual poem I'm not sure the essay would work, but he comments on it, revealing his ability to step back from the artistic piece and be reflective. (PT)

IDEA ESSAYS

Erika N. Cleary
College: Brown University

In the winter twilight of downtown New Haven I wait for my bus. Azure in the east, a purple-hued gold in the west, the sky draws my glance upward. Uncontrollably, my thoughts shift. My stomach growls, heart pulses, and lungs suck in the air. I am separate, individual, mortal. It's scary—the power we, as humans, have over others in society and the weakness inherent to our existence.

Grown men collect cans in the gutter, representatives of humanity's imperfections—pain, injustice, unrealized human potential, a living death. The dead outnumber the living in a ratio of four to one. My great-grand uncle supposedly had long thin feet which looked like spears. I've seen the white hair, mischievous smile, and kind eyes reproduced in photographs; I've heard the stories of his wild sense of humor. I've missed something by being born in 1968. It's not my fault . . . the people I will never meet, the experiences that will never be my own. I wish to see the city of Athens as it existed before the ancient structures were ruined, to have eyes able to see infrared and ultraviolet light, to go beyond the realms of human knowledge, experiences, and possibility. Yet I am human, and like others, must waste time sleeping, eating (I must consume life to sustain my own), excreting, and clothing myself. Alas, this mortal coil and finite mind cannot be changed of their fundamental nature.

The teachings of the Catholic Church manage so beautifully to rise above the material to the spiritual. It is a shame I can't bring myself to take such comforting views as my own, even after ten years of Catholic schooling and eighteen years in the midst of a caring, loving, and devoutly Catholic family. But I've always been the doubter, never accepting something in blind faith or without a reason. Belief in God, in the execution of Divine Justice would create an objective order and purpose in a world which I see as coincidentally formed and chaotic, where glimmerings of goodness, love, peace or meaning in life are

225

subjective, existing only in the mind of the individual. I do not label myself—I am not ready to proclaim myself an atheist, or even an agnostic. My life in mathematical terms might be 18/∞, far too small a number to allow me to subscribe to any particular belief system. For now I will be Nietzschean Ubermensch, standing on my own physically, psychologically, and intellectually; I will try to live the most worthwhile, interesting, and cognizant life I can.

I am jolted out of my reverie as my bus lurches to a stop at the corner. I notice the sky has turned to midnight blue and I am glad that I had time for ten minutes of uninterrupted thought to reestablish who I am and what I am feeling.

COMMENT:

This drifts, but effectively. The reader feels she has much to say, more than is shown here. She creates a mood and reveals a questioning mind. (JMcC)

Jennifer L. Cooper
College: Harvard University

I have of late been thinking about numbers quite a lot, the number one in particular. The abstract quality of numbers fascinates me, and I've been trying to relate them to other abstract concepts, like wholeness and love and perfection.

For example, a glass—Glass A. If Glass A has a small chip in it, it isn't *less* than one glass. If it has a small lump on it, it isn't *more* than one glass. The glass is still one; it is one of itself. It is a perfect Glass A.

This inspires further thought. It is impossible ever to have duplicate Glass A's. The ideal glass exists only in theory. How, then, can two things ever have enough in common to be called two? Put two glasses together and all you have is two ones. The ideal two does not exist. There is no such thing as the ideal two.

I found this concept very disturbing. The ramifications of the nonexistence of the number two would be extensive. How could there be true love without two? I asked friends, teachers; no one had the answer.

Fortunately, I came across a solution to this problem just recently, in e. e. cummings' poem, "if everything happens that can't be done." He sets up the idea of the individual one with lines like "there's nothing as something as one" and "one's everyanything." He then reveals that two ones are involved with each other—in love. He unites these ideas, wrapping it up beautifully in the last stanza:

> we're anything brighter than even the sun
> (we're everything greater
> than books
> might mean)
> we're everyanything more than believe
> (with a spin
> leap
> alive we're alive)
> we're wonderful one times one

One *times* one! It makes so much sense. We don't generally think of multiplication using two *objects*. Usually, we think, "One apple one *time*"—equals one apple. However, Punnett squares have shown that multiplying one horse by one donkey will yield one mule. Decidedly different from either of the originals, it nevertheless combines characteristics of both into one being.

So it must be with people. The love of two individuals, while independent of one another, blends together to form one love— *their* love. People speak of "our love" or "the love between us" or "the love that we share." The two ones multiply to equal one, but that final one is different, seems richer, *fuller* than either of the originals.

The implications are intriguing. I had no idea that numbers could mean so much. It's a paradox, because mathematics is the ultimately logical system, totally intolerant of interpretation. I think these ideas merit further development—after all, I haven't even begun to think about zero.

COMMENT:
Good essay in that it demonstrates the mind/thoughts of the author. The structure is well developed and the leading up to and conclusion of and going from cummings' poem is good style. Having the ending open is also a good idea—it shows that the thought process of this person is alive and still functioning. (HDT)

The logic is wonderful. So is the citing of e.e. cummings. The originality is superb. (PLF)

Nikolas R. Elevitch
College: Yale University

I like hanging around swamps, especially at dusk. But when the glow is down to a never-more stare, which I quickly break by throwing a rock into the mud-pools, the silence turns immense. I grow uneasy; itches and thoughts creeping, and I find myself on the right-hand side of the equation trying to throw some of the silence back to the other side. It is kind of cold. I murmur to myself, and I should go home and eat.

But I must tell you why you too should come to the swamp.

If you're aware enough to hear the mosquito whine in your ear, then watch closely for the will-o-the-wisp. It hovers over the water—a light said to be formed from methane gas pockets that break to the surface. To me it is a fabrication of the time of day, quality of the air, and excitement of the imagination. It is a great focal point, nothing nebulous like the landscape fleeing by on a country car ride. Complacency el maxo. Nolo contendre. To me it is a creature that does not think.

And if it has any purpose in life, you aren't going to discover it. Why is it there? Removed from the hyperbolic curve of my thoughts, it sits on as asymptote of uncertain origin and undefined existence. It is a break from the evolution of nature; you see a realm unpermeated, unspoiled.

So you may never reach it, only approach. But suppose you knew nothing, not even its name, as if seeing it for the first time. What would you think? You would most likely stare in wonder.

I clasp my knees in the fading light and think back to my dream the night before in which I attempt to break the world record in the long jump. I bend over on the line, grab my ankles, and jump forward. While in the air I pull my ankles up behind me, hold them there, and slowly float past the record, past the sand pit, along the track, and out into the autumn night of the surrounding forest.

I soar into a moonlit bog in the middle of the forest and drift over to the will-o-the-wisp. Its fiery glow pulses and fades with its diminishing supply of methane. It is the solute, and the air the solvent, as it melts away in the reaction, the air taking its heat.

"O, Oracle," I say, "should I be linear to discover you? Would I reach you that way? Or should I sit on the side of the swamp with my knees clasped, piecing images together, dreaming, and then writing about you on paper? Tell me which approach is better, show me a sign. Give me a variable in an equation."

I wonder whether this allusion to science is part of a real existence or just a different kind of dream. It isn't going to answer—maybe I'll never know. This pondering brings on a flood of memory—laws of science, equilibrium constants, formulas . . . and gravity. I succumb to that and plunge into the swampwater. Immediately, the will-o-the-wisp disappears. I yell to the hungry night air. "Damn it! It's ice-cold!"

Matthew Fleischer
College: Yale University

Certain people have shaped me. Hesse, for one. And my parents, two or three friends, my brother. Shel Silverstein is not among them. I've never met him. Doubt that I will. Of course, we might—"Pleased to meet you, Matt," he'd say softly, then he'd sign my napkin or bookmark and we'd part. No exchange of ideas or philosophies. Not even a really bad pun. Still, I might grab pen and paper and write him a letter address to "Shel, care of Harper & Row." He'd write back and BAM!—a whizbang epistolary friendship. It hasn't happened yet, though, and so I can't claim that the bald fellow staring grimly at me from his comfortable perch on the back cover has influenced me in the least. Shel's subtle, talented hand and mind, however, have indeed.

Everyone needs a little escape—or at least *I* think everyone does—and Shel's world of Exactlywatts and the Quick-Digesting Gink is probably mine. It's not strictly a world of humor, but rather, it's a world of points and thoughts and you and me—all, granted, essentials of humor—that makes me marvel instead of laugh. Marvel first at Shel's abilities, and then at the idiosyncracies and lunacies that make me ME. His work has a peculiar lived-in quality—like he's lived in my house and seen it all.

Shel's poems and drawings are universal in appeal, and for good reason. His creations are fanciful yet beguilingly simple, and he communicates like the master cartoonist and wordsmith he is. He has chosen two media—cartooning and poetry—that allow him to take an extremely telling thought, esconse it in an unsophisticated line drawing of a few lines of poesy, and let it touch down softly but surely on his "audience's" heads. And he is quite accurate with it. For the USY[1] convention I am organizing, I am using Shel's story *The Missing Piece*—a tale of valuing what you already are—as study material. His books, it seems, are good for things besides reading for company when no one else is home.

Shel's Silverstein's books haven't shaped me (gee!—what a

sight it would be to see the sort of me I would be if that wasn't
true. WHEW-EE!), nor have they struck some latent wish of
mine to be exactly like Shel Silverstein. A *Light in the Attic* and
Where the Sidewalk Ends and the others are my guides; guides
in a different way than Hesse's *Siddhartha* is my guide. These
works are and will be in the fore of my bookshelf, reminding me
as I become a big, bad college student, and then an even more
horrid ogre of an adult, that there are places and creatures like
the boring Land of the Happy and The Worst, and that if I ever
quite lose enough of the child in me, I will probably end up
getting to know them very well.

1. USY-United Synagogue Youth

COMMENT:
Too often a writer tries to overdo it and tries to be funny, or,
tries to be cute. Luckily this essay is not one of those attempts.
It is well put together, grabs the reader at once. The writer also
allows us to see the influence of literary figures on his own self.
(JLM)

Annelise Goldberg
College: Yale University

PERSONAL STATEMENT

At the age of four the fact that I would one day fall from the
platform into the tracks below seemed beyond question. The
only point which needed further clarification was the exact
distance that there would be between the oncoming subway
train and me. While keeping a firm grip on my mother's hand,
I thought about my various escape options, for certainly I had
no intention of letting the train triumph. The first escape route
to be considered was my mother and so, cocking my mary-janed

232 SUCCESSFUL COLLEGE APPLICATIONS ESSAYS

foot to one side, I gazed up appraisingly; was speedy action, saving her youngest child, and only daughter, from the snarling teeth of the train, one of her many virtues? Much as I loved my mother, I thought not—she was much better at reading stories.

Ah, well, if my mother wasn't going to save me then I'd have to think of something else. Still attached, I ventured a brave toe to the yellow line and, holding my breath, peered down into the tracks. Underneath the platform was a very shallow cavity. Pulling in my stomach, I concluded that a person as small as me might, if she tried very hard, be able to stow herself safely in this alcove until the train had passed. After I was very sure that the train really had passed and wasn't just lurking close by but out of sight to trick me, I would venture out of hiding, looking brave—a Hero. Heroes, I thought, invariably liked Chiclets. Certainly my mother, wishing to reward me for my great presence of mind, would shower me with Chiclets of every flavor imaginable. Of course, being a Hero, I would only eat them one box at a time.

All of this planning had made me hungry for Chiclets. Glancing up and down the platform, I spied a Chiclet machine and asked for a penny, which was given to me. The next problem that I had was that of choosing a flavor. Settling on Tutti-Frutti, I carefully put my penny in the proper slot and got a small pink box containing two Chiclets.

The chasm which I would have to cross in order to board the train seemed big and black—perhaps I would fall through. My mother said that she didn't think so but still I lingered; I felt pleased with where I was and thought that perhaps it would be all for the best if I stayed with my Chiclet machine. I hadn't figured the chasm into my escape plans. But my mother was stepping aboard and, just to keep track of her, I decided to go along, my mother being one of my more valued possessions.

Once aboard I totally forgot about the train's sinister side and became fascinated with the other people in the car. One lady had purple shoes and a fake leopard skin vest on. Another had a hat with artificial fruit on top. A man slept, snoring, and another man was picking his nose. Where were *they* going? I stretched and my feet almost touched the floor . . . soon I'd be grown up.

After counting the number of red shoes in the car I got bored and went to look out the back window at all the tracks that we were leaving behind us.

At that time subways were connected with Chiclets, shopping for winter coats, trips to the Central Park Zoo, and my mother's job. I liked the idea of having a job and hoped that I'd get one that was fun, like being a zookeeper (How did the zookeeper get in the cage without the lions getting out? How many baby aspirins does a sick walrus eat?)

Later on I discovered that some of my friends came to school on the subway. For me, school and the dentist were both in bus territory. People on the buses were different and not as many of them slept.

More time passed and I found myself going to dance classes on the subway. My parents split and my brother and I became experts on the West Side line. At least three times a week I'd ride on the subway en route to my father's house. Waiting for the train I'd marvel at the once beautiful mosaics, now caked with dirt, that lined the walls. Once New York had been very proud of its subway system. This made me feel sad. Beggars would come through the cars and Wall Street executives would board the train, going home after a "hard day at the office." I became skilled at reading the newspaper over other people's shoulders and discovered that the numbers accompanying graffiti names referred to the streets that the artists lived on. Sometimes someone would strike me as interesting, or sad. Often people looked as if they were thinking hard. On some trips I thought hard and on others I read the posters and faces. Sometimes I slept and my fear of falling between the platform and the train lessened as I grew larger. However, the empty tracks still looked ominous and I retained healthy respect for the yellow line. Gradually, I started to cross chasms alone. I had heard that if you took a pee on the third rail you'd be electrocuted. I wondered what I'd do if I saw a hundred dollar bill lying in the tracks.

Going to a friend's house in Chinatown I would take the Lexington Avenue line and get off at Worth Street, a station which is housed in a Romanesque building. Wondering when the building had been erected, I gazed up at numerals which I was unable to decipher. Finally I came into the knowledge that *x* is not only the last letter of lox but also the numeral ten.

Often, I pretend that I'm someone else when I ride the subway. Sometimes people talk to you or you to them and sometimes you just stare at each other, each feeling that you are absorbing the other's soul.

On the way home from Sloan-Kettering the apparent normalcy of the subway and its passengers soothes me. I have just seen the cells and face of a girl no older than I who is dying of cancer. Would I be able to work with terminally ill people every day?

My blood boils when my ass is pinched. When I get off at the recently retiled 49th Street station, on my way to Schirmer's for flute music, my stomach gives a funny turn and I feel protective toward my dirty mosaics.

When I read about Odysseus, I look around to see who resembles Poseidon. Othello once rode across the car from me. Last week, in response to a poster, I decided to leave my organs to medicine.

I look at the waterfall in a glossy advertisement for KOOL cigarettes with reminds me of the sea, keeper of my other loyalties. The beaches on Cape Cod are rather deserted in October. Only a few fishermen are out fishing from the shore at that time of year. In I plunged, clothes and all, remembering the summertime taste of salt water.

Once I tried to compute the number of hours that I had spent on the subway but got tired before finishing. I've seen a lot of things and people that I would never have encountered any other way. My background contains European Catholic and Jewish forbears and New England stepparents, but no "believers": It was the smudged foreheads on the subway that introduced me to Ash Wednesday.

I'm glad that I have grown up in New York, but I think that it's time for me to leave for a while, to live in other ways and in other places, even if I eventually wind up returning to this one. I'd like to stay somewhere else for long enough to lose the feeling, which I have had when travelling across the United States and on my brief visits to foreign countries, of being a foreigner in a foreign place.

Wandering through the Met, I can be a coatless child or a Bendel's lady. I value the feeling of uniqueness and the power to choose how I live, both of which my environment has nurtured as inalienable rights. Living amongst many people of different professions, viewpoints, and origins has exposed me to multiple insights and perspectives and made me realize that there are many Answers. All lifestyles and professions have their own depths of competences and responsibilities. I'm looking for my own blend. Many options are attractive to me.

I look at things and wonder how and why they work. What are the intricacies, how is the effect achieved? With these questions forever in my mind I, like many others, seek an education.

The subway is a small-scale version of what I find exciting and special about New York City. I can ride it to go see Goyas or simply to watch the tracks that I'm leaving behind . . . I do both.

COMMENT:

What is remarkable here is her ability to string the beads of memory into a lovely necklace. She re-creates a child's perception of the subway and then takes the subway through the rest of her life. She takes a simple aspect of her life—riding the subway— and uses that to thread the beads into the necklace. (PT)

Colin Hamilton
College: Amherst College

LOOKING AT HILLS

It's mid-August, around 95 degrees in the shade. I'm tired, stiff, and riding my bike through Iowa. I'm not alone; there are nearly 9,000 people for company. Every year about this time, people gather from around the country to join in RAGBRI—the

Des Moines *Register*'s Annual Great Bike Ride Across Iowa. People with no experience with RAGBRI may be quick to ask the question why, for there are no rewards—none that can be pinned or shelved. But what I'm gaining is immeasurable. The bonds I'm forming with my friends will keep us together no matter where we may be taken in the upcoming years. I'm learning about the generosity of rural Iowans who feed and shelter us. And riding, sometimes eight hours a day, I'm learning to look at hills.

The American Heritage Dictionary sums up a hill as "a well-defined, naturally elevated area of land smaller than a mountain." That doesn't give them enough credit. Hills are as diverse as those who wish to conquer them, each hill posing a unique problem. Each hill makes the rider calculate his speed and endurance, to focus his mind on a strong approach. Each hill will force the rider to respect it.

Iowa's hills, in particular, are misunderstood. To believe the media would be to believe Iowa is one flat corn field, occasionally graced with a pig or cow. Instead, the cows and pigs, which are frequent enough, stand on plenty of hills, rolling and mounded.

As we left the western border, we encountered short, steep hills which demanded a racing start so we could easily climb at least the first half. Then a struggle ensued while I hoped my momentum would carry me to the top. More often, I was left inching up the final yards.

East of Eldora, we faced curved hills, on which I could never see if I was at the beginning or the end. On these I had to constantly adjust my speed to respond to the terrain, conserving my energy in case I was suddenly struck with a sharp incline with no chance for a running start. But I also wanted to maintain an intense pace because ahead lay rest, drinks, food, and showers.

Eventually these hills softened into long, mild inclinations which dragged on for a mile or more. In the beginning, the inexperienced rider, like myself, welcomed these hills, anticipating no rushing, imminent challenge. Before long though, I respected their ability to sap my strength. On the third and fourth days of the ride, it was far more common to see people walking these hills than the steep ones which we topped in only a minute.

Maybe more frightening than any hill is its antithesis: the decline. Rushing down a slope at 30 miles an hour with only two thin, floppy strips of rubber between me and a serious accident gave me a perspective far more real than any dictionary definition. On these slopes balance is everything, but at such high, unsteady speeds so little of it remains I could barely risk my head to see what I was riding from; I could only look dead ahead to where I was riding to, very quickly.

Occasionally, as we peddled across the state, we met a hill which could be seen from miles away, looming menacingly, glaring down at us even as we crested the surrounding hills. These are the hills that festered in our minds, always influencing our conservation of energy and the planning of our rests. I learned to establish an equilibrium between preparation for these hills and putting them out of my mind. If I became too obsessed with them, I lost my concentration and with it my ability to conquer the smaller hills. But if I ignored the monstrous hills until I was suddenly on one, I was mentally and physically unprepared for the challenge. Sometimes the hill was more gentle than expected, other times far worse. And sometimes, as I approached, the path turned to the right or left and I'd be on the next stretch.

It is now December and I'm standing at the base of what appears to be a formidable hill, one which has dominated my horizons a long time. The road into it seems to head east, but it is curved and I can't tell how far it will take me. There are many paths which would allow me to turn off, but they too are curved and hilly, although they may appear at first to be flat.

This is a hill almost all my friends have come to. Some have chosen to turn off; many are struggling with it now; many are forced to walk. Some will turn back and others, through hard work, preparation, and skill, will climb to the top where the views are good and there are endless roads to choose from.

I know it will be tough, but I have a running start and am usually a strong rider.

238 · 100 SUCCESSFUL COLLEGE APPLICATIONS ESSAYS

238 · 100 SUCCESSFUL COLLEGE APPLICATIONS ESSAYS

COMMENTS:

At first glance, long, but I was fascinated with this wonderful ability to bring the reader along. Colin has a real ability in written expression, and even though lengthy the essay works well. (JLM)

Long. A bit tedious in the telling, but a clever idea; a unique way to reveal Iowa, biking, and the author's approach to life and future goals. Seems worked on, fabricated, rather than spontaneously, naturally creative language. But good. (MAH)

Alan P. Isaac
College: Williams College

PERSONAL STATEMENT: RUMORS OF INNOCENCE

STAGE: Lighting is dim. Soft spotlights on characters onstage. The two characters, racially indistinguishable, sit on a church pew downstage center. Upstage is completely dark.

B: Does it hurt?

A: Not anymore. Not too much, at least.

B: It's sad, isn't it?

A: Not really, but once in a while, I would get snatches of memory, then a pang would suddenly surface from some well inside, cause a splash, then quietly die down.

B: Any regrets?

A: No, just second thoughts.

B: But, how do you feel? What do you do?

A: I sigh, then go with the next task.

B: It's not so bad, is it? I suppose every turning point makes you the person that you are. The self is formed this way, the mundane experiences are nothing more than the self expressing itself. But, really now, how much time do those turning points take when you put them all together?

A: No, we can't stop too long for anything . . . But innocence is so hard to sacrifice without some regret.

B: Everything we choose to make holy was never ours in the first place. Time comes when we have to give it up.

A: I suppose . . . I often wonder: What is there after innocence?

B: (*Pauses to think*) Why, . . . I guess, your whole life.

A: It was so safe in that bubble. When I was a child, in church I used to look up at the ceiling and stare at the lights up there. Each light was surrounded by all sorts of colors. They were all so pretty, I thought. I picked the three biggest and prettiest. They were Jesus, Mary, and Joseph. They were all up there protecting me. I was happy they did.

B: So, are they still up there?

A: I found out that it was just my eyesight failing me at such a young age. I needed glasses, that's all. I was my body's promise to gradually waste away. It was a nice thought, anyway. I still take off my glasses to see them now and then. (*Looks up.*) They look different now.

B: Are you still a Catholic?

A: (*Smiles.*) Yes? No? In my sense, yes. In my parent's pre–Vatican Two sense, no. But I found that Catholicism was one way. You can't follow The Way if the self is not filled with it. Each person has to find his or her way.

B: A way to what?

A: (*Pauses.*) I don't know . . . Salvation?

B: If there's no salvation? What then?

A: (*Pauses*) Well, . . . I guess there's nothing left but compassion . . . and God, maybe?

B: You still believe in God?

A: Yes, but I had to kill God before I could even begin to believe in a god. Empty myself of Him. What was left was . . . me. I had to realize myself first before God, since God will always be. I, on the other hand, will not. I have time, nothing else. Remember? We had to kill Christ first to gain eternal life.

B: But against God, don't you feel insignificant?

A: But, I don't hold myself against God, but with God. I don't try to objectify a deity. I don't make a box to deposit all my morals in.

B: How was it when you killed God?

A: Frightening. It wasn't God that I killed, though, but an idea of a god. I had to break that idol like I had to break the world my heritage had built for me and around me. One time my mother and I were having an argument. In the middle of it, she demanded: When are you going to start thinking and acting like a Filipino? I thought that a better question to ask was: When am I going to start thinking and acting? You see, I didn't want a world that was built for me, but a world built by me.

B: It's pretty scary out there. What do we have?

A: Choice.

B: Control.

A: Dreams.

B: Compassion.

A: And when all else fails, try dignity. It works sometimes.
(Silence.)
Are you finished praying?

B: I don't think I've ever stopped. How about you? Does it still hurt?

A: No. Not too much.

B: So, . . . what is left after innocence?

A: Why, your whole life.

*(They look at each other, rise from the
pew. They slowly part still looking
at each other as*
                        Lights fade.)

COMMENTS:
An excellent, rather unique portrayal of this student's philosophical and religious views. It is a bit risky—as essays for
college admission go—certainly not standard. At times, it seems
too narrow; at other times, too abstract. Actually it is probably
both. The essay reveals a very clever, perceptive, mature author. (TG)

A creative, powerful essay—a beautiful handling of the "loss
of innocence" or "quest for independence" theme. Another
common subject matter presented in a crisp, clear, individual
manner. (JWM)

Ameen Jan
College: Princeton University

THE TRAMP

The river is cold as fall changes to winter, and its water glides
softly over the sharp rocks on the bed. The bank on both sides is
pebbled, and further up gets forested with willows; the leaves
have turned through orange and red to brown at this time of
year, and each minute adds to the collection of these on the
ground underneath. Chill winds blow in the early morning,
when the sun is not strong enough to break through the clouds,
and a light drizzle starts to fall on the downy leaves up the bank.
Soon droplets begin to form on the leaves still attached to their
boughs, and as they collect, the foliage starts drooping lower
until the accumulated water drops off the edge.

The tramp gets up at this time, for his face is cold. He quickly gathers his meager belongings in the bundle of tattered clothes that he carries with him, and makes his way to the bank of the river. He quickly rinses his face with a handful of water, for it is freezing cold, and runs his fingers through his matted hair (or at least makes an attempt of it). The morning ablutions are done.

Under a spreading willow, which still retains some of its foliage, a few yards up the river he seeks temporary shelter. He reaches into his coat pocket and draws a half-eaten can of beans and a bent spoon. He crumples the lid over with the utmost care, for its edges are sharp, and reaches into its contents. The congealed mass of food is slowly dislodged from the sides of the can, and the tramp starts to chew on the cold morsels.

The end of morning meal signifies the start of a day-long trek upriver to the town. Perhaps he can get a job there, maybe as a laborer, for the harvest is over and so is his last job as a picker at a farm. He would wake up early if he had a warm bed to sleep in and a roof over his head; he would work hard all day, laying bricks or carrying luggage at the railway station or running errands for a store. He would work hard if he could get a proper meal at a proper time, and have a routine set for him. Maybe he could even have a few friends, others like him roaming the country in search for jobs, and landing the same employment. He could progress, if given the chance, and prove his worth to the world . . .

By around noon the sun breaks through the clouds and the drizzle stops; the wet leaves and the soggy ground start to dry, and the atmosphere assumes a slight degree of warmth. The leaves on the ground start to scatter as they dry, for the tramp's shuffling footsteps dislodge them from their bed. The river sparkles up ahead as the sunlight is reflected off its surface, but underneath it is cold and forbidding. There is nothing to be seen in the distance, but for the naked willows and the interminable river.

COMMENTS:

An excellent essay if descriptive writing is the object. The essay is especially good as it conveys the thought that this situation will continue as it is—as does the river—the use of nature as a dominant element in this essay is effective. Enough of the tramp carries arrows to get the idea—and nature and its continuance dominate the mood and thought of the tale. (HDT)

The description of the physical surroundings is great, but the direction of the narrative is fuzzy, leaving a sense of confusion. (PLF)

Anne M. Knott
College: Yale University

TEN WAYS TO CELEBRATE LIFE

Set aside the homework long enough to go outside and smell the sweet springtime and see how blue the sky can be.

Take a walk in the greening woods and fields, make boats to float down the swollen creek, and listen to the birds singing.

Sit with a friend in a restaurant booth and order a chocolate milkshake with two straws.

Go to the arboretum and run through the woods and meadows until you collapse, climb trees, sing, roll down hills until you are dizzy, and let loose all that pent-up energy.

With the sun beating overhead, dive down down down into the clear cold lake and come back up slowly through the fractured sunlight.

Sleep out on a summer's night and count shooting stars and constellations. Wonder at life so small in a universe so big.

On a crisp fall day, go with many friends to roam the apple orchard, climbing trees and finding the biggest and best apples, tasting them all, and afterward of course getting fresh hot cinnamon doughnuts and cider.

Put on all the warmest clothes (not forgetting boots and mittens) and venture out with friends into the swirling blizzard to build a snowman and tackle each other in the snow.

Come in all ruddy-cheeked, put on warm dry clothes that are too big for you, and curl up by the fire with popcorn and hot cocoa while the snow melts on the kitchen floor.

Crunch through the snow with frosty toes caroling with friends, make sugar cookies, smell the evergreen, keep secrets, and sing out the Christmas cheer.

___

COMMENT:

I want to really like this essay answer of Anne's, but am not sure that her attempt works that well. The person she is indirectly describing here (i.e., Anne herself) is probably a warm, sensitive young woman who does indeed have a special zest for living; but we aren't convinced of that because the message of this "poetry in prose" is rather detached from a description of self. I suppose a reader (and maybe an all-too-cynical one), I'd find myself asking, "Is she 'for real'?" If the essay question had asked the applicant how to best celebrate life, the answer would be a truly marvelous one. (RJO)

Nisha Kumar
College: Harvard University

7:31. The mini-schoolbus, as it has done for the past six years, rattles up the street, and the bus driver honks impatiently in front of my house. I search frantically for an earring and a shoe, snatch breakfast from my mother's waiting hand, and dash out. Though the actual buses have changed, the mustard yellow paint, the eight vinyl seats patched with black friction tape, and the grimy floor have not. Yet this atmosphere has not coincided with my time (minimum forty minutes daily) spent on them.

I learned that no stereotyped bus driver (quiet, comatose) exists. Steve had shoulder-length hair, cursed excessively, and blasted heavy metal in the morning. He is now a member of the band "The Steel Warriors." Roofus, a reverend in Harlem, New York, would not budge until everyone had fastened his seatbelt. We despised this notion, and consequently, him. Always chuckling, Renee had quick sense of humor: "Why don't you move a little slower, honey?" she would quip as one of us trudged off the bus. But Jay was my favorite: He waited patiently, no matter how much time I needed to come out, and he always had an irrelevant anecdote about a car show in which he had participated.

But my fellow students enlivened the rides more. Faced with an alternative of silence, Gina, Sharon, Guyetri, and I quickly became friends. We have chatted about schoolwork, teachers, and possible prom dates. "You want to go with him?" I would skeptically ask Sharon.

"Nisha, he is hilarious . . . You should hear him in history class," she would respond. The bus also bred hostility, as Jon Schwartz and Rob Weiss, two arrogant upperclassmen, had insisted they sit alone.

"Don't even think we're about to sit with one of you," they would sneer. Then, we protested them; now, we emulate them, aggressively defending our right to sit apart from underclassmen. We are veterans, so we deserve to.

My other "busmates"—Alan, Stacy, Jennifer, Anita, LeAnn, and Eric—and I have developed a camaraderie, despite our intellectual and social differences. My charades skills have improved immensely, and I have become the bus's best "Punchbuggy" player ("Punchbuggy" is a race to spot a Volkswagen Beetle, declare its color, and punch the person of one's choice). Stacy and Jennifer provide the latest gossip: "Can you believe Alissa broke up with him?" they demand, surprised. Eagerly recalling reruns of *The Brady Bunch*, we interrupt each other, "No wait—remember the one with Davy Jones . . ." and then burst into his song, "Girl, look what you've done to me . . ." Alan and I compare breakfasts: In two years, we have never had the same one. We tolerate each other's books crowding the aisle as well as short tempers. Ironically, we discuss least that which we share most—school!

Whenever the bus rides have seemed too long, or the conversation too dull, I have looked forward to driving (I shall begin in March). Nevertheless, I will miss the rides: the movie discussions, the secrets exchanged, and even the breakdowns in the snow. Besides, you cannot play "Punchbuggy" alone.

Zoe Mulford
College: Harvard University

Belgians grow in circles
like mushrooms in the rain.
Looking down from a window
on a schoolyard at recess
the girls appear in little rings
like a yeast colony—
conversational huddles
that grow and regroup
and divide like cells.
To center a circle
you go around and kiss each person
even the ones you don't know.
Always kiss
     hello goodbye goodmorning goodnight.
As cheek brushes cheek
you verify
     I am a person
     You are person
     We have a basis for communication.

It took me a while to catch on,
coming from a world of determined individuals
who disdained cliques,
studied at the lunch table,
looked up suspiciously
if you said good morning.

Here the girls thought I was standoffish
when I only said it once.
My host-mother shook her head.
    Well, she's an artist.
    Her mind is elsewhere.
    She's ignoring us.
Now I kiss
    hello goodbye goodmorning goodnight.
Cheek brushes cheek.
I ask "ça va?"
really wanting to know.
I learn peoples' names
who they're related to and how,
what they've been doing.
In a room cold with grief
the family circle gathers to kiss for the last time
an uncle dead of leukemia.
Women weep together.
I stand bewildered with the close relatives
as all I can offer is respectful silence
filling a space in the ring.
In a room warm with birth
they gather to kiss for the first time
a long-awaited nephew.
I smile and coo with the rest
and study this new little foreigner
who will learn
as I am learning
by watching.

In kitchens full of soup-smells
where the steam from the pressure-cooker
condenses on the windows
and November's nasal-drip
spatters on the red roofs.
Circles of old women gather for coffee
to talk birth and death and weather
mothers and daughters and women's work,

and I sit with them listening
and asking questions.
I piece together the cycles,
marking the place I would fit in
were I not flying away again in July.
Letters from my mother
talk of adapting the tribe for modern life,
forming supra-family neighborhood support networks.
I am taking notes for her.

Circles can strangle
as well as protecting.
They've burned witches here.
Strong women have been broken over the dishpan,
noble men stifled in the mines.

Kristen Mulvihill
College: Brown University

CONFIRMATION (FAITH JOURNEY?)

All of the other little angels were wearing white. Why wasn't I?

To be honest, it didn't much concern me. I felt I was worthy of the color; however, it was not symbolic pageantry that mattered, but rather good intention. Who ever said white made one holy? Besides, it *was* past Labor Day and I didn't want to commit a "sin" in the name of the Father, the Son, or the Holy Spirit.

You may have surmised by now that I am entering into a realm, sometimes better left untouched, as I reflect upon an event, which although performed with good intention, served only to overshadow the true significance of the occasion, as well as to challenge my personal beliefs.

I remember Confirmation. How could I ever forget it: the

long ceremony, the dignified bishop, the parishioners at their holiest.

But what was most important on that auspicious occasion was the true meaning of Confirmation, the "for what" and "for whom" it was intended. As to just what the exact purpose was, I am still pondering. However, as to "for whom" it was meant, the answer is as clear to me today as it was then: for the parents, of course, and for the Church that took the opportunity to show its holiness and to demonstrate humility.

For the parents, it was a sign of hope. The mothers were so proud, their eyes filled with tears of joy. And why not? Each of their daughters were wearing white, a color most suitable for their sixteen- and seventeen-year-old "innocent girls." The fathers were also elated. For many of them it was a first: "the first Sunday Mass in seventeen years." It was, too, a chance to rename their sons, to give them holy titles other than doctor or counselor. They were so proud of *their* sons—so proud in fact, it's a wonder none of them chose the name Jesus for their son. Then again, humility is a characteristic common to all good Christians.

This humility was best exhibited by the bishop, God bless him, who wore a large ring, which he, out of graciousness, permitted all to kiss. He wore a robe, laden with gold. However, it too was quite modest, as it had no waistline and was anything but revealing. He brought with him an assistant, a middle-aged, rather handsome priest. Looks did not go to his head either, as he was sure to smile at each female candidate as she approached the altar. He too was most humble. Upon numerous occasions, he helped the bishop straighten his foot-tall crown, handed him his long gold staff, and generally did anything his excellency requested, as long as he could look holy doing it. Undoubtedly, he eagerly awaited the day when, after the requisite period of study in Rome, he could fully relieve his excellency of his duties and assume the role of imparting the Holy Spirit into another generation.

The highlight of the event was the bishop's address, his words of divine advice to the "children" of our parish. It was indeed a speech I will never forget or forgive. He was especially kind to the female candidates as he spoke of "*the* grand future" ahead of us, of which he seemed to feel we were most worthy—"the vocation of wifedom and motherhood," as he so graciously phrased it. Deeply moved by this statement, I noted, with not too little irony, that chauvinistic stability that has characterized Holy "Mother" Church since the days of Peter and Paul. Isn't it nice to know some things never change.

The male candidates, of course, fully appreciated the speech. They seemed to be completely relaxed, brought to such a deep state of religious contemplation that they closed their eyes in silent, sleepy meditation.

Perhaps the parents related to the speech best of all, as they had experienced all of the self-fulfilling, religious experiences of which his excellency spoke: marriage, penance, and naturally planned parenthood.

Yes, Confirmation was for me a "true awakening." I regret to say it was neither what I expected nor desired.

Ironically, it contradicted rather than reinforced the values taught to me in Confirmation class. Yet, somehow, the disappointment of that day has taught me to rely upon my own beliefs. It has caused me to appreciate further the difference between the shallowness of pompous pageantry and the depth of simple ceremony.

COMMENT:

She hits much too hard at times (such as in criticizing the priest for smiling), but overall the essay succeeds because it brings out her personality. She takes quite a chance in writing this essay, but one which I believe is worth taking. This is a person I would like to meet.

This is a rare example of a cynical or sarcastic essay that succeeds as a college application essay.

Ruth M. Ohm
College: Brown University

WHAT WOULD LIFE
BE LIKE WITHOUT *LAUGHTER*?

Imagine sitting on a park bench on an afternoon in mid-November, next to a man dressed in somber gray, smoking a dark cigar. He is quiet. All the people in the park are silent mirror images of this solitary figure. The temperature hovers just above freezing. A slight drizzle of rain drifts from a dank and sunless sky. Smoke curls slowly upward from limp fingers and a bit of ash falls onto the man's lapel. As he lifts his hand to brush it away, you see his face, tired, worn, and wrinkled by years of ceaseless disappointments. Sadness erodes his flesh as the pounding of waves carves deep crevices into the shore. This is life without laughter.

A woman with wisps of unwashed brown hair stands at the ironing board, watching endless game shows of manic people and worrying about cold lasagna for dinner, the worn spots on her husband's shirt collars, and the bad grades her children are getting in school. She looks up once as the plastic announcer tells her how essential his product is for a carefree life, burns her finger, swears softly to herself, and returns the iron to the yoke of a blue work shirt. This is life without laughter.

On a desolate beach, a small girl leaves her broken kite caught in a tangle of planking, and watches the waves slowly shift the sand. The beach is littered with useless objects, rusty bits of tin, and leftover wraps from long-ago picnics. She notices an old man sitting among large rocks and wrapped in a coat full of holes. Sheltered somewhat from the wind, he gazes blankly at the pale rays of the late afternoon sun. The wind whistles in the distance and sea gulls off the shore insult one another over bits of decaying fish.

Look at the boy and his dog, shuffling through dead leaves, going nowhere in particular, isolated, bored, and listless. He calls to his dog, who has disappeared into an alley and is rooting through spilled garbage. He looks up at the darkening sky as a lone drop of rain falls onto his face. His vision blurs momentarily. In frustration, he kicks at the curbing and only succeeds in bruising his foot.

Now go back to that afternoon in the park. The month becomes early October. Add laughter as a group of warmly dressed children play catch, and jump rope, and counting games. A brisk wind plays with the red and gold and russet of leaves on the ground and the children cry with delight. The man smiles as he remembers his own youth and from a pocket he finds a balloon to give to the littlest boy. In the middle distance, a young woman shows her daughter how to make her kite soar and glide with the wind. A boy in a checkered red coat throws a stick to his dog who energetically bounds after it. The dog returns the stick, wagging all over in gratitude.

This is life with laughter.

James P. O'Rourke
College: Harvard College

PERSONAL STATEMENT

"Is this a high school or a museum?" I wondered. I had just walked through the doors of Regis High School and formed my first impression of the institution. The impersonal hallways and stone staircases gave me a cold feeling of insignificance. The sounds of the city outside came in through the walls and I realized I hadn't just chosen a school to attend—I had changed my way of life. Gone was my placid grammar school, set in the midst of acres of rolling Pennsylvania farmland. I would only continue to eat and sleep in my relaxed town of Titusville, New Jersey. My daily reality would now be a hurried four-and-a-half-hour commute to and from Manhattan, and the rigorous demands of an intense curriculum.

Almost four years later, I emerged from the daydreaming en route to Manhattan, amused at my freshman misgivings. The 6:59 express train had just departed from Princeton Junction, New Jersey. On board, I took in the familiar surroundings. Like every other day, the commuters had jammed through the doors to get seats for the long ride. After folding raincoats and stowing briefcases, the commuters settled themselves with their newspapers.

I too settled into my seat and reviewed my Classical Political Thought assignment. I began to read Plato's *Republic*. I was fascinated by Plato's ideas. He masterfully expressed much of what I found or suspected to be true in life. I read over the section on the education of the philosopher-ruler. Plato was so right . . . dialectic and rational discussion will always be important for those who want perspective and truth. But how many people share Plato's view in life? How many commit to the same priorities?

I sat there feeling something between despondency and frustration. Perspective was vitally important to me, and the challenge of communicating it to those seated around me seemed impossible. My mind began to shift from the analytical to the imaginative. I began to fantasize that the time had finally come to share my philosophy of life.

I imagined turning to my right. My first partner in enlightenment would be the kind-looking, middle-aged commuter seated next to me. I would begin confidently, picturing myself as Socrates questioning Cephalus or Thrasymachus.

"Do you know there are 130 people in this car . . . most of whom sit merely a few feet away from us. We sit next to these people every day. Do you realize that Plato—one of the greatest thinkers of all time—believed that dialectic could eventually lead people to the discovery of ultimate reality . . . The Good. Through the virtues of wisdom, justice, and discipline we attain knowledge of this Good. It, the Good, then permeates one's entire life, enabling him to do everything better. His whole person with all his faculties are raised to a higher level. If all this can happen through rational discussion of significant ideas among men, can you imagine the enlightenment potential just sitting in this one car? We could all be so much better off if we only conversed with each other on important issues."

I had made my pitch, I had taken my risk and shared with this decent-looking fellow what was important to me. Plato would have been proud. I awaited his reaction and response with eager anticipation as I studied his facial expressions. He looked at me quizzically, quickly but politely excused himself, stood up, grabbed his raincoat, and left the car. He did though continue to look back over his shoulder.

I came back to reality. The decent-looking commuter was still seated beside me, now showing signs of an impending morning nap. No damage done, but no meaningful communication effected in reality.

COMMENTS:

I would give this student an "A" if I were grading this as an English composition. It is cleverly conceived and well written. It wouldn't impress me, however, as an admissions tool in that it fails to reveal much about the author. (TG)

A "catchy" opening that immediately draws the reader into the life of Jim O'Rourke. References to Plato could have come off as forced and pseudo-intellectual, but the clear descriptions of the train and daydreams pull it into a well-written essay revealing an inquisitive mind. (JWM)

ESSAYS ON
WORK EXPERIENCE

Janet Dix
College: Brown University

"So, you have no previous work experience?"

"Nooo . . ."

"And this would be your first job?"

"Yesss . . ."

"Great, you can start Monday! I'll call you sometime during the week with hours. By the way, Janet, my name's Stephen."

All I could think was, but doesn't it say "Etienne" on his nametag? I couldn't believe that after wandering around the mall for 45 minutes, I had a job. Friends had told me job-hunting horror stories about applying at Christmas time and being turned down for the summer. Amazingly enough, 12 hours into summer, the day after my last exam, there was a job.

Now, I'm not sure what my original picture of a Barnes & Noble employee looked like, but the difference between it and my current picture is comparable to the difference between a Van Gogh sky and a Bloom County comic strip. They are a collection of people whom I, under normal circumstances, would never have encountered, but now, after only a short while, I'm not sure I could get along without. Together, we teeter the line between truly bizarre and just plain entertaining. When Stephen explained to me that he shaves his legs because it cuts down on wind resistance while cycling, you could have heard a cotton ball hit the carpet in the store. Several of the more insecure males made a beeline for the door.

I imagine WORK, in capital gothic lettering, to be a sentence to be faced; a grim milestone to remind me that childhood was gone, and I now stood before a concrete wall of RESPONSI-BILITY, also in capital gothic lettering. After all, my father goes to WORK every day, and his favorite clothing color is dark gray. His second favorite clothing color is gray. I figured that once I walked through the doors of Barnes and Noble, I would shed my trappings and suits of youth and become mature. I couldn't have been more wrong.

At Barnes & Noble, languid days are spent taking "vertical

257

naps" on the extension ladder, or planning book cart relay races. Rearranging the "whale" is a favorite pastime, especially good for Friday nights, because every book from the huge central display must be moved to the floor directly in front of the door. This maneuver effectively blocks the door, and prevents customers from coming in and ruining our fun.

However, customers do manage to call, and they are quickly classified. Easy phone calls are highly anticipated, seldom received. "What time are you open 'til," is a favorite. A hard phone call is much more challenging:

"Last month, my cousin from South Dakota was in, and he said that halfway down on the left wall was a stack of pink books, and next to the stack of pink books was a yellow book with blue writing. Well. I want the one across the aisle from that!"

An equally challenging but more simply worded phone question:

"I'm looking for a book." Long pregnant pause here. It's almost as if they expect you to tell them that Barnes & Noble is now selling natural vitamins instead of books. One has to reassure them. "I don't know the title, but the third letter in the author's name is X."

Those customers who sneak by our clever road block are classified also. An easy customer buys a book and has a bill totaling $3.76. He hands me $4.00 and apologizes because he doesn't have a penny. On the way, he actually picks up a book that he didn't even knock off the shelf.

A difficult customer selects $700.00 worth of books. Each book has all or part of its price sticker missing. Near the bottom of the pile he discovers a sodden piece of wood pulp that his daughter has chewed on. It used to be a book, and now he doesn't want it anymore. He attempts to pay with a MasterCard that has exceeded its credit limit. "Call for verification" flashes across the machine's screen. At this point, demonstrating some sort of herding instinct, all the customers in the store lumber up to the register like frightened wildebeest, ready to pay. Within seconds, all of them, including the original difficult customer, are clamoring and threatening to tell the manager of the terrible service. The manager, who has gone to the deli for a snack, walks up to the window, thinks better of coming in, and keeps walking as if he works in the video store next door.

Where could you go for an entree of books with a side order of comedy? Where could the management of a store operate like a five-wheeled vehicle and still survive? Where you can find me even when I'm not working? Barnes & Noble, of course, of course!

COMMENTS:

Janet manages to invest in the Barnes and Noble microcosm while sharing her worldview. That latter is funny, irreverent, and at times transcendent (as Van Gogh sky). Some of her narrative is a little forced; one strongly suspects that the *real* Janet is as much future customer as mischievous clerk. In the end, however, she dismisses the myth of adversary and reveals the insight of a very able and viable young candidate. (SAB)

This is interesting and well written. It is written from experience in a humorous way. Any reader who has spent any time browsing in bookstores could identify with the incidents described and so would catch the interest of admissions people. (BPS)

Richard L. Harrington
College: Amherst College

In an interview with our school newspaper, Kevin Patrick, a friend of mine, once remarked that a newspaper route is the perfect job because "you make enough to save, but not enough to spend." Though I have managed to spend money, also, I have found my paper route to be nearly ideal.

The summer after my sixth grade year I attended a private camp in Minnesota instead of the local YMCA camp I had formerly gone to. It was superior in every way, and I vowed that I would go there the next summer, too. Unfortunately, this private camp cost twice as much as the Y camp; my parents couldn't afford to send me there. When the paper route in my neighborhood was going to be given up, my parents encouraged me to take it, and I did. I made my first delivery October 1, 1981, and I paid for one-half of the camp bill for the next four years.

It seems now as if I have been doing the paper route for just short of forever, and it has come to be part of my daily routine. Fortunately, it's a varied routine, with an interesting group of customers: white and black, young and retired, factory workers and businessmen, engineers and ministers, physicians and an architect, more than a dozen college professors, two former Notre Dame All-Americans, and a couple of little old lady basketball fanatics. On more than one occasion, I have accidentally set off burglar alarms and passed quickly on to the next house. Once, in a fit of heroism, I saved a house with a blaring smoke alarm . . . from burning toast! I have waded through South Bend's notorious lake effect snow and found customers waiting with hot cocoa. I've had chances, too, to practice my geometry by figuring out the shortest secant to two intersecting circles in order to avoid the impeccably precise Rain Bird sprinklers. I've been given cookies, brownies, a Toro Weed Trimmer from a man who was moving, and, after an especially hard winter, twenty dollars on impulse from a customer seriously stricken with spring fever. Over the years, I have watched with interest the arrival of customers' new cars, new babies— and new dogs. Most important, I treasure the time alone to think. While making my rounds, I have memorized lines from *Macbeth* and music for choir. For the most part, though, I simply think and daydream about everything conceivable.

Even though I like the time to myself and the daily exercise, the money, and the sense of responsibility, are probably the most important aspects of the paper route. The publisher has twice honored me as a *Tribune* Scholar, and once as Carrier of the Year. And, besides camp, the paper route has allowed me to purchase some small luxuries which my parents would not or could not pay for. My freshman year I bought a French bicycle and contact lenses, and my sophomore year I procured a small stereo. Last summer, a friend and I took off a week and went camping in Michigan. I never knew how much vacations cost before then. But more important than the material objects, what I have learned from the paper route and the money it produces is a sense of responsibility to the company, to my customers, and to myself. I was responsible for delivering papers to 93 customers in all sorts of weather, 362 days a year. I have had no respite, for Saturday and Sunday editions arrive in the early morning, and I must also rise before six o'clock on school days to attend Concert Choir at 6:45. I have learned to budget my time, for, with the paper route and, lately, editorial meetings after school, I have no time before supper to study.

Unfortunately, Kevin, along with most of my classmates, now flips burgers. But he was right about the paper route—it is perfect. I work hard, meet wonderful people, and make decent money for the time I put in. And I don't get greasy.

Celia E. Rothenberg
College: Wellesley College

Detasseling, simply defined, is the removal of the tassel from a corn stalk so that pollinization of the plant can occur and hybrid seed corn can grow. Among midwestern high school students detasseling is infamous because it requires extremely long hours in the July heat, tolerance of "corn rash" and bugs, and a lot of physical strength. I signed up in response to a dare from someone who believed that I would not be able to last the full six weeks. Perhaps it was the growing recognition of my own strength, my pride in being one of the twelve detasslers (out of the original seventy) who were asked to work the entire detasseling season, or the antagonistic nature of the dare that propelled me through all six weeks, but what I learned from that experience has changed me as a person.

Detasseling helped me to look beyond the surface of people who are different kinds of achievers from those I encounter every day. Attending University High School, I have learned to respect academic accomplishments above other types of achievement. Yet many of my fellow detasselers had completely different sets of values and goals that I came to admire. Many of them were working in order to eat, or to buy essential books and supplies for school. Being singled out as a "brain" from the first day because of the stereotype the students held of students from my high school was difficult. Yet I earned the respect of my crew by working hard, and we developed a friendly, working relationship.

My partner, Josh, told me that the money he was making from the summer would be his only money for the rest of the year and would enable him to finish high school; college for him was an impossibility. Yet he never lost his sense of humor. Walking the three-quarters of a mile down each row, he would "rap," "I don't like to pick this corn, but I'm still glad that I was born." He gave me a true sense of what it means to make the most out of very little.

Speaking little English and understanding even less, two Thai girls who detasseled that summer never complained; together they could outwork the strongest and most experienced of the detasslers. Their determination to adjust to new surroundings and to work hard earned the respect of all of us.

The dynamics of the crew reflected the responsibility most of the crew felt toward the job and the farmer whose corn we detasseled. There were days when we stayed after dark working by flashlight to finish a field so that it would not have to be plowed under, which would have meant a significant monetary loss for the farmer as well as a waste of three acres of good corn. Only after we finished did I realize that we had worked since 5 A.M. Since detasseling, I have not been a part of a group that requires every member to be as responsible as each crew member had to be then.

While discovering the strengths of so many different kinds of people, I also discovered some of my own strengths. I discovered my ability to respond to physical as well as academic challenges. I realized that I am able to depend on my own inner resources. This discovery of my own physical strength and my ability to endure came as a revelation to me.

Learning to judge people by different standards carried over into the school year when I realized that I did not have a date to the Junior Prom. Not used to staying home, I considered my options and discovered someone who was also dateless. A gifted math student, PLATO programmer, and someone who always carried a calculator, he seemed to have little in common with me. Even so, I asked him to Prom. Detasseling proved to me that different types of people can learn from each other, and we did. A very special friendship evolved after Prom, perhaps partly because of our differences and partly because we had taken the time and effort to discover that beneath the surface we share many things in common.

The concept of detasseling and what it requires is understood by few; yet those who have experienced it share a special bond. After detasseling we did not see each other again as a group, but we parted with respect for one another. I left valuing new things about myself and other people. And I also won the dare.

COMMENTS:

The amazing thing about Rothenberg's detasseling essay is that it worked despite leaning on populist platitudes about the American Dream. It works because it is beautifully organized and the argument proceeds in concrete portions. It works because the writer manages to stay within the actual experience instead of sugarcoating it. It works because the determination and sentience for the writer is real. (SAB)

This essay is very well written. Through a summer job, which some college students might regard as somewhat demeaning, this student shows ability to adapt and versatility so necessary to adjusting to college situations. The writer shows a willingness to work hard for what she wants and through this she learns much about herself and others she worked with. She demonstrates through these experiences her ability to adjust (adapt) to new experiences, ideas, and people when she gets to college. (BPS)

ESSAYS ON WRITING

Anonymous

LITTLE BUGGY

It started, I guess, with that little buggy—really *started*, I mean, though the roots had been laid down almost since birth—in around the third grade. I could tool around in that thing, and when I was in it I was indestructible, and with a touch of a button (and there were always plenty of buttons) I could have anything from a pumpkin pie, no crust, to a super solar space modulator beam; and I could zip around, zip forward, zip backward, and I could zip up and down and through the water and in deepest space and through time and the dimensions.

I really liked that little car. I used to think about it as I drifted off to sleep. That was when the idea came to me: The floor beneath my bed would open, dropping me into a flowing crimson river; and as I traveled at breakneck speed toward certain doom, I would press a button and the bed would, yes, *change* into that little car.

So I wrote it down.

I wrote it during classes and after school and while I watched *The Six Million Dollar Man*. I started with the flowing river beneath my bed, and quickly graduated into my adventures against Mouse Man and Super Mouse and The Mouse that was Nasty. And after I beat the mice, I fought the men, like Owl Man and Evil Man and Nasty Man. Then I hit the really big time, in this little book, and fought people with names like The Black Shadow and Jim McCoy, agent of S.K.U.L.L.

And when fifth grade was over, I'd finished my first book. Eighty pages if it was a paragraph, was my book, written in careful letters on wide-ruled paper.

Then I started thinking. How to follow up my masterpiece? A friend and I were churning out 'King Comics Corporation" at the rate of two or three comics a week . . . but these were simply excuses to draw two men hitting each other. I wanted a lot. I wanted realism. I wanted . . what did I want?

I wanted to write a Choose Your Own Adventure book, and, come the end of sixth grade, I had written two (one called *Great White* and the other oh-so-tentatively titled *The Presidential Factor*) and had gotten a friend to start working on publishing them for me. I didn't gross ten dollars, selling those things to classmates, even though the teachers let me Xerox them at half-price. Still, I was inspired. For my first "real" book.

It hit me at the end of tenth grade, after I had recently written enough short stories to fill two anthologies. I had just written a ninety-page story, and I thought: hey. What not expand it?

So I started, and found out I didn't know what the hell "expand" meant. Was I meant to bloat it? Add extra characters?

So I started from scratch. The main character in my stories had always been an extension of what Stephen King calls the "I-guy." And, it seemed, I just wasn't strong enough as a personality to carry a book-length project. To keep a simple outline, I developed an idea that basically bracketed episodes. I wrote the start and the end in fifty good pages, then went back and began to fill it in.

As I went I sort of lost track of the gimmick of the novel, and it became loose and confusing. I finished, sent it to a contest, sent it to an agent, and was duly rejected. By both. It hurts a little, still, the little twinge at finding a one-page rejection, always with the finishing sentence: *I can tell you're a writer with promise.*

But here I am, working on my new masterpiece, with two good working titles and a main character that should allow for hundreds of pages of interesting revelation. It is *Brittle Leaves and Skeleton Trees*, sometimes called *Without Style or Grace*; and who knows? Maybe it'll be on the stands in not too long. And if it won't; well, there's more to come. Plenty more to come.

COMMENTS:
There is a pleasantly vibrant evocation of childhood imagination in this essay. There is also, at times, a kind of transparent respect for slickness. A writer need not advertise the *quantity* of writing but rather reveal its *quality* by what it stated. This essay

wavers between the phantasmagoria of imagination and meretricity. (SAB)

This is good. It is interesting and well written. The person obviously has a talent for writing and the experiences demonstrate a persistence that will lead to success. We just might see something "on the stands" written by this person. (BPS)

Michael Chaskes
College: **Wesleyan University**

WHY I WANT TO BE A WRITER

I do almost all my writing in my bedroom. The prewriting I actually do *in* bed, lying down, with my eyes closed. That way, no one can tell if I'm asleep or just thinking. Sometimes when I do that I really do go to sleep, but that's part of it, you see.

While I sit and write, I look out the window. The blinds are Venetian, and even when they're totally closed I can still see out of them. The blinds make big horizontal stripes over the sky, and as birds swoop down, they are continually obscured, then visible, then obscured, then visible. The birds land on branches; then sometimes I can see all of them clearly, but usually I see only part of them, and sometimes none of them.

When I get tired of writing, I pick up a book. I have a lot of them in my room. Then I'll read, or just stare at the cover. Sometimes my favorite part is the author's biographical sketch. In his, Woody Allen says that "his only regret in life is that he's not someone else." I don't find that funny at all.

Sometimes, I'll get a drink and a copy of the paper or *Newsweek*. *Newsweek* always depresses me. I think it's because they always think they know exactly what's going on, even when the people involved don't.

Or maybe that's not it. I don't know.

There's also an alarm clock in my room. I hate the clock almost as much as I hate the calendar. It only tells two kinds of time to me: "plenty of" and "almost out of." I think "plenty of" is worse because it's an illusion, and when I think I have "plenty of," I look back at the clock a little while later and I'm already "almost out of." I don't like the alarm too much either, it's too loud.

Well, maybe none of that tells you why I want to be a writer, but that's really it, or most of it. Or some of it. Sometimes I feel like the best place to do all my writing would be outside somewhere, by a lake in Maine or something, like an artist with an easel, my typewriter and I, all the time. But then it would rain, and all my work would get wet and ruined. So I just stay in my room. I have trouble seeing out of the window, but everybody has to make do, don't they?

COMMENT:

Michael's essay reminds me of Andy Rooney. He speaks of simple, every day things in simple ways, but his observations are offbeat, refreshing, and honest. The best part of this essay is that it lets the reader into the private life and thoughts of the writer, into his personal self, just as Holden Caufield did. It is totally fitting that the essay was handwritten and not typed, because of the unavoidable tone of formality that accompanies a "perfectly presented" piece. (AST)

Nikolas R. Elevitch
College: Yale University

I DO MANY THINGS, but there's no question that the most important to me is writing.

The other things I do I like for different reasons. I like running, for example, because it is a way for me to make noise physically and competitively. Writing is also venting, but it comes from the quiet voice, quiet breathing, and the loud mind.

I like playing in a rock band because that too is noisy. I can use my hands playing the bass guitar and work with Philip, the drummer. The drums and bass have to be tight, fit in a groove, be the pulse of the music. But what I like most is the way Philip and I build off each other. Philip might introduce a quick off-beat roll and lead into hitting the upbeats between the quarter notes. I have to adapt to this change, but at the same time, I follow through with a rapid walking line from 4/4 to 7/8. Philip keeps hitting those upbeats and the groove changes, the song rises to a new level, a new rhythm.

This partnership is not unique to a band. What brought out and developed my ability to write is a partnership I had with my friend Rob. We would have rap sessions in which the purpose was to create a continuous flow of laughs (keep the other guy laughing).

A good metaphor for our rap sessions is our first Ping-Pong game. Rob was about to serve the ball, but ended up serving a volley of images. He paused to help me imagine Ronald Reagan falling asleep on his desk and accidentally leaning on the red button. I said that the maid would come and ask what he wanted. (So much for the power and control of the President.) I then closed my eyes for no reason and snored, and he did too. We did this for a minute and then began something else. We would do this all the time, while eating, watching TV, etc. Actually there was rarely a serious moment. We constantly searched for things out of context to chuck into the buildup, things funny just because of the way they bounced off each other, weird and from the blue.

But when I want to do something all by myself the most important thing to do is write. Once accidentally I set at a typewriter and played with words, chucking things on the page just for the sake of getting it out and feeling the keys go click, and out came a mixture of words built up from one another. To my surprise, this first poem later went on to be published in the *Boston Literary Review*. It was so easy to get on paper the images floating around in my mind that I wrote many more poems throughout my junior year, getting three accepted for publication. The big obstacle for me had been getting these images to work well together. They played off the subsconscious, each other, and the sounds of the words themselves.

I spend time alone writing in a room at the top of a building that I walk to at night with a flashlight. I can look out at the Hudson River, the lights on the other side, and the trees blowing in the darkness on my side. Out of the 200 scientists that work there, maybe one diehard remains, his lonely car in the parking log. I close the door and sit at the typewriter and start:

My activity is mud wallowing.

To begin again:

I left home but didn't know where to go. I remember what my dad told me the night before, 'Son, you must get a mate.' I am an animal, I know that. But I was intent upon following the food supply, not a mate. Or at least my instinct. But not a mate. I am lonely and strange. Last night I did go straight to the fridge for a Coke, but I only did it because I rolled a 6-sided die and came up 3.5. Maybe I should just plop down here on the street and renounce everything, submitting myself to destiny. Someone will care for me. (I fell face down in the mud, my pants leg catching a nail on the doorstep and ripping.) I submit myself to the street—*as it is*. Let myself be carried away with main street America. By the dice. My life might turn up all 3.5s, summed up in one word. Probability.

I stop. I realize that I'm going in circles. But I've uncovered something along the way. So all I can say is that when I write, I investigate ideas and feelings, my own and other people's. I bandy with the images in my brain and learn about, for example, my frustration with main street America, and the monotony of my walking toward destiny as it shows in real life through daily repetition. I fall in the mud. I even take on the world.

Carol Zall
College: Princeton University

The Essay. It is supposed to make me come alive as a person. Expressing my goals, values, and personal development would be helpful. In fact, the pamphlet I have just read on writing college essays gives me an easy tip: "Try for essays that provide insights into *all* these areas: 1) your intellectual and creative interests; 2) your personal strengths; 3) how well you write; 4) what's special about you." Sure. Right-o.

It is not that I find writing difficult. In fact, writing is one of my greatest pleasures, and has been ever since my poetic debut in the third grade with "O Frog." "Where do you get your croak?" I lamented. "Or your black-spotted cloak? Or black beady eyes? Or toenails that look like twisted bow ties?" Masterful, yes. But the point is, if I am provided with a subject, I will happily set pen to paper. However, assessing one's life can be rather tough.

Then there is the question of what to focus on. I could wax philosophical and give my views on the morality of war. But, I did that this summer in a letter to a friend and nearly killed the relationship. (I started casually enough: "Dear Bob, how are you? The weather here is just fine." Then I threw him the curve. "Just a few thoughts that were going through my mind—Is War Moral?" This was followed by a four-page dissertation on the subject.) Fine, forget the intellectualism. How about discussing the meaningful aspects of my experiences—the satisfaction that comes from tutoring, the new and different people whom I met while working at a "fast food joint" and the insight I gained from the experience (how to fill a straw holder, how much ice to put in the cup, how much a Whopper-without-the-meat costs), even the way I like to think while I ride my bicycle. But—no, it is all too mundane, the same meaningless "meaningful essay" which everyone will write.

Maybe the fact is that I think too much. My mind is constantly working, churning up ideas on an endless number of subjects. One day I can become artistic and take out my paints.

Another, I ponder the implications of nuclear war and call a citizens' group to find out what I can do. There are so many things that interest me, so much in which I can find meaning, that it is impossible to choose one event and let that represent me. It is not that I lack direction—I do know my main area of interest—but rather than my outlook embraces all of life. To me, everything seems interconnected, bound together in one overwhelming network. There are no isolated disciplines, all knowledge is inextricably interwoven. And so, even if I think about physics one moment, and the meaning of life the next, and third-grade poems after that, they are all tied together by the common thread; they are all part of my exploration of life.

Nearing the end, I am wondering if the essay is not a little *too* unconventional. However, I like what it represents: a willingness to take risks, a regard for both humor and serious thought, an interest in life, and a certain confidence that living is always an adventure. Sounds like me.

COMMENT:

This essay falls into the trap of telling the reader what the writer wants him/her to conclude. "My mind is constantly working, churning up ideas on an endless number of subjects." "However, I like what it [the essay] represents: a willingness to take risks, a regard for both humor and serious thought, an interest in life, and a certain confidence . . ." The truly outstanding essays present such a compelling picture of the writer that there is no need to prompt the reader toward the desired conclusions to be drawn. (AST)

PLUME

HELPFUL TIPS

(0452)

☐ **HOW TO GAIN AN EXTRA HOUR EVERY DAY by Ray Josephs.** This is the book that can give you the extra hour you *wish* you had. Acclaimed as the bible of effective time-management in Japan, this completely updated edition presents over 1,000 tips for eliminating routine tasks and distractions in every part of your life. (267838—$11.00)

☐ **THE 90-MINUTE HOUR** *Using Time Extension to Get the Most Out of Every Hour* **by Jay Conrad Levinson.** Here is the first time-management book to combine technology with the latest psychological research in order to reduce the stress level of a heavy work load. This revolutionary approach demonstrates the difference between working hard and working smart. (265967—$9.00)

☐ **THE COMPETITIVE EDGE** *Essential Business Skills for Entrepreneurs* **by Fran Tarkenton and Jospeh H. Boyett.** All entrepreneurs want to learn how to utilize creatively the resources at their disposal to increase productivity, profitability, and market performance. This indispensable guide focuses on every weapon you need to make that happen. (266823—$8.95)

☐ **THE GREAT MARKETING TURNAROUND** *The Age of the Individual—and How to Profit from It* **by Stan Rapp and Tom Collins.** Filled with case histories and dollars-and-sense inspiration, this new triumph will show business readers how to cast off outmoded marketing strategies and begin to implement the great marketing turnaround in their own organizations. (267498—$12.00)

Prices slightly higher in Canada.

Buy them at your local bookstore or use this convenient coupon for ordering.

NEW AMERICAN LIBRARY
P.O. Box 999, Bergenfield, New Jersey 07621

Please send me the books I have checked above.
I am enclosing $_____ (please add $2.00 to cover postage and handling).
Send check or money order (no cash or C.O.D.'s) or charge by Mastercard or VISA (with a $15.00 minimum).
Prices and numbers are subject to change without notice.

Card # _____ Exp. Date _____
Signature _____
Name _____
Address _____
City _____ State _____ Zip Code _____

For faster service when ordering by credit card call 1-800-253-6476

Allow a minimum of 4-6 weeks for delivery. This offer is subject to change without notice